Exploring

COLOSSIANS & PHILEMON

THE JOHN PHILLIPS COMMENTARY SERIES

Exploring
COLOSSIANS &
PHILEMON

An Expository Commentary

JOHN PHILLIPS

krēgel
PUBLICATIONS

Grand Rapids, MI 49501

Exploring Colossians & Philemon: An Expository Commentary

© 2002 by John Phillips

Published in 2002 by Kregel Publications, a division of Kregel, Inc., P.O. Box 2607, Grand Rapids, MI 49501. For more information about Kregel Publications, visit our Web site: www.kregel.com.

Scripture quotations are from the King James Version of the Holy Bible.

Library of Congress Cataloging-in-Publication Data
Phillips, John.
   Exploring Colossians & Philemon: an expository commentary / by John Phillips.
      p.   cm.
   1. Bible. N.T. Colossians—Commentaries. 2. Bible. N.T. Philemon—Commentaries. I. Title: Exploring Colossians and Philemon. II. Title.
BS2715.3.P48 2002   227'.707—dc21   2002006255

ISBN 0-8254-3379-7

Printed in the United States of America

02 03 04 05 06 / 3 2 1

Contents

Preface

S atan is diabolically clever; he was once "full of wisdom" (Ezek. 28:12). He is a fallen creature now but still retains much of his former wisdom, knowledge, and understanding. He is so bent and warped by sin now, however, that he is full of subtlety and malice. Moreover, he nurses a hatred for the human race that beggars description.

He reigns in the unseen world. Countless fallen angelic creatures, some of enormous power, are at his command. Moreover, unnumbered demons own his sway and aid his schemes. He is "the god of this world," "the prince of this world," and "the prince of the power of the air."

He is also the father of lies. As the god of this world, he is the inspiring genius behind all false religions and the energizing force that gives them their power. The idiom of his language is the lie, and he uses the "big lie" boldly. The principle behind the "big lie" is that if someone tells a lie big enough, brazen enough, and often enough, people will believe it. Satan knows, too, the value of mingling truth with error and is a master at it. Also, he knows all about fallen human nature and how to manipulate it. He can dazzle people as an angel of light, terrify them as a roaring lion, or beguile them as "that old serpent."

When Jesus came—truth incarnate, beyond the reach of temptation—God incarnate, invincible and fearless, Satan's grip upon our planet was put to the test. In the end, Satan urged men to get rid of Jesus by way of the Cross, but it didn't work because Jesus came back from the tomb. Jesus ascended into heaven, and once again the world seemed fair game for this master of deceit. Then the Holy Spirit took up the battle. He injected the church into time. The mystical body of Christ was formed to be the instrument of God to hold the Evil One in check and to triumph over all of Satan's seats of power (Matt. 16:13–18).

From the very start, Satan recognized the threat that the church posed to his empire of evil. He determined to stamp it out. For three hundred years, he hurled wave after wave of persecution at the church in an effort to destroy it by force. He failed. The blood of the martyrs proved to be "the seed of the church." All that Satan succeeded in doing by persecution was to fill the ranks of heaven with countless martyrs. They are seated on high in glory and honor; their names are cheered across the echoing, everlasting hills.

Satan thought that the church would be an easy conquest. After all, it was made up of very ordinary people—a village tinker here, a local butcher there, and yonder a fellow who pushed a wheelbarrow through the streets hawking fruit. But, just the same, like the humble fishermen and despised tax collectors whom Jesus had chosen for His personal friends, multitudes of these people proved to be mighty spiritual warriors. Every time they fell on their knees, Satan's kingdom shook. Nor could all of his principalities and powers, his rulers of this world's darkness, or his wicked spirits in high places prevent them from breaking through at will to the throne room of the universe.

There was only one thing to do with this formidable church—corrupt it.

So, he took the truth of God and found agents to deny it, distort it, and debase it. He would alter a word here, snip out a bit there, and add something to that. He attacked the Word of God, the Son of God, and the Spirit of God. At Colosse, he attacked the deity of Christ first. Then came the additions—intellectualism, ritualism, legalism, mysticism, and asceticism. It made the head of poor Epaphras, pastor of the church, swim. He was soon out of his depth. Raw paganism was one thing; obsolete Judaism was another. Those were simple errors. Everything was black and white when it came to those kind of attacks. But the error that had invaded Colosse was too deep, too subtle for him.

Now Paul was in Rome, so Epaphras, faithful pastor and shepherd that he was, decided to head there. He would talk to Paul. It was dangerous, of course, to visit a prisoner in Rome, but what was danger? What he was battling was diabolical. Only one man was intellectual enough and spiritual enough to unravel and refute the tangled web of truth and error that was snaring the simple souls whom Epaphras was seeking to shepherd for Christ.

So off to Rome he went. And, sure enough, Paul was willing, able, and eager to help. He seized his pen and went to work. To Satan's horror, what resulted was another divinely inspired, God-breathed, inerrant, flawless, living, powerful epistle to be added to the Word of God.

That was Satan's biggest blunder. He threw everything he had at the infant church by way of error and deceit. He forgot that God still had His apostles on earth, able to write Scripture, expound truth, and expose error by direct revelation and inspiration of the Holy Spirit! So every possible distortion that Satan could dream up has been answered apostolically! He has no new ideas! All he can do now is rehash and juggle the same bankrupt lies and hope that people don't know their Bibles well enough to see through them.

Exploring
COLOSSIANS

Outline

Part 1: Introduction (1:1–14)
  A. Paul's passion for people (1:1–2)
  B. Paul's passion for prayer (1:3)
  C. Paul's passion for principle (1:4–5)
  D. Paul's passion for progress (1:6)
  E. Paul's passion for preachers (1:7–8)
  F. Paul's passion for perspective (1:9–14)
      1. His petition (1:9–11)
      2. His praise (1:12–14)

Part 2: The Truth About the Christ (1:15–29)
  A. The deity of Christ (1:15–19)
      1. The person of God revealed (1:15)
      2. The power of God revealed (1:16–17)
      3. The purposes of God revealed (1:18–19)
  B. The death of Christ (1:20–22)
  C. The demands of Christ (1:23–29)

Part 3: The Truth About the Cult (2:1–23)
  A. Experiencing the truth (2:1–7)
  B. Exposing the lie (2:8–23)
      1. Secular reasoning (2:8–10)
      2. Sundry rituals (2:11–17)
      3. Special revelations (2:18–19)
      4. Stricter rules (2:20–23)

Introduction

Colossians 1:1–14

     c. For spiritual victory (1:11)
       (1) Its secret (1:11a)
       (2) Its scope (1:11b)
  2. His praise (1:12–14)
    a. To God for remaking us (1:12)
    b. To God for rescuing us (1:13)
     (1) Jesus as savior (1:13a)
     (2) Jesus as sovereign (1:13b)
    c. To God for redeeming us (1:14)
     (1) The price that was paid (1:14a)
     (2) The pardon that was procured (1:14b)

I. INTRODUCTION (1:1–14)

Colosse was a small market town in Asia Minor (modern Turkey) located about one hundred miles east of Ephesus. It was situated on the south bank of the Wolf River (the Lycus), a tributary of the Maeander. The town was located at the mouth of a narrow glen. To the south stood Mount Cadmus (called "Father of Mountains" by the Turks). The sister cities of Laodicea and Hierapolis were in the same valley, each about a day's journey from Colosse. Both were larger and more important although Colosse had known its day of glory. The main road from Ephesus to the Euphrates ran through the town. It had known the tramp of the armies of the mighty Xerxes and the younger Cyrus. In apostolic times, it had ceased to be a town of much importance. Its population was a mix of Phrygians, Greeks, and Jews.

The whole area bore the scars of past volcanic activity. Within several years of the writing of this letter, Colosse was destroyed by an earthquake. It was already only a footnote on the page of history. Probably we should never have heard of the place if Paul had not addressed this immortal letter to the church within its gates. As brief as it is, this letter—little more, really, than a mere memo—ranks among the giants. No one ever wrote greater or grander things about the Lord Jesus than Paul does in this epistle. Colossians 1:15–17 ranks alongside Philippians 2:5–11, Hebrews 1:1–14, and John 1:13–14.

  A. Paul's passion for people (1:1–2)
    1. As a minister of the faith (1:1a)

Paul, an apostle of Jesus Christ by the will of God.

Paul was a latecomer to the apostolic circle. He first saw the risen Christ for himself on the Damascus Road (Acts 9:1–16), and he never forgot the blinding vision given to him there. Peter, James, and John had known the human Jesus in the days when He sojourned on this little island planet in space. Paul knew Him only as "the Lord from heaven" (1 Cor. 15:47). That view of Him colored all of Paul's thoughts of Christ. Long before Epaphras showed up with his tale of woe, Paul had known the Lord as "the most high God, possessor of heaven and earth," just as Abraham had (Gen. 14:18–20), and as the Creator of the universe, just as David had (Ps. 19:1–6).

Paul was an apostle, made a member of that unique and exclusive order by "the ordination of the nail-pierced hands." His particular calling was to be the apostle to the Gentiles. As such, he had a passion for people everywhere. The whole world was his parish, lost souls in all lands were his special charge, and the church of God was his dear love.

Paul begins by reminding the Colossian believers of his own high rank. He had not founded their church directly, although doubtless all of the churches of Asia were the ultimate fruit of his ministry at Ephesus. One of the leading brothers in the Colossian church was Philemon, a wealthy man, and one of Paul's own converts. Possibly there were others. Just the same, Paul was about to contradict forcefully the false teaching that was taking root in this church, so he began by reminding the Colossians of who and what he was—"Paul, an apostle of Jesus Christ by the will of God."

He certainly was not an apostle by the will of Peter or John; still less of James, the presiding elder of the Jerusalem church, who would have loved to rein Paul in. Because Paul was an apostle "by the will of God," he was independent of men. No one could promote him or demote him. The proof of his calling was in the long string of churches founded by him and his converts, which stretched all of the way from Illyricum (modern Yugoslavia) to Lystra and Derbe in Galatia.

It was imperative that the Colossians understand that Paul was writing to them in his official capacity and that they had better pay heed to his words because he not only had the position of an apostle but also the power of an apostle—and that included the power to smite, as Elymas the sorcerer discovered (Acts 13:4–12). Nor did he need to be present to put forth that power. He had warned the Corinthians about that (1 Cor. 5:1–5). He put the Colossians on notice that they would be foolish to take his letter lightly.

2. As a member of the family (1:1b–2)
    a. The brotherhood of Christians (1:1b)

Paul . . . and Timotheus our brother, to the saints and faithful
brethren in Christ which are at Colosse.

Paul was "a people person." He loved people, longed to see them saved, and worked tirelessly to promote their spiritual welfare. Paul likely had been both disinherited and disowned by his family for his Christian faith (Phil. 3:8). No matter! He had another family because all of God's people were his brothers and sisters. Every time he led someone to faith in Christ, he enlarged the size of his family! He loved them all, wrote to them, prayed for them, and visited them.

Thus, Timothy is "our brother." Where else in all of the world can we find a family like it? The world, with its clubs, lodges, and fraternities, has nothing that remotely resembles the family of God. Prince or pauper, banker or beggar, it makes no difference. There is a bond in Christ that is greater than any brotherhood forged by men.

When I was in the British Army in Palestine, I found myself stationed on Haifa docks. I arrived at the base in the middle of the week, a total stranger in a foreign land. On Sunday, I left the camp in the morning to see if I could find a fellowship of believers. I wandered up the slope of Mount Carmel until my eye caught sight of a small building just down a side road. It bore a small sign that read "Gospel Hall." I knew what that meant. It was a gathering of believers, commonly known as "Plymouth Brethren." I had been raised among them. I knew all about them. I had come home!

I did not arrive back on the base until late that night. Some of the men in the barracks wanted to know where I had been all day.

"I've been to church."

"At church? All day?"

"Well, no, not at church all day. I had lunch in the home of a Palestinian Arab and spent most of the day with him and his unmarried sisters and widowed mother. I had supper in the home of a Russian Jew, and after the evening service at the church, I was invited to the home of a British civil servant who holds a high position in the Palestine Railway."

The men were incredulous.

"How long have you been in this country?"

"About six or seven days."

"Are you telling us the truth?"

"Yes. You can come with me next Sunday if you like."

The men continued to be incredulous. One of the men finally said, "That must be some kind of a lodge you belong to!"

It was no lodge. It was the family of God.

I remained in Haifa for nearly two years, and every Sunday was the same story of love, generosity, and open-handed hospitality. Links of love and fellowship were forged that lasted for many years.

So Paul exulted in the brotherhood of Christians. It was a truth to be tested to the utmost at Colosse, where many people were succumbing to the persuasive teachings of a cult. Families would be split over the issues. Church fellowship would be put to the test.

"Paul *and* Timotheus." That is how Paul expressed his appreciation for the brotherhood of Christians. Paul was putting his name to a letter that would outlast all of the suns and stars of space. He was signing a "God-breathed" epistle, one of only twenty-one such letters ever to be written. Here was a writing destined to become part of the living Word of the living God, an instrument to bring light and life to millions of people for thousands of years, a document to outlast empires, and a letter that will be of absorbing interest to God's people in all of the ages of eternities yet to be. And what does Paul do? He summons his young convert and colleague. He hands him his pen. He says, "Here you are, Timothy. Sign here. Now! Your name is linked with mine forever and wherever this letter will be read." That was brotherly love. "Paul *and* Timotheus." Such was Paul's love for people! "Timotheus, our brother." Such is the family of God!

b. The body of Christ (1:2a–d)
  (1) The family description (1:2a–c)
    (a) Who we are (1:2a)

To the saints and faithful brethren in Christ.

That is who we are! We are saints. We need to emancipate that word *saints* from the false concepts which have clung to it as a result of centuries of false teaching. A "saint" in the New Testament is not some person who has been canonized by the Roman Catholic Church, immortalized in a stained glass window, and whose relics are worshiped and supposed to perform miracles. A saint is simply any sinner who is saved by grace. The word used is *hagios.* Essentially, the word means "separated." Among the Greeks, it carried the idea of being dedicated to the gods. In the New Testament, it has to do with being consecrated to God. In the plural, it is used of believers. It is one of those universal words by which God's people are designated in the New Testament—we are believers, brethren, disciples, Christians, and saints. The idea of holiness clings to the word *hagios,* but we are rendered holy, not because of our own merit, but because, as believers, we are washed in the blood of Christ, indwelt by the Holy Spirit, and made recipients of the imputed righteousness of Christ.

How different from Rome's way of making saints! The process is both involved and protracted. The prospective saint must set the stage during his lifetime by living a life of conspicuous virtue or extraordinary asceticism so that over the span of the ages legends can grow up about his or her name. It helps the process considerably if miracles can be attached to the person's reputation or if the candidate for sainthood founded a monastery or died as a martyr. The prospective saint, in any case, must die because no one can be canonized by Rome during his own lifetime.

Upon death, according to Catholic dogma, the saint-to-be goes to purgatory to pay for the residue of his sins. When the mythical fires of purgatory have had sufficient time to do their work, the candidate for sainthood can be raised to the ranks of the beatified. He (or she) is not yet a saint, but progress has been made.

Next, the candidate for sainthood must posthumously perform at least two verifiable miracles, such as will satisfy the ecclesiastical authorities. A special court of enquiry is then convened and lengthy investigations conducted. Traditionally, these inquiries can last several hundred years. Enough time must elapse for a mystical halo to gather around the candidate's name. Once enough people are convinced, the prospective saint is well on the way.

At this point, the Pope must convene a special meeting of the church at which, after due ceremony, the candidate is formally recognized as a saint. The faithful can now pray to him—which, of course, makes the unwarranted and wholly unscriptural assumption that the dead man (or woman) has many of the exclusive attributes of God. It assumes that this "saint" is omniscient and omnipresent, that he (or she) can hear and unravel the prayers and petitions of thousands of people, in all parts of the world, offered in a babel of tongues, all praying to him at once. The Bible knows of no such "saints."

Down through the centuries, Rome accumulated some twenty-five hundred of these canonized saints. They have been duly venerated and petitioned, more or less faithfully, by the devout. *Time* magazine said that there are currently about a thousand men and women on the road to sainthood, all at various stages of spiritual evolution.[1]

About the same time as the *Time* article, however, much to the confusion of many of the faithful, the Vatican decided to purge the ranks of the saints. Accordingly, some saints were deposed although they had been revered for centuries. Among the old faithfuls now ignominiously demoted (and presumably returned to the purgatorial fires) was the popular St. Christopher, patron saint of travelers, whose image was often displayed by Catholics on the dashboards of cars, and St. Valentine, patron saint of lovers. One wonders about the deluded millions of people who over the centuries have prayed earnestly to these "saints" and their fellow unfortunates who have been thus summarily banished from the heights.

God, by contrast, makes saints of us all the moment we accept His Son as Savior! Moreover, our sainthood is not based on any good works that we may have done but on the ineffable righteousness of Christ. No mythical purgatorial fires are needed to burn out the remaining dross still clinging to us in the hour of death. The blood of Christ cleanses us from *all* sin.

(b) What we are (1:2b)

To the . . . faithful brethren in Christ.

That is what we are—"faithful brethren." Paul introduces us to two such worthies in this epistle—Epaphras and Onesimus—both of whom he calls "faithful."

The dictionary gives some interesting definitions of the word *faithful*. It means to be "steadfast in affection or allegiance," to be "full of faith," to be loyal, to be "firm in adherence to promises, or in the discharge of duty." It means "to be true to the original." Each of these definitions can be applied to the believer. The Greek word that Paul uses is *pistos,* which carries the idea of being trustworthy and reliable.

Of all of the definitions and shades of meaning implied by the expression

---

1. "The Long Road to Sainthood," *Time,* 7 July 1980, 42, 43.

"*faithful* brethren," surely the one that has the most appeal is "true to the original." We are to be genuine reproductions of Christ.

(c) Where we are (1:2c)

To the saints . . . in Christ which are at Colosse.

What a challenging statement! Every believer has two addresses and lives in two places at the same time! He is "at Colosse" (or Chicago, or Cairo, or Calcutta, as the case may be) and he is "in Christ." The two locations, one earthly and the other heavenly, must always be kept in proper balance.

These particular believers were "at Colosse," a run-down, Greco-Asiatic town of little or no real importance. They were at home in its streets and bazaars. They were familiar with its surroundings and scenery. They knew all about its river and the nearby farms. They knew about the limestone caverns and the nearby tourist attraction where the Wolf River plunged underground into a natural tunnel to emerge farther downstream just before joining the Maeander. They were "at Colosse," with its local politics, its pagan vices, its pervading parochialism, its age-old idolatries, and its drabness and decay. They were "at Colosse," where the local church was of recent growth, a little community of believers dominated by a few familiar persons—people such as Epaphras; Philemon, his wife, Apphia, and his son, Archippus; along with the recent addition of the runaway slave Onesimus. They were "at Colosse," a place which would become famous throughout the world and for the rest of time because the little church there was torn by schism.

But they were also "in Christ," to use one of Paul's favorite expressions. They were ensphered in Christ, wrapped up in Him to enjoy all of the riches and resources of the Godhead which are His. Nobody could rob them of that. They would go about their business and they would visit relatives, friends, neighbors. They would suffer the snubs and sneers of some people. Their children went to school in Colosse. They kept house at Colosse, visited the doctor and did their shopping at Colosse. And all of the time they were "in Christ." Some of them, in particular, carried the fragrance of Christ with them everywhere they went. What a challenge it was for Colosse that these people, being "at Colosse," were also "in Christ"!

But we must keep this truth, as all truth, in proper balance. Some people are so taken up with being "in Christ" that they forget that they are also "at Colosse."

Such people become preoccupied with being "in Christ" and become mystics, impractical, remote, and "so heavenly minded as to be of no earthly use." Others are so preoccupied with being "at Colosse" that they forget that they are "in Christ." They become materialists, worldly, and carnal, so taken up with work, or sports, or family as to have little time left for the work of God.

(2) The family doxology (1:2d)

Grace be unto you, and peace, from God our Father and the Lord
Jesus Christ.

Here begins a typical Pauline sentence! Paul often puts such sentences together. They are long and involved with clause flowing into clause and thought doubling back on thought. Such sentences are as *distinctively* Pauline as his signature. They remind us of the dual nature of divine inspiration. It is true that "holy men of God spake." Their words and sentences were theirs, reflecting their own personalities, thoughts, and backgrounds. But they spoke "as they were *moved* [borne along] by the Holy Ghost" (2 Peter 1:21). Peter's style is different from John's. Paul's style is distinctively his—indeed, he could change styles, depending on whether he was writing a letter or a dissertation, whether he was reminding or rebuking. Nevertheless, the Holy Spirit so controlled what was written that the very words used by the writers were "God breathed" (2 Tim. 3:16). The mystery of this intermingling of the human and the divine in inspiration is similar to the similar mingling of the human and the divine in the incarnation.

"Grace!" "Peace!" Thus, the early believers wedded the Greek form of greeting (Hail!") with the Jewish form of greeting ("Peace!") to make the Christian form of greeting—a reminder that the "middle wall of partition" between Gentile and Jew had been abolished in Christ (Eph. 2:14). Grace is the root from which salvation springs; peace is the fruit that salvation brings.

This grace and this peace come from "God our Father." Contrary to popular belief, God is not the Father of all men. He is the Father of all them that believe, of those who are born into His family by the regenerating work of the Holy Spirit (John 3:3; 1:11–13). The Father bestows His own grace and peace upon His own.

The King James text includes the words *and the Lord Jesus Christ.* Some people dispute the inclusion of this phrase here. However, it is included in the greeting in the companion epistle to the Ephesians (Eph. 1:2), so it is not out of place here. It is another of those incidental New Testament assumptions, taken for granted by its authors, of the deity of Christ. So in his opening statement, Paul puts an opening warning shot across the bows of his Gnostic opponents in Colosse.

So, then, in his opening greeting Paul reveals his passion for people, both as a minister of the faith and as a member of the family. He affectionately draws God's people into the circle of his love, into the certainty of sainthood, into the circumference of fidelity, and into the center of God's blessing.

    B.   Paul's passion for prayer (1:3)
        1. How thankfully he prayed (1:3a)

> *We give thanks to God and the Father of our Lord Jesus Christ,*
> *praying always for you.*

Paul never stopped praying. Probably the only One who prayed more than Paul was the Lord Himself. How that should speak to our own careless, prayerless ways! If the Son of God needed to pray, and if the great apostle needed to pray, how much more do we! It was Paul's great passion for people that gave him such a corresponding passion for prayer. No sooner did Paul think of Titus on his way to Corinth, perhaps, or of Phebe on her way to Rome, or of James back there in Jerusalem, or of Demas heading off for Thessalonica in a backslidden condition, or of Tychicus making his way to Ephesus, than he prayed for them. At the time he penned these words, he was under house arrest at Rome and chained to a Roman soldier. That could not stop him from praying. The moment he thought of Lydia, or the little slave girl, or the jailer back there at Philippi, he prayed for them. The instant he thought of Philemon back there in Colosse and of Onesimus, letter in hand, heading home to meet his master, he prayed for him. That was Paul's way. He prayed without ceasing as surely as he told us to do the same (1 Thess. 5:17; Rom. 1:9).

Nor did Paul's prayers cease at the circumference of the vast circle of those whom he knew personally or those whom he knew only by name. Most of us have a list of people who command some kind of place in our prayers. The list, as likely as not, contains the names of family and friends, a neighbor or two, some fellow Christians, and some missionaries we have met. We may extend it to include people mentioned in prayer letters that come flooding in. Often, these are people in foreign lands, people with unpronounceable names and whose circumstances it takes an effort to visualize. We do our best, but it is uphill work.

Paul took it all in stride. As far as we know, Colosse had never been part of his itinerary. Most of the believers there were people whom he had never met. Some of their names had doubtless been brought to his attention by Epaphras. Yet, Paul could tell them that he prayed for them—all of the time. What a rebuke to us all!

The point that comes through here is Paul's thanksgiving for every blood-bought Christian at Colosse. He was genuinely grateful to God for every one of them. Had they been his own next of kin, he could not have cared for them more. They were the salt of the earth, the light of the world, the saints of the Most High, and the aristocracy of the universe. He thanked God for them.

Little does this world know what it owes to the presence in its midst of God's dear people. Take Sodom, for instance. Its perversions had reached the point where God had determined to pour out His wrath upon it. But down there in that polluted city, vexing his righteous soul from day to day because of the foul lifestyle of the wicked, lived a believer. His name was Lot. Before He acted in judgment, God stirred up Abraham to pray for Lot. Then He sent two angels to warn him and, indeed, in the end, practically to drag him out of the evil place. "This fellow!" That was the contemptuous epitaph of the Sodomites for the one believing man in their midst. They were enraged to think that as one of the city-state's officials he could possibly introduce legislation that might curb the open practice of their vile lusts. Even his sons-in-law, native-born citizens of Sodom, thought that Lot was crazy when he came to warn them that their doom was upon them. Yet, it was Lot and Lot alone who stood between the people of Sodom and the impending judgment of God. The angel sent by God to call down fire and brimstone on Sodom, in urging Lot to make good his escape, declared, "Haste thee, escape thither; for I cannot do any thing till thou be come thither" (Gen. 19:22).

So Paul thanked God for His people. All too often, we gossip about them, ignore them, or slight them. Paul prayed for them. He knew the great value to God of even the feeblest believer. It was better for Sodom to have a backslidden believer like Lot in its midst than no believer at all. The same is true today. God cannot and will not pour out His wrath upon this world until He has raptured His church. To men, the church often seems to be feeble enough, divided enough, and useless enough. To God, it is infinitely precious. As long as the church is here, the world is safe from the end-time judgments to come.

2. How thoughtfully he prayed (1:3b)

We give thanks to God and the Father of our Lord Jesus Christ.

The emphasis here is on the fact that God, our God, is none other than the Father of the Lord Jesus. Throughout His earthly pilgrimage, the Lord Jesus acknowledged God to be His Father and Himself to be God's Son. The very first recorded words that fell from His lips spoke of God's being His Father: "wist ye not that I must be about my Father's business?" (Luke 2:49). The last thing that He said to His disciples before returning home to heaven had to do with "the promise of the Father" and with those mysterious "times and seasons" that "the Father hath put in his own power" (Acts 1:4, 7). The gospel particularly reveals the coeternal, coequal relationship that existed between the Father and the Son.

Our prayers can be addressed equally to the Father and the Son—another way of affirming the deity of Christ. Only *God* can hear and answer prayer, for only God has the necessary attributes of omniscience, omnipresence, and omnipotence to respond to millions of prayers offered in countless tongues daily, amid the onward march of events and from countless locations and dealing with myriad situations.

We note, too, that Paul prayed to "the Father" of our Lord Jesus Christ, not to His mother, another popular Romish error. Paul would have us know that we can approach both God the Father and God the Son directly, without the need of an intermediary, such as Mary, a saint, or an angel.

Equally important here is the word *our*—*our* Lord Jesus Christ. The cultists at Colosse had a "Christ," but their Christ was not *our* Christ. Their Christ was some mythical Demiurge, some intermediary angelic being.

Similarly, all of the cults today have a Christ, but in each case, he is not "our Lord Jesus Christ." One cult has a Christ who was a polygamist, secretly married to Martha and Mary at the wedding at Cana of Galilee. That is certainly not *our* Lord Jesus Christ. Another cult has a Christ who is only "a" god, a Christ who is not God the Son, the second person of the Godhead, but who is, so they say, none other than Michael the archangel. Their Christ did not rise bodily from the grave, but his body was dissolved into gas. That is not *our* Lord Jesus Christ.

Our Lord Jesus Christ is God over all, blessed for evermore, eternal, uncreated, self-existing, Creator of the universe. Our Lord Jesus Christ stepped out of eternity into time to be born of the Virgin Mary, conceived of the Holy Ghost, to be both God and man. Our Lord Jesus Christ "went about doing good." He spoke infallibly and inerrantly, as no man ever spoke. He walked upon the waves and stilled the storm. He fed the hungry multitudes with a little lad's lunch and turned water into wine. He cleansed the leper and healed the sick. He cast out evil spirits and raised the dead. Our Lord Jesus Christ died an atoning death. He was buried. He rose again in triumph and ascended bodily into heaven. He is now seated in Glory at the right hand of the Majesty on high, where He ministers as our Advocate with the Father and as our great, high Priest. Our Lord Jesus Christ is coming back, first to rapture the church and then to rule the world. Praise God for "our Lord Jesus Christ"!

3. How thoroughly he prayed (1:3c)

Praying always for you. . . .

Always! What a remarkable statement! What a way to pray! Paul knew how to break through the opposing ranks of principalities and powers, of wicked spirits in high places, and of the rulers of this world's darkness. He knew how to put to flight all of those diabolical, spiritual forces ranged against us and how to prevail in prayer.

Paul knew how to come boldly into the Holiest by the blood of Jesus. He knew how to pray, how to present before the throne the names and needs of all of those in whose welfare he had an interest as one of the Lord's undershepherds.

How did he manage to get through the prodigious prayer lists that he must have compiled? Look at him! There he goes on one of his interminable journeys. He is tramping up hill and down dale, mile after mile, day after day. How does he fill the endless hours? He prays! Or there he goes on another of his voyages by sea. He will be shut up on that little ship for weeks on end. What will he do? He will pray! No idle gossip for him, no time to spare for games. There's too much for which to pray. Or here he is, imprisoned—at Caesarea, at Philippi, or at Rome. The days are long. He cannot go anywhere. At times, perhaps, he cannot sleep. What does he do? Does he toss and turn; does he fret and fume? No indeed! He seizes the golden moments, one by one, as they pass him by; he loads each one down with a prayer. That, surely, was how he did it—"praying always for you," he says. "Constantly praying for you" is another way to put it.

C. Paul's passion for principle (1:4–5)
   1. Saving faith (1:4a)

We give thanks . . . Since we heard of your faith in Christ Jesus.

Faith! Hope! Love! The three great cardinals of Christianity as seen by Paul, comparable to John's great words—love, light, life.

The Christian message revolves without apology around certain great truths. We proclaim these truths in the face of all unbelief because they are true regardless of whether people believe them. Truth is truth no matter how strident, organized, and persistent the denial. The world remains round no matter who says that it is flat. The earth still revolves around the sun no matter how loudly Pope Urban VIII proclaimed "ex cathedra" and hence infallibly (!) that it does not.

One of the cardinal doctrines of the church is the doctrine of salvation by faith. In his opening remarks to the Colossians, Paul mentions their "faith in Christ Jesus" because the cultists were introducing false teaching about this. The important thing about the believer's faith is that it is "faith in Christ Jesus." The amount of faith to begin with is unimportant—faith as a grain of mustard seed is all God looks for. What is important is the object of our faith. Faith has a tendency to grow as we find out that the object of our faith is sound.

Gold from black sand! That was what the brochure said. It was convincing enough. The place was a remote region in the Canadian Northwest. Enough technical details were given to make the brochures sound convincing, something much more real than the alchemy of the Middle Ages, which promised gold from iron. And the salesman, well, he was the one who made it credible. He was known around town. He had been on the mission field, had a good character, and was obviously sold on it. It was a sure thing—people could expect to double, even quadruple, their investments. People took out their life savings and put them into the scheme. The whole thing turned out to be a fraud, however, and the salesman either a scoundrel or a dupe. Those who invested in the scheme lost every penny. They had faith. But it was misplaced.

Faith in the wrong person or the wrong thing is worse than no faith at all. A person may put his faith in a quack doctor or a dubious cure. He will pay dearly for it in the end. There is more hope for a doubting Thomas than a duped Judas.

We all have faith, and we exercise it every day. We have faith in the doctor who diagnoses our ailment. We have faith in the druggist who makes up the prescription. We have faith in the bank where we deposit our hard-earned pay. We exercise faith in the architect and the builder when we enter a house. We demonstrate faith in the engineer when we cross over a bridge. We rarely think about it in those terms. Faith is such an everyday, commonplace part of our lives.

What is it that transforms our ordinary, mundane, simple faith—everyday faith—into *saving* faith? Its object! Simple faith becomes saving faith when it becomes "faith in Christ Jesus." There is nothing mysterious or mystical about it at all. Faith in *Him* is faith that saves for the simple reason that He is the Savior. Some people are troubled because they do not have enough faith or because they do not feel anything when they put their trust in Christ. That is usually because they are putting their faith in their faith, or they are putting their faith in their feelings. Paul commends the Colossians because of their faith in Christ.

2. Supernatural love (1:4b)

We heard of . . . the love which ye have to all the saints.

Love for all saints! That includes love for old Brother Backbiter and for quarrelsome Sister Axegrinder and garrulous Brother Tongueswagger and for weak Sister Mudwallower! As someone has said:

> To dwell above, with saints above,
>   That will indeed be glory;
> To dwell below, with saints we know,
>   Well, that's another story!

It is a great thing to have love for all of God's people. The Lord Jesus loved everybody. He loved Pilate as much as he loved Peter. He loved His brother James as much as He loved His disciple James. He loved Malchus as much as He loved Matthew. He loved Bartimaeus and Barabbas as much as He loved Bartholomew. He loved Saul as much as He loved Simon. He loved Nicodemus as much as He loved Nathanael. He loved Judas as much as He loved John. He loved Caiaphas as much as He loved Cornelius. He loved everybody.

Paul was made in much the same mold. He loved the people of God. He loved dour James, "old camel knees" as he was called, the presiding elder of the semihostile Jerusalem church, as much as he loved Timothy, his young convert and colleague. He loved poor lost King Agrippa as much as he loved his dear doctor Luke. He loved Festus and Felix as much as he loved Aquila and Priscilla, his companions on the mission field.

So Paul was impressed and pleased by the report that he had received of the *agapē* love that the Colossian Christians had one for another in their small corner of the world.

3. Sustaining hope (1:5)

For the hope which is laid up [apokeimai, "treasured up"] for you in heaven, whereof ye heard before in the word of truth of the gospel.

Hope! The order is important here—first faith, then love, and then hope. Faith comes first, notwithstanding Paul's declaration elsewhere that "the greatest of these is love" (1 Cor. 13:13). Faith has to do with the *content* of salvation. Faith is "in Christ Jesus." Faith has to do with the bedrock certainties of salvation purchased for us at Calvary at infinite cost and made available to us in Christ. Faith is what links us to the Word of God, to the work of Christ, and to the witness of the Spirit.

Love comes next. Love has to do with the *character* of our salvation. Love is what God is. Love became incarnate in Christ. The first of the fruits of the Spirit is love. Truth must be held in love. Love never fails.

When J. G. Paton applied to the British government for permission to go to the New Hebrides islands to convert the cannibals to Christ, he was at first denied. Finally one of the lords of the British Admiralty relented. He suggested that Paton be allowed to go although the islanders were reputed to be the most savage people on the face of the earth. "Perhaps," said the naval spokesman, "the cannibals will eat him. That will give us an excuse to blow their islands out of the sea." Paton laughed. He said that he had some gunpowder of his own he would like to try first. He was referring to Calvary love. How gloriously effective that "gunpowder" proved to be is one of the great stories of the missionary enterprise of the Christian church.

Hope comes last. Hope has to do with the *consummation* of our salvation. We tend to discount hope. If we ask a person, "Are you saved?" we are not much enthused if he says, "I hope so." The world's hope is much in that vein. A person receives word that he has incurable cancer or that he has just lost his job. A well-meaning friend assures him, "Everything's going to be alright." Who says so? Often that is just an optimistic statement designed to make the other person feel better. It might have no basis in fact at all. The words are often meaningless.

Christian hope is not like that. It is solid and substantial because it is embedded in eternal truth. Our hope is treasured up in heaven. Hope looks ahead. Hope has to do with the future, and what a glorious future it is! Our hope is guaranteed by God Himself in His infallible Word. The Rapture itself, toward which we look with eager anticipation, is described as our "blessed hope" (Titus 2:13).

There are instances where the word *hope* comes into its own, taking precedence over faith or belief. Here, for instance, is a little boy who has behaved badly. His mother says, "I shall tell your father what you said the moment he gets home. He will deal with you." You might ask that little boy, "Do you think that your father will spank you when he gets home?" He might say, "I *believe* he will." He is not likely to say, "I *hope* he will." His future is not very bright. Hope, by its nature, deals with the future, but with a happy future. Christian hope looks forward with eager anticipation to what is stored up for us in heaven.

Paul, then, has a passion for principle—for the faith principle, the love principle, and the hope principle—because our salvation embraces all three principles. And all three were under attack at Colosse.

D. Paul's passion for progress (1:6)
   1. He wanted the gospel to take root globally (1:6a)

. . . the gospel; which is come unto you, as it is in all the world.

Paul longed with all of his heart to see the gospel take root worldwide. He was born a *Jew*, was raised in a *Greek* city, and was a *Roman* citizen. Paul knew that neither Jewish light, nor Greek logic, nor Roman law could meet the needs of the human heart. Only the gospel can do that.

And the gospel had arrived at Colosse. More! It was rapidly taking root "in all the world" as well. The book of Acts tells only a tithe of the story. The Scriptures are silent as to the eastward march of the gospel to Babylon, beyond the Euphrates, and on to India and the Far East—although it is likely that Peter went to Babylon (1 Peter 5:13) and that Thomas went to India. Paul had his sights set on Spain.

Some years before he wrote this Colossian letter, he had told the Romans that he himself had "fully preached the gospel of Christ" all the way from Jerusalem to Illyricum (modern Yugoslavia)—a wide swath of some fifteen hundred miles. The gospel had come to the Colossians the same way it had found its way to Rome—quite independently of Paul or the other apostles. From Rome, roads led in all directions, from the golden milestone in the Forum to the ends of the Roman world. The gospel was spreading into Africa, Asia, and Europe. It was on the march.

On the banks of the Thames in London, across from the Houses of Parliament, is a famous statue. It was made when Britain's empire embraced a quarter of the world. The statue was carved to honor the memory of the British Queen Boadicea. When Julius Caesar landed his legions on the shores of Britain, they were met by bands of fanatical Britons, determined to fight for their lives and homes. One of these bold island defenders was this intrepid British queen. She failed to save her land from Caesar's more disciplined troops, but the memory of her wild charges and her great war chariot survived. So her statue stands today in the heart of London. Boadicea herself is depicted whipping her horses as her chariot rushes on. Her tribute is blazoned into the motto that is part of the statue: "Regions Caesar never knew thy posterity shall sway."

The same could have been said of Paul and the early church. Paul was in Rome not long after Caesar's legions had been challenged by the British queen. The gospel had invaded Rome. It was expanding rapidly in all directions. Regions that Caesar never knew, continents of which Paul had never dreamed, would hear the Word and come beneath its sway.

Paul had no doubt at all about the outcome. The Great Commission was "to all the world" and "to the uttermost parts of the earth." The witness of the Spirit could certainly be no less widespread than the witness of the *stars,* of which we are told "their sound went into all the earth" (Rom. 10:18). The Holy Spirit is "the Lord of the harvest." So Paul, true prophet that he was, could daringly use the present tense: "their sound is come unto you as it is in all the world," heedless of the fact that the process of global evangelism was as yet in its infancy. It was as good as done! Certainly, when Paul wrote, the world that he knew was already being invaded on all fronts, and bold evangelists were targeting "the regions beyond."

The early church was a missionary church. Almost every book in the New Testament was written by a foreign missionary. Every epistle in the New Testament addressed to an individual was addressed to the convert of a foreign missionary. Every epistle addressed to a church was addressed to a foreign mission church. All of the apostles, except one, became a missionary; the one who didn't become a missionary became a traitor. The disciples were first called "Christians" in a foreign land.

No wonder Paul had no doubts about the outcome! The Devil is afraid of the church. He mobilized the might of Rome itself to fight it only to discover that the more he persecuted it, the more it spread. Paul knew that from personal experience. In his unconverted days, he had spearheaded the attack upon the fledgling Jerusalem church, stirring up "a great persecution against the church which was at Jerusalem." The effort had been counterproductive. The believers "were all scattered abroad," and they "went every where preaching the word" (Acts 8:1–4). No indeed! Paul had no doubts that the gospel would reach into the entire world.

2. He wanted the gospel to bear fruit locally (1:6b)

> . . . the gospel; which . . . bringeth forth fruit, as it doth also in you, since the day ye heard of it, and knew the grace of God in truth.

The gospel bears fruit. It changes lives. Those whose lives have been changed tell others. And so it spreads.

But so does Satan's counterfeit gospel. He was already busy at Colosse, planting his tares among the wheat. He had designs on the whole harvest field. Paul had battled error before, in Galatia, for example. Asia Minor (modern Turkey), where Colosse was located, had been the scene of some of Paul's most successful gospel campaigns. By the end of the first century, it was the brightest spot on earth for gospel testimony. When John wrote the Apocalypse, however, some few decades later, and sent those letters from heaven to the seven churches (Rev. 1–3), the decline had already begun. Today, the false religion of Islam holds sway throughout the region.

Paul viewed the situation in Colosse with concern. Colosse was only a little city and the church there was only a little church, but it had a big problem. Satan's game plan at Colosse was not to persecute the church but to pervert its doctrine.

Paul, in prison, did what he could. Indeed, he did all that a mortal man with a flaming passion and clear vision and resolute determination, and with the Holy Spirit to guide him, could do. He seized his pen. And a pen in the hand of an inspired apostle was a weapon to make Satan himself turn tail. Paul did not want to see the gospel checked, even in a small backwoods market town like Colosse. He wanted it to take even deeper root and extend its fruit-bearing boughs over the wall and spread them out near and far. He would deal with the cult in a moment. But first he would encourage "the saints and faithful brethren" not to get sidetracked. Fruit bearing must go on.

E. Paul's passion for preachers (1:7–8)
    1. Epaphras, a fruitful messenger (1:7a)

As ye also learned of Epaphras. . . .

Paul was very good at encouraging other preachers. He scorned all of that petty jealousy that afflicts so many people who are engaged in the Lord's work. It did not bother Paul that Peter was more admired in some places than he was, or that some people considered Apollos to be a much more eloquent preacher than he. "Bless the man!" Paul would say. "Thank God for him. I wish the church had more like him."

Speaking of the Colossians and their fruit bearing seems to have turned Paul's thoughts to Epaphras. The Colossians, it would seem, had heard the gospel from him. "As ye also learned of Epaphras," Paul says. It was a great joy to Paul to see the Lord of the harvest thrusting out laborers into the harvest. Paul had done enough pioneering missionary work to be able to appreciate what Epaphras had accomplished in Colosse. Invading a pagan city with the gospel was both a difficult and a dangerous task. Paul could recall what he had faced himself on various pioneering missions. He had been mocked at Lystra, maligned at Ephesus, and mocked at Athens, and the day would come when he would be murdered at Rome. Indeed, even as he wrote to the Colossians, he knew enough of Nero's uncertain temper to know he could be martyred at any time. Pioneering with the gospel was man's work. Paul had nothing but praise and respect for men such as Epaphras who would dare to plow and plant a pagan field for God. Epaphras had been "a faithful messenger." Their conversion and their congregation was proof of it.

2. Epaphras, a fellow missionary (1:7b)

Epaphras our dear fellowservant. . . .

The word used means "fellow slave." The apostle associates Epaphras with himself, Paul, the great apostle to the Gentiles and, thus, endorses the work that this brother had done as evangelist, pastor, and teacher to the Colossian church. He, Paul, might be a chosen and God-ordained apostle (a rare breed of men), but as far as the actual work of planting churches was concerned, he and Epaphras stood shoulder to shoulder. They were on the same level—fellow slaves! Not only was this heartwarming praise for their pastor-teacher but also it struck a blow at any notion that there should be some kind of hierarchy in the church.

It must have been a proud moment in the church at Colosse when this letter was opened and read and the church secretary came to these words—Epaphras, our dear fellow servant. How that word *agapētos* ("beloved") must have rung out. It is the very word used of the Father in heaven for the Son on earth (Matt. 3:17). When Epaphras himself saw what Paul had written about him, tears must have come into his eyes. For we can be sure that he had been made the target of many a snide and sneering remark by the cultists. They would have to put him down to raise themselves up. Well, he could never be another Paul, but he had done what he could. Paul's unstinting word of praise must have been the very balm of Gilead to his soul.

3. Epaphras, a faithful minister (1:7c–8)

Epaphras . . . who is for you a faithful minister of Christ; Who also declared unto us your love in the Spirit.

It is possible that Epaphras might have been entertaining some doubts as to the kind of reception he might receive when he arrived back at Colosse. Doubtless some people had already labeled him a talebearer. The cultists, in particular, would be busy blackening his name and taking advantage of his absence to undermine his authority. They knew perfectly well why he had gone to Rome. And, as is always the case, there would be those willing enough to listen to both their slanders and their exotic teaching.

Paul cut the ground from beneath them. "He has been telling me all about your love," he said. If Epaphras had been informing Paul about the activities of the cult, as doubtless he had, he had also been lavish in his praise of the love that the Colossian Christians had been showing both to one another and to him.

Sure, Epaphras had told Paul the other side of the story. He had told him about the crafty teachings of the Gnostics. But his motives had been pure. He was driven to it by the highest kind of love, by a love for and a concern for their souls. He could think of no better way to express his love for them than to solicit Paul's help in dealing with their destroyers. Some years before, Paul had warned the elders of the sister church at Ephesus that the wolves were coming (Acts 20:29–31). Well, they had already come to Colosse, and "grievous wolves" they were at that. Epaphras was not simply "crying wolf!" when he hurried off for help. The wolves had come to the Wolf River and on to Colosse. Paul thoroughly approved of Epaphras's coming to him for help. He did not hesitate to put all of the weight of his authority behind Epaphras.

F. Paul's passion for perspective (1:9–14)
   1. His petition (1:9–11)
      a. Our spiritual vision (1:9)

> *For this cause we also, since the day we heard it, do not cease to pray for you, and to desire that ye might be filled with the knowledge of his will in all wisdom and spiritual understanding.*

Paul was stirred deeply by the glowing report that Epaphras was able to bring to him of the love that the Colossian Christians displayed. He burst into prayer! It helped put things in perspective. Paul's outlet for any deep feeling was to pray.

This, another of Paul's famous prayers, gives us an interesting glimpse of Paul's perspective. His own circumstances, be they threatening or thrilling, were always overshadowed by his heavenly vision. He saw everything from heaven's point of view.

We could profitably note the kinds of things for which Paul did *not* pray—at least it is rarely, if ever, mentioned that he did pray for them. He did not pray to get out of prison or to be saved from execution. He did not pray (at least in his recorded prayers) for financial support or about his chronic ill health. He did not pray for people that God would prosper their businesses, heal their ailments, or forward the secular and material interests of their children, or even save their relatives. Doubtless, there were times when he prayed for such things. But these things were reserved for his private prayers. We find them conspicuously absent from his public and recorded prayers.

For what, then, did he pray? What was his perspective as reflected in the things for which he petitioned the throne of God? We can find the answer to these questions by studying this prayer recorded here in Colossians and by studying his similar prayers in his other epistles.

This particular prayer is in two parts—first, petition and then praise. Paul does not say, "I pray." He says, "We pray." His habit of prayer was infectious. Those around him found themselves caught up by him and swept into the throne room of the universe.

Some resounding prayer meetings must have been conducted there in Paul's hired house in Rome. What did his Roman jailers think about it? There was no escape from Paul. He wasn't chained to them—they were chained to him! So, like it or not, they often found themselves in a prayer meeting. Most unsaved people do not like prayer meetings.

For that matter, most saved people don't like them very much either. Perhaps it is because we manage to make them so dull.

The Roman soldiers who found themselves detailed to guard Paul must have either loved him or loathed him. No doubt, there were some guards who jerked angrily on the chain when Paul began to pray again. Others yawned their indifference and counted the hours to their release. Surely, too, some must have said, "Say, Paul! Put in a good word for me." Probably, too, some of Paul's prison prayers led to heart-to-heart talks with these soldier-jailers and often led to cases of conversion because Paul had a knack for getting some sound doctrine into his prayers.

When we consider, by contrast, the arid, repetitive nature of much of our own praying and the incredibly boring nature of our church prayer meetings, we ought to be appalled. What can we do to remedy this? Surely one way to learn a skill is to spend time with an expert. The two greatest prayer experts in the New Testament are the Lord Jesus and the apostle Paul.

Paul took his arrest, imprisonment, and loss of freedom in stride. Because he could no longer move around, he would meditate. Because he could no longer preach, he would pray. Because he could no longer visit places in person, he would visit them in prayer. Since he could no longer travel, he would travail. Imprisonment gave him days and weeks and months and years—time! Plenty of time! Time to ponder, time to pray. The less time he had for preaching, the more time he had for praying. That is why, perhaps, he could again and again tell the Colossians that he prayed for them "always" (1:3) and without ceasing (v. 9). Only eternity will reveal how those prayers tipped the scales and effected events.

Moreover, thanks to the visit of Epaphras he could not only pray for the Colossians *constantly,* he could pray *comprehendingly* because now he had first-hand knowledge of what was going on. Now he could pray not only intelligently for the church at Colosse but also for the leading of the Holy Spirit as to what he should do about it. Prayer ought to lead to involvement. Should he write to them? If so, what should he say?

The first thing for which Paul prayed, in relation to the Christians at Colosse, was for their spiritual *vision.* He prayed, too, for their spiritual *vitality* and their spiritual *victory.* We note the threefold repetition of the phrase "that ye might"— "that ye might be filled . . . that ye might walk worthy . . . that ye might be strengthened."

Paul began his prayer by requesting that the Colossians might have spiritual vision. They needed knowledge, understanding, and wisdom. Satan always goes after the mind (2 Cor. 4:4). Their minds had to be brought into captivity to

Christ. Ever since the Fall, the mind of man has been particularly susceptible to Satan's deceptions. This fact was evident at Colosse. The Gnostic cult there was going after the minds of the people. So Paul prays for their spiritual enlightenment. Satan always exploits ignorance, so Paul prays that the believers would have knowledge, understanding, and wisdom.

So then Paul prayed that the believers would be "filled with . . . knowledge." The word he used is *epignōsis* (note the root *gnōsis* and its kinship to the word "gnostic"). Doubtless Paul used this word deliberately as an opening thrust at the Gnostic cultists.

The Gnostics claimed to have a special and superior kind of knowledge. The word *epignōsis* was one of their favorite words. It means precise or additional knowledge. Paul was scornful of this false claim, and he refused to surrender the word to the cult. He snatched it away from them and wrote it boldly into his epistle. It was God's word, not theirs. He handed it back to the church. "Be filled with the knowledge of his will," he said.

Paul prayed further that they might be filled with "wisdom and spiritual understanding." Again he used two favorite Gnostic words, *sophia* and *sunesis*. The word *sophia* has to do with the discerning faculty, with cleverness and skill and the right application of knowledge. It is possible to have knowledge without wisdom, to be a walking encyclopedia of Bible facts yet to be foolish or neglectful in their application. The word *sunesis* relates to our discrimination, to the ability to look at things critically and objectively and to discern the true from the false. If someone tells you, for instance, that as a born believer you now need to pray for the gift of the Spirit, *sunesis* would enable you to recognize the flaw in that advice. All genuine believers have the gift of the Spirit as their birthright (Rom. 8:9).

We need then to be "filled with the knowledge of his will in all wisdom and spiritual understanding." The Colossians were being imperiled by cleverly fabricated error. So Paul prayed that they might have spiritual vision, that their eyes might be opened to see the snares being set for them.

> b. Our spiritual vitality (1:10)
>> (1) The walk of the Christian life (1:10a)

That ye might walk worthy of the Lord unto all pleasing.

The word *walk* is used in the epistles to describe the activities of the Christian life. It refers to "the outward life that men see." If that outward life is pleasing to

God, it will be beyond criticism by men. Step by step, we walk through each day. We should see to it that every step is pleasing to the Lord. Because the word for "walk" here is in the aorist tense, it can be rendered "to set out walking." This would suggest making a fresh start, a new departure. It is never too late to make that new departure from our old, worldly, carnal ways and to begin a closer walk with God.

The expression *unto all pleasing* carries the idea of "meeting all of His wishes." The word used is *areskeia.* It occurs only here. This word was sometimes used in a bad sense. It carried the idea of a cringing and subservient spirit, a willingness to do anything to please a superior, even an eagerness to anticipate his most trivial wishes. The apostle rescues the word from its ignoble connections. The child of God is pointed to the Lord Jesus Christ, He who took his place at Calvary and who has the nail prints in His hands. He is invited to anticipate his beloved Master's every wish, to do studiously anything and everything to satisfy the desires of His heart.

(2) The works of the Christian life (1:10b)

That ye might . . . [be] fruitful in every good work.

Evangelicals tend to be suspicious of "good works" because liberals and false religions in general make good works the means of salvation.

We must not look slightingly on good works simply because of their misuse by others. Good works and salvation walk hand in hand. We are justified along three lines. We are justified by blood (Rom. 5:9), which is what makes salvation *possible;* we are justified by faith (3:28), which is what makes salvation *personal;* and we are justified by works (James 2:21), which is what makes salvation *practical.*

In other words, the believer is so grafted into the Vine (John 15) that the life of the Vine flows through him and produces the fruit of the Vine in him. Jesus is the Vine; we are the branches. What He is we are; what He says we say; what He does we do. The Lord Jesus "went about doing good," as Peter told Cornelius (Acts 10:38), so we are to be "fruitful in every good work." Indeed, evangelicals have always been in the lead when it comes to good works. George Müeller and Dr. Bernardo led the way in caring for orphans in their day. The church in the Middle Ages was a haven for the poor and the oppressed. Christian missionaries have led the way in foreign lands in building hospitals and schools. It was a missionary, David Livingstone, who did most to awaken the conscience of the British people to the horrors of the African slave trade.

(3) The wonder of the Christian life (1:10c)

That ye might . . . [be] . . . increasing in the knowledge of God.

The wonder of the Christian life is that we can know God. We can get to know Him *expositionally* through His Word. God has revealed Himself. He has made clear that He wants us to know Him by giving us sixty-six books of divine revelation. He has spoken to us through the Old Testament prophets, in the Person of His Son, and by the writings of the New Testament apostles. God says to us, "I want you not only to know Me but also to get to know Me better." The queen of England has never invited me to get to know her. The president of the United States has never invited me to get to know him. Neither one nor the other has written me a personal letter. But the living God invites all of us to get to know Him!

Moreover, we can get to know Him *experientially*. He who once came daily into Eden's shady vales to walk and talk with Adam and Eve will meet with us, likewise, in the cool of the day, in our daily "quiet times." He has torn aside the veil, flung wide the way into the Holiest, and invited us to come on in! We can come whenever we like, stay as long as we like, and talk to Him about whatever we like. We can sit down where angels only dare to stand. We can open His Word. We can say to Him, "Speak, Lord, for thy servant heareth," and He will reveal His mind and heart and will to us.

That is the wonder of the Christian life. Am I "increasing in the knowledge of God"? Do I know Him better today than I did a year ago? Getting to know God is the highest, holiest, and happiest occupation in the universe—it is the very stuff of which eternity is made.

c. For spiritual victory (1:11)
(1) Its secret (1:11a)

That ye might [be] . . . Strengthened with all might, according to his glorious power.

All of God's boundless resources are at our disposal in our battle with Satan's forces. "In all empowered" is one way that the apostle's thought can be rendered.

God's boundless resources are displayed in the universe. Everywhere we see evidence of His wisdom, His omniscient genius, and His awesome power, power to energize an atom or explode a galaxy. Take our own sun, for instance. It is just a moderate star, as stars go, one of billions in a galaxy that itself is one of billions more. Our sun consumes some one thousand million tons of hydrogen every second. Astronomers say that it has been doing that for five billion years. It is "in all empowered"! It is strengthened from God's boundless resources. It is "strengthened with all might according to his glorious power." In the sun, as throughout the entire created universe, we see God's infinite resources of power expressed physically.

God now wants to express those same infinite resources of power in us spiritually! God does not leave it up to us to achieve by our own efforts some measure of victory over indwelling sin in our lives. We can serve Him in the various ways open to us but not in our own strength. On the contrary, He Himself lives within each blood-bought believer to release all of His own boundless resources so that we can serve Him as He wants to be served. "If God be for us," cried Paul, "who can be against us?" (Rom. 8:31).

(2) Its scope (1:11b)

Unto all patience and longsuffering with joyfulness.

When we think of patience, we think of *Job* (James 5:11). When we think of patience and longsuffering, we think of *Jeremiah* (Lam. 1:12). But when we think of patience and longsuffering with joyfulness, we think of *Jesus* (Heb. 12:2).

We see Him in the Upper Room with His disciples after Judas had left. The remains of the Passover Supper still remained on the table. A new feast of remembrance had been instituted to help believers all down through this present age to remember vividly His death. The disciples were distraught because He had just told them that He was going back home to Glory. Moreover, the shadow of the Cross lay heavy in that room. Gethsemane, Gabbatha, Golgotha, and the grave were all awaiting Him. Yet, pulsating through that room was "joy unspeakable and full of glory" (1 Peter 1:8). The joy of the Lord! The Lord talked about it all of the time (John 15:11; 17:13).

That was the legacy that He sought to impart to His disciples. That, too, is

His legacy to us—joy! (John 15:11; 16:22). It is this joy that enables us to trace the rainbow through the rain, that enabled a blind Fanny Crosby to fill the church of her day with song, and that enabled martyrs to sing in the midst of the flames. Joy is not mere happiness. All too often happiness depends on what happens. This is joy, the second fruit of the Spirit (Gal. 5:22).

Thus, Paul prayed! Vision! Vitality! Victory! Once these things fill us with the fragrance and the fruitfulness of the very life of Christ, the Devil is robbed of all of his power.

2. Paul's praise (1:12–14)
   a. To God, for remaking us (1:12)

*Giving thanks unto the Father, which hath made us meet to be
partakers of the inheritance of the saints in light.*

Paul's prayers often pass swiftly into praise. And, like his petitions, his items for praise are predominantly spiritual rather than physical and material. To begin with, he thanks God for remaking us.

As a result of Adam's fall, something has been lost to us and something has been left to us. We lost Paradise, and we inherited a fallen nature. It would have been of little value for God to restore our lost estates and boundless potential without first dealing with our fallen condition. We would only have lost it all over again. In the book of Ruth, which graphically illustrates the plan of redemption, we see Boaz, the kinsman-redeemer, purchasing both Ruth's person and her property. All that belonged to Ruth was transferred to Boaz to have and to hold for Ruth as the strong one ("Boaz") whose very name implies power.

God begins with us by making us "meet to be partakers of the inheritance." The word Paul uses is *hikanoō*. It occurs only here and in 2 Corinthians 3:6. It literally means "to enable" or "to make efficient." The phrase can be rendered "who qualified us to be partakers." We were disqualified in Adam from handling our inheritance; we are now qualified to do so in Christ.

And what an inheritance it is! It is called "the inheritance of the saints in light" (literally, "in the light"). The primary reference is to our spiritual blessings as believers that enable us to live for God in the darkness of this world. But above and beyond that, Paul doubtless has in mind the wonders of heaven itself that await us on the other side.

God is light. He dwells in a light that outshines the sun. The celestial city that is to be our eternal home and our inheritance besides has no need of natural or artificial light. The sun, the moon, and the stars are redundant over there. "The Lamb is all the glory of Emmanuel's land." Paul knew! He had been there. He had seen, both on the Damascus Road and in the Glory land, the beauty and the brightness of the face of Jesus (Acts 26:13; 2 Cor. 12:1–4).

God has remade us and equipped us to enter into a dazzling inheritance. The word that Paul uses here for "light" is *phōs,* light underived and absolute, the very opposite of darkness. The word is characteristically used in the New Testament to describe God (John 1:4–5; 8:12; 1 John 1:5). One of these days, when we are in our glorified bodies and we shall be equipped to bear such light, God will lift up the light of His countenance upon us and bathe all of our future with bliss.

"He hath made us!" Consider the difference between the prodigal's going-away prayer ("Father, give me") and his coming-home prayer ("Father, make me"), and marvel at the change already wrought in him (Luke 15:12, 19).

Paul had one such remade prodigal with him there in Rome, even as he wrote—a runaway slave and thief by the name of Onesimus. Paul was sending him back to Philemon, right there in Colosse, with a memo hinting that Philemon should receive him, not merely as a repentant slave, not merely as a new brother in Christ, but as though he were Paul himself! That would mean the best robe, the best room, the best place at table, and the best seat in the church! An inheritance indeed! But not before he was first "made meet."

b. For rescuing us (1:13)

> *Who hath delivered us from the power of darkness, and hath*
> *translated us into the kingdom of his dear Son.*

That takes us to Gethsemane. Here comes the traitor with the mob, the weapons and the necessary warrants in hand. Roman soldiers march stolidly behind, the arrest of the Son of the living God being their hopeless goal. Twelve legions of angels with drawn swords strain over the battlements of heaven, eager to put an instant stop to this unbelievable folly. One word from Him and they would have swarmed down the star road of the sky, burst upon the midnight scene, and put an end, once and for all, to this rebel race of beings on this sin-cursed planet Earth. As for those marching men, with their swords and spears—they had no power over Him at all. He did not need the heavenly hosts. One word from Him and His foes fell backward to the ground! He allowed Himself to be taken, however, and said, "This is your hour, and the power of darkness" (Luke 22:53).

And so it was—the hour of the power of darkness. In Gethsemane, He allowed them to arrest Him, sorely shaken as they were. He allowed Judas to plant that infamous kiss upon His check. He allowed them to haul Him here and there all night—to Annas, to Caiaphas, to Pilate, to Herod, and back to Pilate. He let them bully Him. He let them mock Him and malign Him, manhandle Him and maul Him. He let them smite Him and scourge Him and crucify Him. It was their hour and the power of darkness. The darkness deepened. The sun went out. And it all ended in the darkness of the rock-hewn tomb.

For three days and three nights the world went on its way, a vast coffin in which lay the lifeless clay of the Christ of God. Darkness had triumphed. Yet men went about their affairs as though nothing had happened. The soldiers changed guard at the tomb. Pilate wrestled with his conscience and his cowardice. His wife fought with the memory of her dreams. Herod sneered. Annas and Caiaphas, in grisly glee, shook hands over their ghastly triumph. Darkness reigned.

Then it happened! An earthquake heralded it. Jesus rose from the dead. The power of darkness was overwhelmed by the light of a new, eternal day. A vast highway had been built leading out of darkness into the kingdom of God's dear Son.

The word Paul uses is *delivered*. It can be rendered "translated." Behind the word is the picture of an eastern conqueror who uproots his vanquished enemies and carries them away to another place. The same word is found in Paul's statement, "though I have all faith, so that I could remove [*methistēmi*] mountains" (1 Cor. 13:2). This is what God has done. He has rescued us. He has "removed" us from Satan's sphere of darkness and has put us in His own kingdom. The Holy Spirit speaks of it as "the kingdom of his [the Father's] dear Son"—the kingdom of the Son of His love.

c. Redeeming us (1:14)

In whom we have redemption through his blood, even the
forgiveness of sins.

The rivers of blood that flowed from the sacrifices of Old Testament times could not redeem people from their sins. As the apostle puts it, "The law having a shadow of good things to come, and not the very image of the things, can never with those sacrifices which they offered year by year continually make the comers thereunto perfect" (Heb. 10:1). The shadow of a key cannot set a prisoner free. The shadow of a meal cannot satisfy the hunger of a starving man. The shadow of Calvary could not redeem a sinful soul.

But the shed blood of Christ effects redemption. How casually we read these words "the forgiveness of sins"! How we have groaned under the burden of guilt and sin! Modern psychology traces many emotional problems to guilt. The secular psychologist, however, has few, if any, real answers to the problem of guilt, except to persuade the guilty one to shift the blame to someone else.

The guilt remains. The secular humanist therapist knows nothing about "the law of sin and death" (Rom. 8:2), a basic and comprehensive explanation of human behavior. Sin! Guilt! Death! The answer is simple—shift it all to Someone else! Jesus! Take His life in exchange! That is why we can "have redemption through his blood, even the forgiveness of sins."

Forgiveness! Who can forgive sins but God only? And even He can forgive only on the basis of the shed blood of Christ. At such infinite cost we can know "the forgiveness of sins."

In telling us about the Old Testament sin offering (Lev. 4), the Holy Spirit repeatedly talks about the place (the *clean* place) "where the ashes of the offering are poured out" (twice, for instance, in verse twelve alone). Ashes! They tell us that the fire has done its work. It has consumed the sacrifice. The judgment is over. Wrath has been spent. Ashes! You can stir the embers of a fire and rekindle the flames. But ashes cannot be made to burn. Such is God's forgiveness. Our guilt, once dealt with at Calvary, is as dead as the ashes of the sin offering. Dead! Utterly dead! Never again to be rekindled into tormenting, consuming flame.

Such was Paul's prayer for his friends—and for us!

PART 2

The Truth About the Christ
Colossians 1:15–29

II. THE TRUTH ABOUT THE CHRIST (1:15–29)
   A. The deity of Christ (1:15–19)
      1. The person of God revealed (1:15)
         a. The image of the invisible God (1:15a)
         b. The implications of the incarnate God (1:15b)
      2. The power of God revealed (1:16–17)
         a. Jesus Christ created the universe (1:16a)
         b. Jesus Christ claims the universe (1:16b)
         c. Jesus Christ controls the universe (1:17)
      3. The purposes of God revealed (1:18–19)
         a. Who Christ is in these purposes (1:18)
            (1) He heads a new body (1:18a)
            (2) He heads a new beginning (1:18b–c)
               (a) He originated life (1:18b)
               (b) He overcame death (1:18c)
         b. Where Christ is in these purposes (1:18d)
         c. What Christ is in these purposes (1:19)
   B. The death of Christ (1:20–22)
      1. The means of our reconciliation (1:20a)
      2. The measure of our reconciliation (1:20b–21)
         a. It extends to two realms (1:20b)
         b. It extends to total rebels (1:21)
            (1) We are mentally alienated (1:21a)
            (2) We are morally alienated (1:21b)
      3. The meaning of our reconciliation (1:22)
   C. The demands of Christ (1:23–29)
      1. We are to be loyal to Him (1:23)
         a. A definite loyalty (1:23a)
         b. A deepening loyalty (1:23b)
         c. A determined loyalty (1:23c)
         d. A dispensational loyalty (1:23d)
         e. A doctrinal loyalty (1:23e)
      2. We are to be living for Him (1:24–29)
         a. Identified with His Cross (1:24)

   b. Identified with His church (1:25–29)
     (1) Its ministry (1:25)
     (2) Its mystery (1:26)
     (3) Its message (1:27)
     (4) Its mission (1:28–29)
       (a) Reaching men for Christ (1:28)
       (b) Reaching men through Christ (1:29)

II. THE TRUTH ABOUT THE CHRIST (1:15–29)
  A. The deity of Christ (1:15–19)
    1. The person of God revealed (1:15)
     a. The image of the invisible God (1:15a)

Paul, having finished his opening remarks, now comes to grips with the main issue at stake in the Colossian church—false teaching about Christ and His church. In chapter 1, Paul reaffirms the truth of the absolute deity of the Lord Jesus Christ as Creator and Sustainer of the universe. In chapter 2, he deals with some of the more subtle attacks upon the deity of Christ and the doctrine of salvation.

He wastes no words. Christ is "the image of the invisible God," Paul says. God is a spirit, as Jesus told the woman at the well (John 4:24), and "a spirit hath not flesh and bones, as ye see me have," as the Lord told His astounded disciples in the Upper Room when He appeared to them in His resurrection body (Luke 24:39). To prove the physical reality of his resurrection body, He invited them to come and handle Him and satisfy themselves that He was no ghost.

Because God is a spirit, it follows that He is immaterial and invisible. Everything about God is marvelous and mysterious to us. Our minds cannot cope with the concept, for instance, of One who has always existed, who is eternal, and who never had a beginning. We find it equally difficult to conceive of One who is a pure spirit and who has no need for a body. A spirit being exists on a plane and in a dimension quite outside the realms of our normal experience. We can visualize God as One who never gets tired, never gets hungry, never gets ill, never grows old, and can never be tempted. We can even visualize One who dwells in quite a different relation to time than we do, One who transcends time, who describes Himself as the I AM, for whom past and future are enfolded in the eternal present. We can likewise visualize One who is absolutely holy, incapable of sin and of unfailing love. But eternal and invisible? Here our finite minds draw back.

The driving force behind the incredible folly of idolatry is man's inability to grasp a God who is invisible and immaterial. Men want a god that they can see and feel, although in the end they have to make one with their own hands of metal, stone, or wood. Interestingly enough, the word translated "image" here in Colossians 1:15 is the same word translated "image" in Romans 1:23 to describe pagan idols—"they . . . changed the glory of the uncorruptible God into an image made like to corruptible man."

The Lord Jesus, the second person of the Godhead, satisfies our longing for a God who has all of the wisdom, love, power, and holiness that we associate with God but who is also One we can see, touch, hear, and talk to. He is the "image of the invisible God," the One who gives visible expression to the invisible God. The Lord Jesus is, to borrow J. B. Phillips' expression, "God in focus." We see God in Christ. Jesus said, "He that hath seen me hath seen the Father" (John 14:9).

The ancient Greeks, famous for their science, philosophy, art, and politics, were fools when it came to the knowledge of God. Their great city of Athens was renowned for its learning, yet it was wholly given over to idolatry. Their religion peopled Mount Olympus with gods made in the image and likeness of men. They took the lines of human personality and extended them into infinity and conceived God as being a much larger edition of their own selves. The process was sound enough. The problem was that they projected into infinity the lines of fallen man and as a result came up with fallen gods—gods who lusted and hated and warred and indulged themselves on a grand and terrible scale.

Then Jesus came. He was God and always had been God. Only now He was "God manifest in flesh." The birth of Christ marked a moment unprecedented in the annals of time and eternity. When any other babe is born, a new person is created and a new personality begins to form. When Jesus was born, however, it was not the creation of a new personality at all; it was the coming into this world of a Person who had existed for all eternity. God became Man without ceasing to be God. The human and the divine were blended into One. The eternal Word "became flesh" to dwell among us, so that we might "beh[o]ld his glory, the glory as of the only begotten of the Father, full of grace and truth" (John 1:14). We can take the lines of His unique and perfect personality and project those lines into infinity—and *that* is what God is like. He is just like Jesus. What God is, Jesus is. What God does, He does. What God says, He says. There is not one iota of difference between God in heaven and Jesus on earth. Thus, He could say to Philip, "He that hath seen me hath seen the Father." For thirty-three and a half years, the Lord Jesus lived on this planet as Man inhabited by God. He set before us a flawless, moment-by-moment, audiovisual, full-color, three-dimensional demonstration of what God is like. He was "the image of the invisible God."

The blending of the human and the divine in the person of the Lord Jesus was like the seamless robe that He wore, woven throughout to be one indivisible whole. It is impossible to say where the humanity ends and where the deity begins or to say where the deity ends and the humanity begins. The major heresies of the church have resulted from attempts to define the one at the expense of the other.

In the Gospels, we meet One who was very human indeed. He was born, He grew up, He went to school, and He worked as a carpenter. He became tired, hungry, and thirsty. He experienced all of the emotions of the human heart apart from sin. He asked questions. He enjoyed companionship. He was wholesome, delightful, and perfectly balanced at all times. He was a wonderful and attractive human being to whom all kinds of people were drawn.

At the same time, He was God. The demons instantly recognized Him as such and were terrified of Him. He had power to turn water into wine or to multiply the few loaves and fishes of a little lad's lunch into a banquet for a multitude. He could walk upon the waves and still the storm. He could cleanse lepers, heal all kinds of sickness, and raise the dead. And He could do all of these things as a matter of course. His enemies could plot against Him but could not harm Him until He voluntarily allowed them to do so. Even then, although they nailed Him to a cross, they could not kill Him. "No man taketh [my life] from me," He said, "I lay it down of myself" (John 10:18). Nor could they keep Him in the tomb. On the very day He had foretold, He rose from the dead.

Yet nobody can draw the line between His deity and His humanity.

We see him, for instance, sound asleep in Simon Peter's boat. That was His humanity. The next moment, He stood amid heaving waves and howling winds and commanded them to be still. That was His deity. Where does the one end and the other begin?

We see Him at the tomb of Lazarus. He witnessed Martha's grief and Mary's tears and He, too, wept. That was His humanity. The next moment, He summoned Lazarus back from the dead, undaunted by the fact that corruption had already begun its terrible work in his corpse. That was His deity. Where does the one end and the other begin?

This mysterious mix of the human and divine passes human comprehension. We know He was a perfect human being. We know, too, that He was eternal, uncreated, self-existing, the second person of the Godhead. It was not that as

God incarnate now He was being Man, now He was being God. He was both—all of the time!

An illustration of this truth is in the veil of the Old Testament temple. We have the Holy Spirit's word for it that the temple veil was symbolic of Christ (Heb. 10:19–20). It was made of linen and displayed three colors: scarlet, blue, and purple. The colors of the veil depicted Christ. The scarlet reminds us that He was Man—"the last Adam," to borrow Paul's significant phrase. The name *Adam* simply means "red." Blue is the color of heaven, the place from whence He came. Thus, the blue reminds us that He was God. But what about the purple? If we take a given amount of the scarlet dye and an equal amount of the blue, then pour the one into the other and mix them until we can no longer tell where the one ends and the other begins, we have the purple. The purple is something new. It results from a perfect blending of the other two.

Just so with the Lord Jesus Christ. He was Man. He was God. In Him the two natures perfectly blend. He was inseparably (and now eternally) *both.* As Paul puts it here, He is "the image of the invisible God."

b. The implications of the incarnate God (1:15b)

Who is . . . the firstborn of every creature.

The title "firstborn" here does not mean that He was born first or created first of all created beings. The context makes this point abundantly clear: "By him were all things created," Paul says (v. 16). No text must be divorced from its context. If verse fifteen means that the Lord was a created being (as the Arians taught), then according to verse sixteen, He must have created Himself—which is an absurdity. The words "the firstborn of every creature" can be rendered "the firstborn over all creation," making Him superior to and distinct from the entire sphere of created beings and things. The title means that "Christ, existing as he did before all creation, exercises the privilege of primogeniture as Lord of all creation. . . . He was there when creation began."[1]

Any Jew in the church at Colosse when these words were read would have no difficulty understanding them. Gentile believers, influenced by Gnostic teaching, might not have grasped the truth so quickly. The Gnostics placed Christ in their theoretical angel hierarchy either at the bottom of the list or far down the

---

1. F. F. Bruce, *The Epistles to the Ephesians and the Colossians* (London: Marshall, Morgan and Scott, 1957), 194.

line of angelic ranks. At first, they might have thought that Paul was simply putting Christ at the head of the hierarchy. Jews would have known better. They would have been familiar with Psalm 89:27, where the title "firstborn" is used prophetically of Christ. In any case, Jews were well familiar with the Old Testament concept of the firstborn.

In Old Testament times, the expression "firstborn" had little to do with being born first. Reuben was born first of Jacob's sons, and this fact was acknowledged by the dying patriarch. But he had long since forfeited any right to the dignity the duties and the high destiny associated with the rank and the high privilege of the firstborn. Merely being born first meant nothing (Gen. 49:3–4).

Throughout the Old Testament the one who was born first was regularly set aside in favor of one who was born later. Thus, God set aside Ishmael and chose Isaac, and He set aside Esau and chose Jacob. "The elder shall serve the younger," God foretold to Rebekah before either Esau or Jacob was born. Similarly, God set aside Saul and chose David. Spiritually, He sets aside "the old man" in the believer and chooses "the new man"—Adam is replaced by Christ, the "flesh" is replaced by the Spirit.

The "firstborn" in the Old Testament was primarily a title indicating rank and privilege. In the patriarchal family, three things accompanied the title. With the position of "firstborn" went the property; the one who inherited the title received a double portion of the inheritance. That is to say, he received twice as much as any of the others. The "firstborn" also received the priestly right, the right to lead the family in worship. And he also received the progenitor right—to be in the direct line to the birth of Christ.

In the case of Reuben, he was disinherited, and the "firstborn" rights and privileges were divided three ways. Joseph received the double portion of the inheritance—two of his sons, Ephraim and Manasseh, became tribal heads. Judah received the progenitor right because Christ was descended from his seed. And, eventually, Levi received the priestly right. All of this indicates clearly that the idea of being "the firstborn of every creature" had nothing to do with being born (or even created) first. It has to do with rank, priority, and position. God's dear Son is thus set apart from all others. He ranks first. He takes precedence over all. He is not only "[God's] dear Son" (v. 13), He is God the Son.

Here, in Colossians 1:15, Paul links "the firstborn" with creation, vast, awesome, and far-flung, proclaiming the might and majesty of the Creator and totally subservient to Him. Some scholars have thought that He is called "the firstborn of every creature" because He took creature form to create, just as later

He took human form to redeem. Be that as it may, He stands at the head of all creation, linked with it but apart from it. Elsewhere in Scripture, the Lord is called "the firstbegotten" in connection with the hosts of heaven (Heb. 1:6), in connection with the family of faith (Rom. 8:29), and in connection with the ranks of those raised (Col. 1:18; Rev. 1:5). In each case, the Lord is identified with others but as being in a class by Himself.

As "the firstborn of every creature," He was related *to* the creation because He was its mighty Maker, yet He was distinctly removed *from* it for the same reason—He made it. This is a very different Person indeed than the downgraded angelic being of the Colossian cultists. It is also a different Christ than that claimed by modern cultists.

> 2. The power of God revealed (1:16–17)
>   a. Jesus Christ created the universe (1:16a)

> *By him were all things created, that are in heaven, and that are*
> *in earth, visible and invisible, whether they be thrones, or*
> *dominions, or principalities, or powers.*

This statement flatly contradicts Gnostic teaching concerning the impossibility of any link between God and matter. Paul now declared the Lord Jesus to be the Creator of the universe, One possessed of infinite power and infallible wisdom.

This, furthermore, is a statement concerning origins. We do well to remind ourselves, in the face of high-powered evolutionary propaganda, that science knows nothing of origins. Dr. Asa Gray, once called the greatest botanist in the history of American science, declared, "A beginning is wholly beyond the ken and scope of science which is concerned with how things go on and has nothing to say as to how they begin."[2]

T. H. Huxley, the friend and promoter of Darwin, sometimes called "Darwin's bulldog" because he liked to snap at the heels of the theologians, said much the same. Huxley popularized Darwin's theory. He saw in it a working hypothesis for atheism. Before he died, however, he was obliged to declare, "It appears to me that the scientific investigator is wholly incompetent to say anything at all about the first origin of the material universe."[3]

2. Asa Gray, *Natural Science and Religion*, 1880, 38; cited in *Therefore Stand*, by Wilbur M. Smith (Natick, Mass.: W. A. Wilde, 1959), 274–75.
3. T. H. Huxley, *Natural Science and Religion*, February 1886, 202; cited in *Therefore Stand*, by Wilbur M. Smith (Natick, Mass.: W. A. Wilde, 1959), 274–75.

Much the same thing was said by Sir Oliver Lodge, a British scientist knighted by the crown for his contribution to science. He declared, "Ultimate origins are inscrutable. Let us admit, as scientific men that the real origin, even of the simplest thing, we know nothing, not even a pebble."[4]

Science knows nothing of origins. It is simple to illustrate why science can never speak authoritatively about the origin of the universe. R. E. D. Clark cites Ludwig Silberstein as picturing a scientist coming into a room where there was a clock with a swinging pendulum. Let us assume that he has never seen such a clock before but that he is immediately interested. He observes the swing of the pendulum and the movement of the hands. He takes some measurements and comes up with an equation. It is evident that things are gradually slowing down and that eventually the pendulum will cease to swing. His equation can tell him just when that will be.[5]

He now decides to investigate the past. How long has the clock been running? How did the pendulum start swinging in the first place? He changes certain factors in his equation and begins to probe back in time. For a while, the information that he receives makes sense. The farther back he goes, however, the more obvious it becomes that the incoming data no longer makes sense. The swing of the pendulum becomes greater and greater, now it is hitting the ceiling with each swing; now it is swinging in two directions at the same time! He concludes that this is an absurdity. There must be some other explanation.

He comes to the conclusion that although he is able to measure the laws that now govern the swing of the pendulum, those laws do not explain how the pendulum first started to swing. On the contrary, something quite different from what is now happening must have happened at some point in the past and at a time before the data coming from his equation began to be ridiculous.

But what was it that happened? He does not know. The familiar laws of energy and motion do not extend that far. He can, of course, come up with a theory. He can say, "I think this is what happened. And I think it happened before such-and-such a time." But he cannot speak with authority about these things. He might be wrong. The only way he could speak with authority as to the beginning of things would be *if someone who was there when it happened* were to tell him. In other words, this kind of information is derived not from a process of *reasoning* because the required facts are not available but from a process of *revelation*.

---

4. Sir Oliver Lodge, *Man and the Universe*, 6th ed. (London: n.p., 1909), 19, 29; cited in *Therefore Stand*, by Wilbur M. Smith (Natick, Mass.: W. A. Wilde, 1959), 274–75.

5. R. E. D. Clark, *Creation* (London: The Tyndale Press, 1946), 10–11.

It is the same with the universe. We can measure the laws that now govern in the material world, but these laws do not explain how it all started. As scientists themselves admit, science knows nothing of origins. The fact is that something quite different from what is now happening must have taken place to get it all started.

Like our pendulum theorist, scientists have come up with suggestions. Some astronomers believe in the "Big Bang" theory; even so, they can say neither what caused that first massive explosion nor where the primeval matter came from. In any case, scientists often change their minds and alter their theories. It all boils down to this: whenever a scientist pontificates regarding the *origin* of the universe, he is no longer speaking as a scientist; he is speaking as a philosopher. He is not saying, "This is what we know." He is saying, "This is what I think."

Some years ago, my brother, a medical research scientist well respected by his peers as an authority on diseases of the liver, told me that in his field of investigation they had what they called "five-year half-life." He explained that every five years half of the things now believed to be true are proven false and are replaced by new theories! That is how quickly new research changes current opinion.

As with our pendulum theorist, so with our scientists. The only way anyone can possibly know how the universe began would be if someone who was there when it happened were to tell us. Well, Someone was there when it happened. The Holy Spirit was there, and He tells us that Jesus Christ created the universe. This is not a matter of *reasoning* but of *revelation*. "Jesus Christ created the universe!" It is a statement concerning origins, and "science knows nothing of origins." This position upsets the secular humanists because no one can contradict *on scientific grounds* the statement that Jesus Christ created the universe.

The popular scientist and author Robert Jastrow tells us how annoyed secularists are by all of this. Jastrow—an internationally known astronomer, founder of NASA's Goddard Institute for Space Studies, professor of Astronomy and Geology at Columbia University, professor of Earth Sciences at Dartmouth College, and author of a number of best-selling books—is an articulate spokesman. He speaks eloquently about the current scientific impasse over the question of origins. In his book *God and the Astronomers,* he admits that strange developments are going on in astronomy that are particularly fascinating because they have *"religious implications,"* and because of the irrational way scientists have reacted to the unwelcome conclusions.[6]

---

6. Robert Jastrow, *God and the Astronomers* (New York: W. W. Norton and Co., 1978).

Astronomers, he says, have thought their way back, step by step, to a point in time about twenty billion years ago when the universe was born in a fiery explosion. The implications of the "Big Bang" theory annoy many astronomers, especially because the theory of a cataclysmic explosion has completely displaced the more popular and more comfortable "steady state" theory, which held that the universe itself was eternal and had no beginning.

Faced with the cumulative evidence for the "Big Bang" theory, Jastrow says, secular scientists either tried to pretend that the evidence did not exist, tried to gloss it over, or hoped that something else would turn up. Dr. Jastrow likened the scientific community to a group of mountaineers who had finally scaled the Himalayas of human ignorance. They had finally pulled themselves over the last ledge only to be greeted by a group of theologians who had been there for hundreds of years!

Apparently Einstein was the first scientist to react, disturbed because the circumstance of an expanding universe implied that it had a beginning. "To admit such possibilities seems senseless" was his offering on the altar of truth. Arthur Eddington, the famous British astronomer and mathematician, refused point blank to believe it. He wrote that "the notion of a beginning is repugnant to me. It leaves me cold." These men and their peers and disciples shrink from the next question: If the universe had a beginning, *how* did it begin?

The answer of the Divine Eyewitness is unequivocal: Jesus Christ created the universe. "By him were all things created."

Think about what that means! In Paul's day, the Lord Jesus had only recently been on earth. Many people were still alive who had known Him; heard Him speak; seen His miracles; and knew about His death, burial, resurrection, and bodily ascension into heaven. He had lived in one of their villages. He had tramped their highways, preached in their synagogues, and visited in their homes. Paul, once a thoroughgoing unbeliever, had finally met Him face-to-face. He had seen Him in all of His glory. He knew Him as "the Lord from heaven." He now had no doubts at all. Jesus of Nazareth was God, over all, blessed for evermore, the second person of the Godhead, self-existing, uncreated, and the Creator of the universe!

Many people today have a concept of the Lord Jesus that is too small. This fact was brought home to me very forcibly some years ago when our son was still quite small. We had been reading the Bible story of Elijah's being caught up to heaven in a chariot of fire. After a few moments, I asked the little fellow if he would like to go to heaven one day. He said, "No!" He was quite definite about it. "No!"

We looked at the young heretic (!) for a moment and then asked, "Why don't you want to go to heaven?"

He said, "Because Jesus is there." He wasn't being smart. He was quite serious.

"Why don't you want to go to heaven if Jesus is there?"

Back came the answer, as serious as could be, "He wears a dress!"

It did not take long to put two and two together. The little boy had been to Sunday school, where on the classroom wall was a picture. It was supposed to be a picture of Jesus. It depicted a man with long hair and an anemic expression on His face and wearing long, flowing robes which, to a four-year-old, looked just like a dress. He decided that if *that* was Jesus, he wasn't interested.

We smile at the story, but the same kind of thing happens to us. We know, of course, that Jesus did not have long hair and He didn't wear a dress.[7] We know, too, that all artistic portrayals of Jesus are purely subjective and imaginary. Many of them are displeasing. Just the same, people see these artistic renditions and record a mental picture of "Jesus" in their subconscious minds. They think of Him in terms of these pictures as someone who lived a long time ago in a faraway land, someone who is not at all relevant to the modern world of nuclear science, instant communication, microbiology, and computer chips.

But that is just where they are wrong! Jesus Christ created the universe. He knows all about these things. Apart from Him, none of them would exist. He gave no outward sign of acquaintance with these things when He lived on earth, but that was because He had not come to dazzle men with the wonders of science. He had come to offer men the even greater wonder of salvation, and to do that it was not necessary for Him to be an atomic scientist. It will be a different story when He comes back to reign.

Although at His first coming He was content to live on earth in the context of that particular period of time, it does not mean that he had no knowledge of things that we now take for granted. After all, He created the universe.

We are living in a very complex universe. No one today can know everything there is to know about even his own particular scientific discipline. Still less can he know everything there is to know. It has been said, for instance, that a physician would need to read the equivalent of one book an hour just to keep up with

---

7. In the Old Testament, long hair was associated with a Nazarite vow. The Mosaic Law required a Nazarite to abstain from drinking wine, to refrain from touching any dead body, and to let his hair grow long (Num. 6:5). We know of only three lifelong Nazarites—Samson, Samuel, and John the Baptist. Jesus was not a Nazarite and did not have long hair.

his own specialty. That means that if you went to the doctor yesterday, you had better hurry back. He is twenty-four books out of date on whatever is wrong with you!

Some years ago, a medical researcher specializing in just one disease of the human body, sugar diabetes, addressed his colleagues at a medical convention. During his address, he admitted that he still knew very little about this disease. "In fact," he said, "every time I get the answer to just one question about this disease, it only raises another hundred questions to which I don't have the answer." My brother, who was at the convention, told me that when the man sat down, the chairman thanked him "for casting so much darkness on the subject!"

So then, we are living in a complex universe. Nobody can know more than a small fraction of the laws of science. But Jesus knows *every* law that is known to science and every law that is not yet known to science. Moreover, He knows these laws not because He has *investigated* them but because He has *invented* them.

Kepler, a famous astronomer of a past generation, after a series of experiments that unlocked the secrets of astronomy, said, "Oh, God! I am thinking Thy thoughts after Thee!" And that is all that anyone, even the most brilliant of men, can do. Jesus Christ created the universe and authored all of its laws.

It is not only a very complex universe but also a very vast universe. For instance, an estimated one hundred billion stars are in our galaxy and about a hundred billion galaxies besides our own are in known space. Furthermore, known space is said to be one billionth of theoretical space. Sir James Jeans, a British astronomer, has been quoted as saying that there are more stars in space than there are grains of sand on all of the seashores of the world!

And Jesus made them all!

Jesus is more than adequate for the modern world. He was more than adequate, too, for Paul's world and for the false philosophy of the quibbling, Gnostic cult at Colosse. Paul now expands upon the concept of Jesus as Creator-Lord to sweep away the Gnostic notion of grades of angels with Jesus being somewhere toward the bottom of the list. He tells us specifically that not only were "all things" created by Jesus Christ but also things "visible and invisible" were created by Him—whether they be thrones and dominions or principalities and powers.

The Gnostics held that matter was evil. Because matter was evil, how could God have anything to do with it? How could a good God create evil matter? They solved this philosophical problem by means of a man-made theory. They interposed between the Creator and the creation an innumerable company of aeons (emanations)—angelic beings. Paul does not dispute the fact that other beings than man are in the universe. Indeed, by rank and by order of creation, they are higher in the scale of things than man (Heb. 2; Ps. 8:4–6). Jesus created them, too! So much for the Gnostic notion that He was a low-ranking aeon.

Then Paul gives a flash of divine light, which helps illuminate the whole subject. One verse of Scripture is more valuable than any amount of philosophical or occult speculation. Paul affirms that ranks exist among the heavenly beings. He describes them here as "principalities," "powers," "thrones," and "dominions" ("lordships"). Elsewhere, we learn that Michael is an archangel, a title that distinguishes him from the others. There are also cherubim and seraphim. The demons, too, seem to be a separate order of spirit beings. They are described as "unclean" and "evil" and possess a craving to be embodied. Then, of course, high above the ordinary ranks of spirit beings is Lucifer, "the anointed cherub," now known as the Devil and Satan.

Here, Paul mentions just four classes of created spirit beings. We learn from the next chapter (2:15) that the "principalities and powers" were despoiled by Christ in His death and resurrection. We learn from Ephesians 6:12 that they are our enemies and that we need the whole armor of God to overcome them. They are fallen angelic beings who help Satan hold this world and its kingdoms in bondage.

It is not clear as to which angelic beings are referred to here as "thrones" and "dominions." Some clue as to the "thrones" may be gathered from Revelation 4–5, where John describes for us the "four and twenty elders" sitting on thrones in heaven. Some scholars have thought that these are merely men, the twelve patriarchs and the twelve apostles. That view is untenable, however, because in Revelation 5, John (one of the twelve apostles) was certainly not seated among the four and twenty elders. These sinless sons of light, enthroned in heaven, seem to be angelic beings who form a heavenly jury. They watch the movements of God in judgment throughout the period covered by the Apocalypse. They express their approval of God's acts, and they worship Him by casting their crowns at Jesus' feet. These four and twenty elders possibly are the ones to whom Paul refers as "thrones."

The "dominions" would seem to be yet another group of unfallen angelic beings. They are mentioned in the companion letter of Ephesians (1:21), where the Lord is said to be seated far above them and all of the other orders of creation. They are mentioned, also, in Jude 8, where apostates are warned against foolishly setting them at naught. The word for "dominions" is translated "government" in 2 Peter 2:10, but the word evidently is used in the same connection and with the same connotation as in Jude. All of this leads to the conclusion that the "dominions" are governing angels. Thus, the "thrones" and "dominions" in the unseen world counterbalance Satan's "principalities" and "powers."

Paul's point is that "God's dear Son" created all of these angelic beings. Paul does not here bother about the false and foolish Gnostic speculations. The Gnostic false teachers at Colosse had their own philosophy of angels, wholly uninspired and totally speculative and worthless. They envisioned varying grades of angels. They exalted these creatures and placed Christ way down among their lower ranks. Paul had no patience with their foolish ideas. The Lord Jesus Christ was not some mythical or hypothetical Demiurge way down the supposed hierarchical ladder; rather, He is the Creator Himself, apart from them and far above them all.

b. Jesus Christ claims the universe (1:16b)

All things were created by him, and for him.

On various occasions, when he lived on earth, the Lord Jesus claimed absolute authority and power over heaven and earth (Matt. 11:27; 28:18; Luke 10:22). He was simply stating a fact. The whole fabric of the created universe belongs to Him. He owns every blade of grass on earth and every speck of cosmic dust in space. Every atom in the universe is His, made by Him and controlled by Him.

All denial of that fact is based on ignorance, often willful and defiant. There is no future in such denial. It is permitted only for a few short years of time.

All defiance of His right to reign is likewise permitted only on the most temporary and transient of terms, and then only in the interests of a vaster purpose, a purpose about which the false teachers themselves knew nothing. It is a purpose worked out in a past eternity before time began. The time is coming when every knee shall bow and every tongue should confess that Jesus Christ is Lord (Phil. 2:9–11). He owns the universe.

Some years ago, I needed a picture of the stars to use as an illustration in a book. I went to the local planetarium to see what was available. The man in charge generously set before me an armful of file folders packed with photographs of the sky. I chose a picture of Orion. He gave it to me and refused any payment. "We don't own Orion!" he said—then hastily changed the subject when I asked him if he knew the One who does!

Jesus Christ claims the universe. The title deeds of space belong to Him, including those of this rebel planet of ours.

We are reminded of that matchless scene in the Apocalypse. John is seen weeping because no child of Adam's ruined race could be found fit to govern the globe (Rev. 4–5). The challenge had gone forth: "Who is worthy to take the scroll and unloose the seven seals thereof?" The call was not designed to find anyone *willing* to rule the world—there would have been a stampede—but to find someone *worthy*. There was silence. That silence was shattered by a sob. John says, "I wept much, because no man was found worthy" (v. 4)—because not a single human being could make the claim, not Abraham, Isaac or Jacob, not David or Daniel, nor Peter nor James nor even John himself. John wept bitter tears for the shame and disgrace of the children of men.

Then Jesus stepped forth and held out a nail-scarred hand. Instantly, the scroll was given to Him. No questions were asked. He simply claimed the scroll, and the title deeds were His.

What would He have said, we wonder, if He had been asked by what right and on what grounds He claimed the right to rule the globe. Surely He would have said: "That world is Mine! It is Mine by right of *creation*—because I made it! It is Mine by right of *Calvary*—because I bought it! It is Mine by right of *conquest*—because I'm going back to take it by force of arms!" Not only does this one world belong to Him but also all of the worlds of space belong to Him to the most distant galaxy and the most far-flung star.

c. Jesus Christ controls the universe (1:17)

And he is before all things, and by him all things consist [cohere].

He is before all things. He takes precedence both in reference to rank and in terms of time. He is before all things. *Is*, not just *was*. The force of that specific use of the present tense comes out in His reply to His critics (John 8:58). "Before Abraham was, *I am*," He said. He did not say, "Before Abraham was, I was"— although that would have been perfectly true. He said, "Before Abraham was *I am*," claiming to be the great I AM of the Old Testament (Exod. 3:13–14). The Jews understood what He meant. He was claiming equality with God, claiming that He, the Jesus of the New Testament, the Jehovah of the Old Testament, is before all things.

He is *before* all things. Back we go in thought. Back to Abraham, who lived four thousand years ago! Back to Noah! Back to Adam! Back to that awesome moment when the silence of eternity was broken with a rush and a roar! Back to that moment when the angel hosts shouted their astonished acclaim. Back, still further back, to a time when not even the rustle of an angel's wing disturbed the hush of the everlasting hills. And there He is! "Before all things," dwelling with the Father and the Spirit as their eternal coequal—God the Son!

"And by him all things consist [cohere]," says Paul. By Him everything holds together.

Take, for instance, the center of the atom. It contains protons, all positively charged. Coulomb's Law, however, states that "like charges repel." If we bring the positive poles of two magnets together, they will not stay together. They pull apart. For years scientists referred to the force that held the center of the atom together as "an unknown, mysterious force." It is now thought that it has held together by "gluons." To study the center of the atom more accurately, a $600 million research center has been built in Virginia. Physicists want to look inside the half-dozen quarks (the basic components of matter) and the still hypothetical gluons (massless particles) that are thought to bind them together.[8] What makes everything "cohere"? We may not yet know *what* it is that makes everything hold together, but we know *who* it is! Jesus!

And not only the atom! He holds together all of the galaxies of space. The forces of motion, magnetism, gravity, and electricity—all of the thundering machinery of the universe—all of it is held in balance by Him. Countless stars and their satellites travel at inconceivable velocities on prodigious orbits, bodies of enormous size and mass fueled by fires burning at fantastic temperatures are rushing through intangible space—all controlled by Him. They travel, too, with such mathematical precision that we can predict the occasion of an eclipse or the visit of a comet years in advance. Such is His control of the universe.

Our sun, for instance, is just a moderate star as stars go, yet it is pouring energy into space with the utmost prodigality, losing weight by radiation at the rate of 4,200,000 tons a second. This enormous output of sheer physical energy is so well controlled that our planet never gets too hot and never gets too cold but remains at the proper mean temperature to sustain life. Life as we know it can exist only within a very narrow margin of temperature. If it were to get hotter for a little longer, the whole world would become a vast Sahara desert; if it were to get colder for a little longer, the whole world would become a frozen arctic. Someone set the thermostat. That Someone was Jesus.

---

8. Michael Jacobs, "$600 Million Accelerators Could Cast Light on Subatomic Secrets," *Insight* magazine, 6 February 1995, 32–33.

He controls the universe just as He did when He lived on earth. The forces of nature owned His presence and His power. Water blushed into wine when He looked at it. Loaves and fishes multiplied in His hands. Raging seas hushed to rest at His command. Howling winds hushed to sleep. At His will, rolling waves became a pavement beneath His feet. An unbroken colt submitted instantly to His touch. Fishes hurled themselves into Peter's net at the sound of His voice. A glance from Him and instantly the cock crew. After His resurrection, He walked calmly through barred and bolted doors and just as easily vanished from view.

He created the universe. He claims the universe. He controls the universe. All of the entities of space, matter, and time are in His hands. Thrones and dominions, principalities and powers, all of the forces of nature, all the factors in the total equation of eternity and time are His to command. So, why pay the slightest attention to Gnostic nonsense? But Paul is by no means through.

3. The purposes of God revealed (1:18–19)
    a. Who Christ is in these purposes (1:18)
        (1) He heads a new body (1:18a)

And he is the head of the body, the church.

For into these spheres in the heavenlies, where principalities and powers, thrones and dominions engage in battle and hold sway, God has injected a new creation—the church, a force with which to be reckoned both on earth and in the heavenly realm.

But let us pause for a moment and go back to that little Colossian church, timing our arrival to coincide with the reading of this inspired epistle from Paul. The return of Onesimus bearing two apostolic epistles was the talk of the town. That Philemon had received his runaway slave back, not just without punishment but with honor, had focused everyone's eyes on the church. The memo to Philemon had attained its object. Now the letter to the Colossian Christians was to be read! Everyone knew why their pastor, Epaphras, had gone to Rome. Anyone could guess that this Pauline epistle would carry enormous weight. The meeting place was packed. There is Philemon, with Onesimus sitting in the place of honor, usually reserved by Philemon for his personal friends or distinguished visitors. Over there in a huddle, and very much on the defensive, are the false teachers and those whom they have won to their side. They are furious at this turn of events. They will be even more put out when they learn of Paul's apostolic, authoritative, and divinely inspired exaltation of the Lord Jesus Christ.

Bishop Lightfoot says that this was the least important church to which a Pauline epistle was sent. But Paul cared little or nothing about the relative size or importance of a church. The church at Colosse had assumed an importance out of all proportion to its size because Satan had made it his base to subvert all of the churches in the area and, beyond that, all of the churches of the ages to come.

Satan had concocted a dangerous mix of Greek philosophy, Jewish religious tradition, and Christian truth. It was a heady brew. His emissaries had already made friends and influenced people around town. They were dangerous men and glib talkers who were persuasive and clever. But Satan reckoned without the Holy Spirit, and these men reckoned without Paul. The result was one of the most magnificent books of the New Testament, one well designed to protect God's people from such subversive doctrines for the rest of time.

We look around the circle of God's people assembled on this great day. The secretary has now read the opening chapter of the epistle. The great truth of the Lord's deity has been stated in unambiguous terms. The Lord's people beam. The cultists scowl. They had posed as intellectuals but they are now confronted by Paul, the greatest intellectual of all time and one who spoke and wrote by divine inspiration and from divine revelation. Those who had been disposed to listen to the claims of the cult must have been filled with dismay. That dismay can only deepen as Paul turns now from the place of the Christ in creation to the place of the church in redemption. The transition is smooth. The Lord Jesus, after all, is not only God's Firstborn but also the church's Head.

"He is the head of the body, the church," Paul says. The word *He* is emphatic. We can put it thus: "He [with special emphasis] is [an undying fact] the Head [the inspiring, controlling, deciding, and sustaining power] of the body [linked to Him, the Head, in organic unity], the church [the instrument through which He asserts his headship on earth and in the heavenlies]."

He is the head. No sovereign pontiff, no patriarch, no priest, no pastor, is the Head of the church. Christ is the Head.

When the church is mentioned, people tend to think of that vast, organized system of religion that began to develop about the second or third century, which became the state religion of the Roman Empire, which is represented today by the Roman, Greek, and Coptic churches, by the various state churches, and by the numerous incorporated, nonconformist bodies throughout the world; which claims to be represented by the World Council of Churches and similar organizations; and which is sadly misrepresented by a miscellaneous assortment of cults. That, however, is not the church. That is Christendom. However, that is what the average person sees and hears, and that is what he thinks is "the church." The hymn writer has phrased it thus:

> For with a scornful wonder
> Men see her sore oppressed,
> By schisms torn asunder
> By heresies distressed.

In his book *The Screwtape Letters*, C. S. Lewis has given us a great description of the church.[9] He depicts a senior devil, Screwtape, writing to a junior devil, Wormwood, to instruct him in the art of temptation. Wormwood, it seems, is in disgrace for allowing his human client to become a Christian. After gloatingly warning Wormwood that he would not escape the usual penalties for such dereliction of duty, Screwtape tells him how to salvage what he could from this deplorable situation.

He informs Wormwood that, at this stage in the new convert's Christian experience, Wormwood's best ally would be the church itself. The new convert, he says, will feel obliged to go to church where he will meet just that particular assortment of his neighbors he has been at pains to avoid.

Then he lets in a shaft of light. He tells his junior partner that, fortunately for the kingdom of darkness, human beings have never seen the church as it is seen in the spirit world—spread out through all time and space, rooted in eternity and "terrible as an army with banners." He added, "That I confess is a sight to make the boldest tempters tremble."

So then what *is* the church? The New Testament gives us three helpful illustrations. The church is likened to a *building* of which Christ is the foundation. It is a building "not made with hands." It is composed of "living stones"—born-again people, people quarried out of nature's dark, deep mine, shaped and fashioned by the Holy Spirit and placed by Him on the rock, Christ Jesus. As each and every part of a building comes to rest upon the same foundation, so each and every believer rests upon the Lord Jesus Christ for salvation, security, and support. As every part of a building has its proper place in relation to the whole, so every believer has his proper place in the church and his corresponding relationship to every other believer.

---

9. C. S. Lewis, *The Screwtape Letters* (New York: Macmillan, 1961).

The church is likened, also, to a *bride* who has Christ as her Groom. The church is viewed as a lovely woman of unblemished character and great beauty. She is arrayed in the righteousness of Christ, and her destiny is to live and reign with Him forever. She is already seated with Him on high in the heavenlies, and all of His resources are hers. She awaits the day when her enemies will be made her footstool and anticipates "the crowning day that's coming bye and bye." No wonder the hosts of hell tremble at the sight of the church. She has the ear of the King.

The church is likened to a *body* with Christ as the Head. A body is composed of many members, some more visible than others but all important in their place. All share a common life, the life of Christ, and all are constantly "washed" by the life-giving blood. So also is the church, the body of Christ. It is made of members mystically united to Christ by the baptism of the Spirit (1 Cor. 12:13).

It was this headship of Christ over the mystical body, the church, that the Gnostics denied and that Paul here affirms (2:19). Paul declares bluntly that as Christ was the *Lawgiver* in creation, establishing each and every law that governs the universe, so he is the *Lifegiver* in redemption and in relation to the church. The church is not simply a super organization; it is a spiritual organism. It enjoys the very life of Christ to whom each individual believer is as vitally linked as each member of a body to its ruling head. Let the hosts of hell tremble at the thought.

> (2) He heads a new beginning (1:18b–c)
> (a) He originated life (1:18b)

Who is the beginning.

The word for "beginning" points to the Lord Jesus as "the origin" or as "the life source." Life from nothing began through him. The amazing entity that we call "life" is complex beyond anything we can ever imagine. Scientists in a hundred disciplines toil ceaselessly to reduce it to a manageable formula. It eludes them and always will.

Some years ago, biochemists engineered a major breakthrough in their research into the nature of life and announced that it was now possible to manufacture artificial protein in the laboratory. The reactions were varied but predictable. The *Saturday Evening Post* conducted a survey of the kinds of things people were saying about this new achievement. Included in the survey were some leading researchers and some prominent church leaders.

The reaction of some of the scientists was typically humanistic. One researcher prophesied optimistically (and wrongly) that the twentieth century would be known as the century when life ceased to be a mystery. With what has to be a classic case of understatement, he said, "Life is only chemistry."

A British researcher was even more boastful. He extolled the evolutionary view that life originated from "purely chemical events." Then he boasted that scientists would be able to create life themselves "within a few decades." His final contribution on the altar of unbelief was this: "I no longer find it necessary to believe in God."

One churchman's response was particularly appropriate. Monsignor Kelly, spokesman for Archbishop Spellman of the Roman Catholic Archdiocese of New York, said that he was not impressed. "Let them come and talk to me," he said, "when they can create life out of nothing."[10]

That is exactly what Jesus did! Life is the most fantastically complex thing in the universe. Years of patient research, using the most sophisticated of instruments that modern technology can devise, only reveal new and even more complex aspects of it. Life itself eludes us. The deepest secrets of even many of the viruses and diseases that attack it elude us. Life in all of its myriad forms sprang into being as a result of the omniscient genius of Jesus. He originated life!

(b) He overcame death (1:18c)

Who is . . . the firstborn from the dead.

Life from the dead began through Him. He not only designed the womb but also destroyed the tomb. He, the source of life, became "obedient unto death," sovereignly dismissed His Spirit, allowed His body to be placed in a virgin tomb while He Himself departed into the underworld to seize for Himself the keys of death and Hades (Phil. 2:8; John 19:30; Rev. 1:18). Then, on the third day, as He had so often foretold, He rose bodily from the dead.

He is called "the firstborn from the dead." In actual fact, half a dozen people were raised from the dead before He was (seven, if we include Jonah). Elijah raised one. Elisha, with a double portion of Elijah's spirit, raised two, and Jesus Himself raised three. So Jesus was number seven. How could number seven be number one?

---

10. Max Gunther, "The Secret Life," *Saturday Evening Post,* 3 July 1965, 25–29.

Paul gives us the answer in his great chapter on the Resurrection. He says of the death of the believer and the entombment of his body, that "it is sown a natural body; it is raised a spiritual body. There is a natural body, and there is a spiritual body" (1 Cor. 15:44).

Those raised before the resurrection of Christ were sown a natural body and raised a natural body; consequently, they eventually died again. The Lord Jesus was sown a natural body and raised a spiritual body. That is to say that His mortal clay was raised with spiritual properties and raised triumphant forever over death. That is why He is "the firstborn" from the dead. All of those who subsequently partake of resurrection share in His resurrection so they are to be raised with spiritual bodies similar to His (Phil. 3:21). This, doubtless, is what happened to those who shared in His resurrection at the time of the Crucifixion (Matt. 27:52–53). Presumably, they ascended with Him to be presented to the Father as the firstfruits of His resurrection (Eph. 4:7–12). They were the "wave sheaf" of the Old Testament feast of firstfruits (Lev. 23:9–14).

The death, burial, and resurrection of the Lord Jesus was a thing apart. He lay down His life and took it again of His own volition (John 10:17–18). He emerged from death's domains more than conqueror, as Paul will soon remind the Colossians (2:15). He lives forever in "the power of an endless life" (Heb. 7:16).

In his defense before King Agrippa, Paul said, "Why should it be thought a thing incredible with you, that God should raise the dead?" (Acts 26:8). Why indeed? When we think of how many factors have to be in place before life even can be possible and how fantastically complex a thing our body is, then it is no more marvelous a matter that we should *live again* than it is that we should *live at all!*

So, then Jesus originated life. He overcame death.

b. Where Christ is in these purposes (1:18d)

That in all things he might have the preeminence.

That He might hold the primacy; that is, the Lord Jesus stands unrivaled. The word *all* is neuter, indicating "the most inclusive inclusion." He holds first place, the highest rank. The word occurs only here in the New Testament. So much then for the Gnostics and their "emanations" with the Lord Jesus being somewhere far down in the lower ranks. It was an insulting view of Christ! Paul indignantly puts the record straight.

A similar word is found in 3 John 9, but it is prefixed by the verb for "love."

John wrote of that old scoundrel, Diotrephes, that he loved to have "the preeminence." He elevated himself to the rank of a petty pope and even tried to excommunicate the apostle John from the church!

The word translated "preeminence" occurs once in the Septuagint version of the Old Testament, where is recorded Haman's misplaced delight at being invited to Esther's banquet (Esther 5:11). That foolish and wicked man did not know that his death was in the invitation. He came home walking on air, full of the news of his invitation to the banquet. The Holy Spirit says, "And Haman told them of the glory of his riches, and the multitude of his children, and all things wherein the king had *promoted* him, and how he had advanced him above the princes and the servants of the king." The Septuagint says that he was given the preeminence, the primacy, the first and highest place of dignity. He was raised higher and higher so that in the end he might have that much farther to fall.

For the ultimate preeminence and primacy, the place of highest dignity of all, which Haman coveted, is reserved for the Son of God. No Diotrephes in the church, no Haman in the world, and no Lucifer haunting the high halls of heaven can take the place that God has reserved for Jesus. That place is His right now. He is already seated at the right hand of the Majesty on high (Heb. 1:3).

Some people give Him *place.* They have opened their hearts to Him and accepted Him as Savior. Other people go further and give Him *prominence.* They order their lives so as to give Him general control, but they have reservations about going all of the way. Some doors are still barred to Him. In some areas they still reserve the right to do as they please. Then a few people give Him *preeminence.* He is King of kings and Lord of lords over all that they have and are.

The world is hostile to the claims of Christ, and it has displayed that hostility from the beginning. The day is coming, however, when every knee will bend to Him and every tongue will confess that He is Lord (Phil. 2:9–11). That day has not yet come, but come it will. Then, at the focal center of things, those people who stand around the Great White Throne will raise their anthems of praise, and those people in the outer darkness at the farthest circumference of things will likewise add their anguished anthems of praise (Rev. 5:9–14). Angels from the realms of glory will praise Him. The elders and the cherubim will praise Him. Principalities and powers will praise Him. Thrones and dominions will praise Him. Fallen angels and demons from the pit of hell will praise him. Satan himself will praise Him. Men and women and boys and girls will praise Him. Saved and lost alike will praise Him. That issue has already been settled in heaven. And, to His joy, some people on earth today praise Him with full and grateful hearts.

c. What Christ is in those purposes (1:19)

For it pleased the Father that in him should all fulness dwell.

The word for "fulness" is *plerōma,* a favorite word of the Gnostic heretics. They used it in a technical sense to express the sum total of divine power and attributes, and they denied that Jesus ever had this *plerōma,* this plenitude, this fulness. They conceived of God as a pure spirit and denied that the Word had really become flesh. They placed a vast, graded hierarchy of spirits between God and Christ. Paul's answer to all of this was blunt and to the point. He labels it nonsense (2:8). "It pleased the Father that in Him [in Jesus Christ] should dwell all of the plerōma, all of the plenitude of God." Paul did not write that as the product of his own intellect and capacity for brilliant thought. He wrote it by direct illumination and revelation of the Holy Spirit.

The word for "dwell" is important, too. It means "to be permanently at home." In other words, the Lord Jesus was the manifestation of God to man. The divine fulness was not something that was added to His being; it was naturally His. It was "permanently at home" in Him. It was part of His essential being—just as all of the divine attributes are at home in Him.

In His incarnation, He was "God in focus." For many years I have had to wear thick glasses. If I take them off, I cannot see either people or things very well. All I see is a blur. I have some general idea of their size and shape, but beyond that everything is hazy and fuzzy. When I put them on, however, then I can see people and things as they are. They are in focus. The Lord Jesus has brought God into focus for us. The fulness of the Godhead is in Him. The Lord Jesus and His Father are one. What the Father was, He was. If we want to know what God is like, all we have to do is look at Jesus. Jesus brings God into sharp focus. As He Himself said to Philip, "He that hath seen me hath seen the Father" (John 14:9).

The Lord Jesus has now gone back to heaven. So where should people down here look now for a manifestation of that *plerōma?* They are to look at us! Just as people could look at Jesus and see God, so they should be able to look at us and see Jesus. That is part of the eternal purpose of God.

B. The death of Christ (1:20–22)
  1. The means of our reconciliation (1:20a)

And, having made peace through the blood of his cross.

Paul has had us up on the heights. Now he takes us down to the depths. He has taken us out among the stars and back before the beginning of time and has set before us the deity of Christ. Now he sets before us the death of Christ. The contrast could hardly be greater. Paul has been reminding us that God has no plan, no program, and no purpose either for our planet or for all of the vast reaches of space that does not find its center in the person of His Son, our Lord Jesus Christ. He confronts us now with the most amazing of all of the purposes of God—His purpose in redemption, His plan from a past eternity to save ruined sinners of Adam's fallen race at infinite cost.

So the spotlight swings from the deity of Christ to the death of Christ, from the dizziest heights to the uttermost depths, from light unapproachable to night unbelievable, and from the thunderous applause of the heavenly hosts to the bitter blasphemies of murderous men. In a single sentence, down we come from the realm where Christ is crowned with glory and honor to the place where He was crucified in weakness and shame.

We are hurried unceremoniously to Calvary to see men nailing their Maker to a tree. And wonder of wonders, instead of God's hurling His anathemas across the world and sending the chariots of His wrath to visit swift and summary vengeance on a guilty human race, we have the opposite. Instead of wrath, we have *reconciliation:* "Having made peace through the blood of his cross, by him to reconcile all things to himself; by him, I say, whether they be things on earth, or things in heaven." Instead of opening up hell to receive guilty, daring sinners, heirs of the Fall, God opens up heaven.

The verses that are now before us deal with the doctrine of reconciliation. Paul discusses the means, the measure, and the meaning of reconciliation.

Reconciliation! Not once in the Bible is it ever said that God is reconciled to man. God has no need to be reconciled to us; we need to be reconciled to Him. The hostility is all on our part. God's hands are outstretched to us in love and always have been. We are the ones who have turned away. The hostility is always on man's side, not on God's side.

This point is well illustrated in the story of the prodigal son. We see that young man, his purse well lined with money received from his inheritance. He is heading out of the gate and down the road and over the hills and far away. He had high hopes regarding the far country. He had a spring in his step, a song in his soul, and a merry whistle on his lips.

A day or so before, he had callously confronted his father. "About your will, Father, I take it that you have included both my brother and me. Well, let's take the position that you are already dead and your last will and testament has been read. Why not give me my portion now while I'm still young enough to enjoy it?"

The old man looked sadly at his son. There would be no point in reasoning with him in this frame of mind. Bitter experience would have to be his teacher. Of course, there was always the Law because in Israel such rebellion against a parent was a capital offense. The father could have had the young man stoned. But that was not the father's way. He opened his safe and counted out the cash; one third of his savings for this young son of his, the remaining two thirds to be kept in the safe for his other son. The boy scooped the windfall into his bag. Tomorrow he would be off.

The next day, he bade a cheery "good-bye" to his dad, grinned at his older brother, and headed down the country road. The "far country" called him with its siren voice. The "far country" was Carthage, perhaps, or Corinth, or even Rome. The distance to the far country, however, is never measured in terms of miles but in terms of morals.

With a wide grin, the young prodigal congratulated himself. His well-lined purse soon opened every door! He found friends everywhere, wastrels and wantons like himself, willing enough to help this young spendthrift part with his money. And, best of all, he had no more family devotions to endure, no more time wasted on Sabbaths and synagogues, no more endless religious taboos. He could do as he liked and go where he wished. He had no more hard labor on the family fields and farms and no more cows to milk, sheep to shear, or bulls to breed. He was free!

Like grains of sand running swiftly through an hourglass, the boy saw his money melt away. He had picked up the tab for wild parties too many times. The day came when his last shekel was gone—and so were his fair-weather friends.

Hunger drove him from farm to farm in search of work. He soon discovered what the far country was really like. Nobody cared whether he lived or died. On and on he tramped, becoming more disillusioned and more desperate every day. As doors were slammed in his face, so his inflated ideas of his cleverness, attractiveness, and worth declined.

At last, he was given a job. But what a job for a well-born, once-wealthy young Jew! He was hired to feed swine. Hunger gnawed at him until at last he flung himself down beside the hogs to get his share of the slops.

By and by, he "came to himself." He began to think about home, about his dear old dad, about his father's servants, and about the good food that always abounded, even in the servants' hall. He thought of the comfortable quarters that his father provided for even the lowliest of his hired hands. He thought of the clean clothes that they wore and of the fair wages they were paid. And here he was, arrayed in rags, perishing with hunger, unloved, unwanted, lonely, and wretched in a faraway foreign land and engaged in the kind of work that his father would not assign to the meanest slave.

He "came to himself." He would go home. He would return to his father, confess his sin, ask his father to give him a job—any job, however lowly and despised. He was no more fit to be a son. He would be content to be a servant. At least there were no swine on his father's farm. It would take him months to get the smell of them out of his nostrils. Moreover, his father was kind. His father would not turn him away.

So he picked up the pig pail and headed for the house on the hill where lived the Gentile lord who had hired him at starvation wages to herd his hogs. He banged on the door. "Here, mister," he called, "here's your slop bucket. I quit. Get someone else to mind your pigs. I'm going home."

We can visualize the lord of the manor coming to the door and eyeing that wretched hippie up and down as he stood there with his foul-smelling rags, his unkempt hair, his unwashed body, and his sin-stained soul.

"So, you're going home!" we can hear him say. "Going home, are you? Having dishonored your father's name and disgraced your family. Going home—looking like the beggar you are! If I were your father, I'd turn the dogs loose on you."

"I daresay you would," we can hear him reply, "but you don't know my father."

Then began the long journey home. With every mile came a memory of some wild party here or of some young woman seduced there. And with every mile came a fresh resolve to face whatever awaited him at home. What would his father say? What would his brother say? What would the servants say? And what should he himself say? He had wounded his father. He had squandered his wealth on riotous living and dragged an honored name into the dust. What could he possibly say? "Father, I have sinned!" That was how, at last, he decided to begin. "I have sinned. Before heaven and in thy sight." That was it. His sin was not only against his father but also against God. God's law decreed death for a rebellious son. "I am no more worthy to be called thy son." That was the crux of the matter. He had spurned his father's love. In his rage and resentment at even reasonable restraint, he had constituted himself an enemy of the kindest and most loving father it was possible to have. "Make me as one of thy hired hands." His going-away prayer contrasts vividly with his coming-home prayer. His going-away prayer was, "Father, *give* me." His coming-home prayer was, "Father, *make* me." It was proof of a repentant heart.

He trudged on and on. The endless miles came and went until at last the landscape became increasingly familiar. He began to notice, too, the curious stares of people whom he passed. Then he came up over the brow of the last hill before home. Way over yonder were the familiar lanes and fields of his boyhood. And there, far away, was the farmhouse where he had been born. He could almost hear the merry voices, the jokes, the snatches of song, as the servants busied themselves with a hundred farmyard chores.

His footsteps faltered. He could picture the noble old man, his father. He could still picture the tears in his eyes when last he had seen him. He thought of his self-righteous older brother and of his bitter, scornful tongue. He came to a stop. He buried his head in his hands. He groaned aloud. He had come this far, but now his courage failed. He sank to the ground, all of his resolve gone. How could he face his father? He looked at his rags. He was disgusted by his unwashed body and deterred by his uncleansed soul. How his father must hate him! The man in the far country was right. He would be driven from the door. He would do better to die in this ditch. He would take one last look at the old home and then creep into that hedge over there and die.

But what was this? A figure had appeared, running, calling. It couldn't be! It was! It was his dear old dad! "For when he was yet a great way off," Jesus said, "his father saw him, and ran, and had compassion, and fell on his neck and kissed him." He had been watching for him all this time. He had not run after him into the far country—he was much too wise for that—but he had prayed for him and watched for him. He had a corner on the flat roof of the house from which he could see for miles down the road to the far country. Never a day passed but the father had climbed to his watchtower to gaze with a longing, aching heart down that road, anticipating the day of his lost boy's return.

That was the point of the parable. The father did not need to be reconciled with the boy. It was the prodigal who needed to be reconciled with the father. He was the one who had turned away.

We are reminded of the humorous story told of a man and his wife driving down the road in their car. The man was driving and his wife was sitting on her side by the window. She noticed a courting couple in a passing car. It set the thoughts running through her mind.

"Fred," she said, "do you remember when we was courting?"

"Yep!" he said, "Sure do!"

"Do you remember how you would hold my hand?"

"Sure do!"

"Do you remember how close we used to sit when we went out in that old jalopy of yours?"

"Yep! I remember."

"Do you remember how you would put your one arm around me and drive with just one hand, Fred?"

"Sure do," he said.

"Well," she said, "how come we don't sit like that no more?"

He said, "I ain't moved!"

God has not moved. We are the ones who "turned every one to his own way" (Isa. 53:6). The father never stopped loving the prodigal. The wildest stories filtered back to that big house on the hill from far-off lands. Outraged fathers, perhaps, wrote angry letters about daughters debauched and ruined by the prodigal son. Angry men threatened lawsuits over impressionable young sons drawn away into wild ways by that young prodigal. The old father back at home watched and waited and went on loving his lost boy.

At the very first sign of repentance, the very first sight of that tattered, faltering figure on that distant hill, and the father was off! Down from the roof, out of the house, out through the gate, and off down the road. Scornful of his old age! Heedless of curious stares! As fast as his old legs would carry him, as fast as his pounding heart would permit. He was off to meet his boy! He ran, his robes flying behind him and his arms outstretched before him. He was going to bring him home! His boy! Rags, ruin, and all!

Nor would he hear a single word about being received home as a hired hand. This was his *son,* lost and now found, dead once but alive again! This called for a robe and a ring and for shoes for those blistered, callused feet. The fatted calf for the feast! A great welcome home! Spread the news! Call in family, friends, neighbors, anyone who would come. His boy had been reconciled.

God does not need to be reconciled to us. We need to be reconciled to Him. The change of attitude must be ours, not His. He hasn't moved! He is "the same yesterday, today, and forever" (Heb. 13:8). Blessed be His Name!

Paul begins with the *means* of our reconciliation. He says that God has "made peace through the blood of his cross." What an astounding statement! One would have thought that God would have waged war over that blood. The Spirit of God says that He has "made peace" through it instead.

At the heart of that statement is God's plan for our ruined race. That plan has its roots in a past eternity. Way back in a dateless, timeless past, God the Father, God the Son, and God the Holy Spirit decided that they would act in creation. With their omniscient foreknowledge of all things, they knew full well that if they acted in creation the time would come when they would have to act in redemption. Thus, the Lord Jesus is described as the Lamb that was slain from before the foundation of the world (Rev. 13:8). The triune God saw sin raise its head in the universe, sponsored by Lucifer, the anointed cherub. They saw our planet invaded from outer space. They saw sin imported to earth by that same fallen being, now known as "the old serpent." They saw sin spread like an ugly blight across the face of the world. They saw it give rise to graveyards, leper colonies, prisons, madhouses, and battlefields. They saw our race throw off the light yoke imposed by divine love and gird on, instead, the harsh chains of lust, hatred, and fear.

Then the problem arose (if it is permissible to think of God's having a problem). God's holiness said, "Punish them." God's love said, "Pardon them." The solution was simple but sublime and costly beyond anything that we can conceive. God passed sentence against the human race, the maximum sentence commensurate with absolute holiness—death, followed by eternal damnation in those dread, mysterious fires prepared for the Devil himself and his fellow conspirators (Matt. 25:41). Then, in the person of the Lord Jesus, God paid the penalty Himself. Whatever it was that happened on the Cross when the Lord Jesus laid down an everlasting life, when He endured the horror of great darkness, and cried out in utter agony, "My God, my God, why hast thou forsaken me?" will forever be beyond our ability to know or understand. The hymn writer has put it thus:

> None of the ransomed ever knew
> How deep were the waters crossed,
> Nor how dark was the night the Lord passed through
> E're He found His sheep that was lost.

Thus, the demands of God's holiness and the demands of His love have been met. The psalmist caught a glimpse of it when he wrote: "Mercy and truth are met together; righteousness and peace have kissed each other" in a psalm written to praise God for the ending of the Babylonian captivity (Ps. 85:10).

At Calvary, two opposite things are displayed. By crucifying the Son of God, our race exhibited how far it would go in rebellion against God. Sin came out into the open. It was unmasked and exposed for what it really is in all of its naked horror. At the Cross, man did his worst; human wickedness could do no more.

Calvary not only exhibited the greatest tragedy in man's dealings with God but also displayed at the same time the greatest triumph in God's dealings with men. For at Calvary God dealt once and for all with the entire question of sin and with the ancient mystery of iniquity. The vast burden of human sin was laid on the Lord Jesus Christ. The Holy One of Israel was "made sin" for us. "God was in Christ, reconciling the world unto himself" (2 Cor. 5:19).

That is why God can and does "make peace through the blood of his cross." The Cross was foreknown from the beginning. It was to be the means of our reconciliation. It is true that the Lord Jesus was "taken" and that "by wicked hands" He was "crucified and slain." It is equally true that He was "delivered by the determinate counsel and foreknowledge of God" (Acts 2:23). The sin question has been settled. That which constituted man the enemy of God has been removed. Now poor prodigal sons and daughters of Adam's race can come home. God runs to meet them. He plants the kiss of peace upon their brow. He brings them into His house. He spreads a banquet before them. He guarantees a warm welcome in His home on high for all eternity (Rev. 3:20).

> 2. The measure of our reconciliation (1:20b–21)
>   a. It extends to two realms (1:20b)

To reconcile all things unto himself; by him, I say, whether they
be things in earth, or things in heaven.

Both heaven and earth have been defiled by sin. Sin did not begin on earth; it began in heaven. It did not begin with Adam and Eve but in the heart of the highest and most glorious created being in the universe. It began in the heart of that very one who was behind the Gnostic heresy and its dark teaching, teaching that was designed to push Christ down, ever down, in the scale of things, and to exalt Satan in His place. So because sin has defiled both realms, God intends to create both a new heaven and a new earth. All trace of sin will be removed, and both spheres will be reconciled to God. The only marks of sin that will be seen in the new creation will be the marks of Calvary in the hands and feet of Jesus.

God's *reign* extends to three realms; His *reconciliation* extends to only two. Jesus will indeed be confessed as *Lord* on earth, in heaven, and in hell (Phil. 2:9–11). Fallen men and fallen angels alike will own Him as Lord. Unrepentant human beings and unredeemable fallen angels and demons, however, will never be reconciled. Their estate, as terrible as it is, is eternal. It is their choice. The sentence is crystal clear: "He that is unjust, let him be unjust still: and he which is filthy, let him be filthy still" (Rev. 22:11). Similarly, the reconciliation of the redeemed is eternal: "He that is righteous, let him be righteous still: and he that is holy, let him be holy still." People go to a lost eternity not because they have rebelled against God but because they refuse to be reconciled with God. God's *reign,* then, extends to three realms; *reconciliation* extends to only two realms. Reconciled people are to be found both on earth and in heaven.

      b. It extends to total rebels (1:21)
          (1) We were mentally alienated (1:21a)

> *And you, that were sometime alienated and enemies in your*
> *mind.*

Nowhere is man's alienation from God more evident than in his thinking and especially in his thinking about God. Ever since the Fall, when our first parents ate of the tree of knowledge, the human mind has been susceptible to error. Satan knows this and always goes after the mind (2 Cor. 4:3–4). God, by contrast, goes after the heart (v. 6).

Man's mental alienation from God is to be seen everywhere. Witness the countless false religions that flourish around the world. Witness the power with which a false philosophy such as evolution holds men's minds captive. Or think how much easier it is to remember a smutty story than it is to memorize a passage of Scripture. How easy it is to conjure up impure fantasies. How easy it is to deceive people.

Fallen man, especially, cherishes many false, distorted, and wicked ideas about God (Rom. 1:21–32). People resist the revealed truth about God with all of the power of their minds, right down to the moment of salvation or the moment of death. Even after a person is saved and indwelt by the Holy Spirit, old errors die hard. Divine truth is distorted, diluted, or denied. Once an idea is lodged in the head, it is hard, if not impossible, to get it out again.

Years ago, one of my little girls was praying after me. The exercise went something like this:

"Close your eyes." She closed her eyes. "Say this after me."
"Say this after me."

"Dear heavenly Father."
"Dear heavenly Father."
"Make me a good girl."
"Make Daddy a good girl!"
"No! Make me a good girl."
"No! Make Daddy a good girl."

I gave up!

What a blessing that the Holy Spirit does not give up when we persist in our errors. He graciously continues to shine light into our hearts to reach our darkened minds.

(2) We are morally alienated (1:21b)

Alienated . . . by wicked works, yet now hath he reconciled.

Sin is the most destructive force in the universe. It debases us and ruins us. When the great artist Leonardo de Vinci decided to paint what became his masterpiece, *The Last Supper,* he sought for a long time to find a man whom he could use as a model for the picture of Christ. He finally found a man, a young man named Pietro Bandinelli, singing in one of the choirs of Rome. He hired him to sit for him as he immortalized his face as the face of Christ.

Years passed. Much of the painting was finished, but still the artist lacked a suitable model whom he could paint as Judas Iscariot, someone whose features bore the indelible marks of sin. Finally he found a beggar, a man of villainous countenance, exactly suited to portray the face of the traitor. He hired the man, who sat stolidly while the artist transferred his features to the face of Judas on the canvas. When he was finished and as he paid the man for his service, he said, "By the way, what is your name?" "Pietro Bandinelli," the man replied. Sin had done its work and left its mark.

Sin debases character and ruins lives. Sin makes us enemies and aliens from God. All that lay between the man with the face of Jesus and the man with the face of Judas was a few short years of sin.

Sin alienates us from God mentally and morally. But still God's love reaches out to us. The Holy Spirit brings His Word to bear upon our consciences. He shines the light of the gospel into our darkened minds. He lets us see how great are the ravages that sin has wrought in us and how greatly we need to be reconciled to God. "And you, that were sometime alienated and enemies in your mind and by wicked works, yet now hath he reconciled."

3. The meaning of our reconciliation (1:22)

To present you holy and unblameable and unreprovable
in his sight.

In the sight of a God, that is, who sees everything, misses nothing, and re-members it all. What a miracle of grace!

Let us picture a scene. Yonder in heaven sits an omniscient God, and here we are on earth, sinners saved by grace. Satan appears in heaven, as he did from time to time in the days of Job. He comes in the same character as "the accuser of [the] brethren" (Rev. 12:10). His purpose in coming to God is to discredit us before all heaven. Moreover, he does not come to tell lies about us. He is too clever to do a thing like that. He knows perfectly well that no lie would live for an instant in the presence of He who is the truth. Besides, he does not need to tell lies about us. All he needs to do, sad to say, is tell the truth about us.

He approaches the throne and says, "Look at that man. Look at his *filthiness.* You know as well as I do the kind of thoughts he entertains in his mind, the kind of pictures his imagination paints. Why, only the other day he was in a hotel room alone. He turned on the television. A dirty movie caught his eye—one of my cleverest little pieces of smutty sex. Did he turn it off? No. He persuaded himself he needed to watch it to see how far the movie channel would go in portraying pornography, to see, if you please, just exactly what people are watch-ing these days. It was pretty raw stuff. Now he can't get it out of his mind."

God answers, "All I can see is the precious blood of Christ. So far as I can see, he is *holy.* That sin is under the blood."

Satan tries again. "Then look at his *faults,*" he says. "He's full of them. He is totally inconsistent. He is full of flaws and blemishes. He is always stumbling and falling. Now he's in Doubting Castle under the thumb of good old Giant De-spair. Now he's in the Slough of Despond. Next he goes in mortal terror of my friend Apollyon. And all the time he says that he trusts You!"

God says, "I see no faults. Sure, he fell into the Slough of Despond, but he scrambled out on the side farthest from the City of Destruction, the side closest to the narrow gate and Calvary's hill. I see no flaws. He is 'in Christ.' He is unblamable, wholly without blemish. When I look at him, I see Jesus, and that's good enough for Me. One of these days, he will indeed be like Jesus for he will see Him as He is (1 John 3:2). Meanwhile, I see Christ when I see him. He is unblamable. He doesn't have his resurrection body yet."

Satan, ever persistent, tries again. "Look at the *facts*," he says. "Why, I could recount to you a thousand instances where this person has broken Your laws, grieved Your Spirit, acted in the flesh, made a worldly decision, or erred from the truth. Where shall I begin? Shall I begin with that nasty little quarrel he had with his wife—all because she had moved his cuff links?"

God says, "There are no such facts. This man is *unreprovable*. Here, look in the books. See, his name has been blotted out of the book of the lost. It has been written instead in the Lamb's Book of Life. The kind of 'facts' you mention have all been blotted out. I have chosen to remember them no more (Jer. 31:34; Heb. 8:12; 10:17). I control all of the factors of time, matter, and space. The moment that sinner became a saved sinner, I willed his sins—past, present, and future— out of existence. He is unreprovable from where I sit in Glory. 'Who shall lay any thing to the charge of God's elect?' (Rom. 8:33). Calvary covers it all. That man has been justified. That is the all-important fact. You have no case."

Such is the redeeming, justifying, reconciling grace of God. That is the meaning of our reconciliation! God sees us as holy, unblamble, and unreprovable! If that's how God sees us, surely that is how we ought to see each other.

C. The demands of Christ (1:23–29)
   1. We are to be loyal to Him (1:23)
      a. A definite loyalty (1:23a)

"If ye continue in the faith," Paul says, moving on from our standing to our state. Paul has confronted us with the deity of Christ. Then in a dramatic move he confronts us with the *death* of Christ, hurrying us on from Glory to Golgotha, from Creation to Calvary. He has shown us the Lord Jesus as Creator of the universe, as Head of the church, and as Justifier in heaven. Already Paul has struck a mighty blow at the Gnostic cult at Colosse. No cult, ancient or modern, can last long beneath such hammer blows as these.

Take, for instance, Rome's claim that the pope is the Sovereign Pontiff, the Vicar of Christ, the head of the church. Or take the Russellite teaching that Jesus was not God, merely "a god," that He was a created being, none other, indeed, than Michael the archangel. Or take the liberal view that Jesus lived before His time and was martyred, that He died as the victim of a malicious establishment, not as the atonement for our sins. All such false teaching is exposed as error by this passage.

Now Paul moves on to the *demands* of Christ. Such monumental truths demand a response from us. Because Jesus is God and because He, God incarnate, took our place at Calvary and died, the Just for us the unjust, to bring us to God (1 Peter 3:18), then no demand that He might make upon us can be too great. As Isaac Watts put it,

> Were the whole realm of nature mine,
> That were a present far too small;
> Love so amazing, so divine
> Demands my heart, my life, my all.

First, the Lord demands a *definite* loyalty. Paul puts it as a conditional clause: "If ye continue in the faith. . . ." The word *if* is used in various ways in the New Testament. The force of the word is always determined by the mood of the verb with which it is used. Two Greek words are used for "if." One of them can be followed by a verb in the indicative mood or by a verb in the subjunctive mood; the other can be followed by a verb in either the indicative, the subjective, or the optative mood. Here the word for "if" can rightly be rendered "if so be," and it is followed by a verb in the indicative mood. In other words, there is no doubt about it. We can supply the ellipsis: "If ye continue in the faith (which you will assuredly do)."[11] What we have here, then, is a definite loyalty. Paul is not casting doubt on our salvation; he is simply saying that a person who is genuinely saved will most assuredly continue in the faith. It is not a question of "*if* you do this or that," you will be saved; it is a question of "*because* you are saved," you will do this or that.

Paul uses the word *if* in this way on several notable occasions. In his great passage on the resurrection of Christ he says, "Now *if* Christ be preached that he rose from the dead" (1 Cor. 15:12). There was no doubt at all that Christ was being so preached. The apostles were turning the Roman Empire upside down with that very message. It was at the very heart of apostolic preaching.

In the same passage, Paul says, "And *if* Christ be not risen, then is our preaching vain, and your faith is also vain" (1 Cor. 15:14). Again, there was no doubt at all about the fact of Christ's resurrection. In both cases, the word for *if* is the same one used here in Colossians 1:23, and in both cases it is in the indicative mood.

---

11. See E. W. Bullinger, *The Companion Bible* (Grand Rapids: Kregel, 1993), app. 118.

So, then, the loyalty of which Paul speaks here is not a *doubtful* loyalty but a *definite* loyalty. Paul had no doubt at all that the Colossian believers would show that their faith in Christ was genuine. The word of assurance by the great apostle expressed his confidence that the Colossians would not succumb to the Gnostic cult.

b. A deepening loyalty (1:23b)

If ye continue . . . grounded and settled. . . .

The word for "grounded" here signifies the laying of a foundation. The word for "settled" stems from a word which means "to be seated." In other words, we are not only to take firm stand upon the Rock but also to settle down there.

Discipline and determination are key factors in the equation of the Christian life. They are like the flesh hooks used in connection with the sacrifices offered on Israel's altar in Old Testament times. Those flesh hooks were employed to keep the body of the sacrificial animal properly positioned at all times in the heat of the flames. Without them there might have been some danger of the sacrifice moving and even falling off the altar.

Throughout history we see this characteristic in the lives of individuals who made a noticeable mark for God. David, for instance, made it a fixed principle never to retaliate against King Saul, who on two dozen different occasions, in this way or that, sought to murder him. On two occasions, he could have killed Saul easily, but he refused to do so (1 Sam. 24:1–21; 26:1–25).

We see the same determination in Joseph, who was resolved to keep himself clean although he was a slave in Egypt and was exposed to fierce temptation (Gen. 39:7–20). Likewise, "Moses . . . refused to be called the son of Pharaoh's daughter; Choosing rather to suffer affliction with the people of God, than to enjoy the pleasures of sin for a season; Esteeming the reproach of Christ greater riches than the treasures of Egypt" (Heb. 11:24–26). Similarly, Daniel, a youthful captive in Babylon, purposed in his heart that he would not compromise his convictions for the sake of worldly gain (Dan. 1:8)

We think of the sufferings that Adoniram Judson endured in Burma; of the loneliness of that intrepid explorer and missionary, David Livingstone, in Africa; of the determination of Hugh Latimer in the fires of martyrdom in Oxford; and of the unyielding boldness of Martin Luther before the Diet of Worms and his resolute refusal to bow or bend before prince or pope.

Paul was made of similar granite and iron. He scoffed at persecution. He spoke equally fearlessly to Jewish pontiff, Roman governors, and Herodian king. He stood firm for God in prison, whether at Philippi, Caesarea, or Rome. He was bold when faced with Nero, disciplined and determined to be true to martyrdom itself (Eph. 6:19–20). Well Paul knew the importance of settling down on the Rock.

Our commitment to Christ must be of the same nature. We are to take our stand on the eternal verities that Paul has been expounding to the Colossians. We are to sit down on them, resolved to stay there at all costs.

c. A determined loyalty (1:23c)

If ye . . . be not moved away. . . .

Paul develops the thought. The expression "not being moved away" can be rendered "not being continually shifted away."

This kind of commitment is basic to achievement in all walks of life. My brother rose through the ranks of the medical profession to become a leading world authority on diseases of the liver. I can remember when as a very young man he decided that he wanted to be a doctor. He was working in a low-paying job as a bank teller in a remote town in western Canada. The major employer in town was a pulp mill. He discovered that he could make much more money doing deadening manual work at the mill than he could ever hope to make with the bank. He quit the bank, took the soulless job at the mill, and scraped and saved to get enough money to go to medical school. He had little encouragement, no influential friends, and no one to smooth his way. He faced a grueling ten years of continuous study.

Our paths crossed several times during his student days. I remember meeting him one day shortly after he had been accepted by a prestigious Canadian medical school. He was well into his studies. I had not seen him for several years. He was thin. His coat was threadbare; and, although it was winter, he had no topcoat.

"How much longer do you have to go, Jim?" I asked.

"Five more years to get my M.D.," he said, "then three more years to specialize in pathology. I want to be a doctor's doctor."

"Do you have many friends?"

"I don't have much time for friends. I study day and night."

"Do you need money?"

"I always need money."

To get money, he worked as a waiter on a transcontinental train all one summer.

"Why don't you settle for less?" I asked him. "You could make a decent living as a druggist."

"I don't want to be a druggist," he said. "I want to be a doctor."

And that was what it took—determined loyalty to the goal he had enthroned in his heart. That is what it takes to achieve success and eminence in any career. My brother was determined to be a doctor and not merely a doctor, but a doctor's doctor, a pathologist. He wanted not to be merely a pathologist but to be a research pathologist specializing in diseases of the liver. But he wanted not only to be a specialist on diseases of the liver but also to become a leading authority in that field. He was determined "not to be moved away," as Paul would put it, "not to be continually shifted aside."

Surely as Christians we must be equally resolved to be the very best kind of a Christian it is possible to be. In the light of the Lord's deity and death, how can we settle for anything less?

d. A dispensational loyalty (1:23d)

The hope of the gospel, which ye have heard, and which was preached to every creature which is under heaven. . . .

The universality of the gospel is what Paul has in mind here. So far and wide were the gospel heralds spreading even in those early days that Paul could speak of the whole world coming under the sound of the gospel. Only three decades had passed since Calvary, and the story of Jesus would still be vibrant in peoples' memories. The first impetus of missionary zeal had not yet died out.

The gospel messenger is the herald of a new dispensation, a highly privileged and unique generation. In Old Testament times, the revelation of God was confined largely to the Jewish people. If God had anything to say, He said it to a Jew. If God spoke to men, He spoke in Hebrew. If a Gentile wanted to know God, he had to go, for the most part, to a Jew. Foreigners had to become Jewish proselytes to enjoy the privileges of the Jewish religion. They had to submit to circumcision, take on the burden of the Mosaic Law, live by the Levitical dietary code, and keep the Sabbath.

Pentecost has changed all of that. For this dispensation, the Jews have been set aside as the monopolists of divine revelation (Rom. 11). Gentiles today occupy the place of religious privilege that for two thousand years was the monopoly of the Jew. After Pentecost, God began to speak in Greek, a Gentile language. For the past two thousand years for the most part, if a Jew has wanted to know God in all of the blaze of New Testament revelation, he has had to come as a rule to a Gentile. The church is largely a Gentile entity. The good news about God is spread abroad by Gentiles.

The gospel is going forth in thousands of tongues. Missionaries today are pressing on with the task to the uttermost parts of the earth. The Bible is being translated into tribal tongues at a speed never before known, with the aid of technologies not dreamed of until now. Means of mass communication are reducing the world to a global village. Even so, for all of our modern techniques and mobilization, it is questionable that we can boast of zeal and success to compare with that of the early church when the memory of the Lord's sojourn on this planet was still fresh and when the Holy Spirit's outpouring was still accompanied by the transitional gifts.

The meaning of Paul's actual words in this verse has been debated back and forth. Some scholars have claimed that Paul was using hyperbole. Others accept the words at their face value. The Savior bade them reach the uttermost parts of the earth. They did what He said. Others think that Paul's words here are explained in terms of the widespread distribution of the gospel by those from so many countries converted in Jerusalem on the day of Pentecost. Lightfoot says that we should not demand mathematical exactness here, Paul was emphasizing the universality of the gospel. Robertson took the view that the gospel was much more widespread than we suspect. Paul, he thought, was urging the Colossians not be diverted down some false path by the heretics.

e. A doctrinal loyalty (1:23e)

The gospel . . . whereof I Paul am made a minister.

This is an important statement because scores of so-called "gospels" are in circulation today. They are false gospels concocted by the father of lies. Paul doubtless had in mind here the false Gnostic "gospel" that was being circulated at Colosse. He, Paul, was certainly not a minister of *that* "gospel." Numerous passages in the New Testament are aimed at various false gospels already in circulation, some of them before the church was a dozen years old. The Galatians had to be warned by Paul against a false gospel (Gal. 1:6–9). Paul was being personally and vehemently attacked at Corinth as a means of discrediting his teaching (2 Cor. 11:3–6, 13–15, 19–23). The Thessalonians had been taught error concerning the second coming of Christ (2 Thess. 2:1–3). Peter, Jude, and John all had to combat error.

Paul was the Holy Spirit's choice to be the theologian of the church. Paul was the one who expounded the three major "mystery" truths of the New Testament—the mystery of Christ's *cross* (in Romans), the mystery of Christ's *church* (in Colossians and Ephesians), and the mystery of Christ's *coming* (in 1 and 2 Thessalonians). The other Pauline epistles are related to these three great primary epistles—because of either doctrinal or moral departure from the truths revealed in Romans, Ephesians, and Thessalonians. In a very real sense, Paul was a divinely appointed and unique minister of the gospel. He was the chief custodian of its doctrinal content.

Doctrine is of vital importance. We are greatly indebted to Paul not only for thinking things through but also for writing things down. Even in his unconverted days as a trained young rabbi, he had an encyclopedic knowledge of the Old Testament. His vision of the risen Christ voided most of his rabbinical theology, however, and he retired into the solitudes of Sinai to seek the Holy Spirit's enlightenment. Calvary had changed everything. He sought out the heights of Horeb, taking his Old Testament with him and keeping the vision of a nail-scarred, risen, and glorified Christ ever before him. He came back with Romans, Ephesians, and Thessalonians in his heart.

It is fashionable these days to depreciate doctrine. "Doctrine is divisive," we are told. People's experiences are allowed to annul doctrine. One of the great questions underlying the book of Job was this: would Job's experience triumph over his theology, or would Job's theology triumph over his experience? Job was shaken by the storms of disaster that swept over him in wave after wave. But he held true to his beliefs. "Though he slay me, yet will I trust in him," he said (Job 13:15). It is a good thing that Job had something more substantial than today's "prosperity gospel" to support him when his whole world caved in. He lost family, fame, fortune, and friends, along with the love and loyalty of his wife. And none of it made sense—especially to his so-called "comforters," who believed that a godly man could expect to be rewarded with riches, good health, and long life. But Job's theology triumphed.

We are being invited (as Eliphas invited Job) to accept exotic experiences and extrabiblical revelations as true and to pin our faith on healings, miracles, tongues, and prophecies that come from who knows where. We would do well to heed

Paul's demand for sound doctrine. We must have a doctrinal loyalty to Christ. Experiences and expositions that fly in the face of sound doctrine are delusory and dangerous.

> 2. We are to live for Him (1:24–29)
>   a. Identified with His Cross (1:24)

Who now rejoice in my sufferings for you, and fill up that which is behind of the afflictions of Christ in my flesh for his body's sake, which is the church.

The statement about filling up "that which is behind of the afflictions of Christ" strikes us as strange. Surely the sufferings of Christ were complete. Surely when the Lord shouted on the Cross, "It is finished," He meant just that. Surely it is impossible to add to a finished work. If something is finished, it's finished.

The Roman church has made great capital out of the notion that the merit of Christ's sufferings must be supplemented by the merits of the Virgin Mary and by the merits of saints canonized by the church. The merits of Christ, plus all of these other "merits," are said to make up a kind of spiritual treasury, the accumulated fund of which can be administered by the church for the benefit of sinners. The Roman practice of granting indulgences is an outgrowth of this kind of teaching. Paul never intended his words to receive such a twist.

What then *is* Paul saying here? Is it possible for us as believers to add something to the merit and suffering of Christ? Can we fill up with our own good works and our own sufferings some lack in what the Savior Himself provided? Of course not! All of our righteousness is "as filthy rags," the prophet says (Isa. 64:6). We have no merits of our own. We are bankrupt sinners saved by grace (Eph. 2:4–9). Then whatever is Paul talking about?

Paul links *his* sufferings with the sufferings of Christ and also with the sufferings of the church, the body of Christ. At this point, it will be helpful to go back and explore Paul's own spiritual history. Before his conversion, he persecuted the Christian community with the ferocity of a wild boar tearing up tender saplings by the root. He himself said that he was "exceedingly mad" against the Christians (Acts 26:11). Then he met Jesus, and all was changed! Then and there, on the Damascus Road, he learned a lesson that he never forgot. Jesus did not say to him, "Why do you persecute *them?*" He said, "Why do you persecute *Me?*" In that moment, he learned about the mystical body of

Christ—that for him to put his hand upon a Christian was for him actually to put his hand on the *Christ.*

Throughout the long centuries of the Christian era, it has been the same. Members of the body of Christ have suffered, and Christ has suffered with them. He has been right there alongside them in the arena as the lions roared, beside them at the stake as the flames leaped up, and there beside them as the inquisitors gouged their flesh with red-hot pincers. The body suffered, and the Head suffered. They are inseparable.

Thus, Christ's sufferings are of two kinds. Christ has suffered *for our sins.* That suffering took place on the Cross, and that suffering is over forever. He died. He rose again. He ascended on high. Now Christ suffers *with His saints,* and that suffering goes on and on. Christ suffered for our sins; that was *redemptive* suffering. Christ suffers with His saints; that is *responsive* suffering.

Paul tells us that *he* was suffering. Even as he wrote this letter, he was chained to a jailer, having been falsely accused of assorted charges, some of them lethal. He could no longer travel and preach, and he could no longer evangelize great cities and plant new churches. His body was a mosaic of whip marks printed on his flesh by many a Hebrew lash and Roman scourge. Moreover he was chronically ill and in need of the constant care of a physician.

As just one member of the body of Christ, Paul was suffering. But no member of a body suffers alone; other members suffer with it. If I cut my finger, my whole body feels it, especially the head, where the nerves register and interpret the pain. Paul was in prison and in pain. The Lord Jesus, the Head of the mystical body, felt that pain. Paul was suffering, and Christ was suffering. They were suffering together. Paul, in his sufferings, was helping to fill up the measure of the sufferings of Christ. Elsewhere, he referred to this kind of thing as "know[ing] . . . the fellowship of his sufferings" (Phil. 3:10).

So, then, we are to live for Christ. If we are called upon to suffer, then that is a privilege. He and we suffer together. One day, all suffering will cease. Christ will come back and put an end to it all.

b. Identified with His church (1:25–29)
(1) Its ministry (1:25)

The church . . . Whereof I am made a minister, according to the dispensation of God which is given to me for you, to fulfil the word of God.

Paul has just said that he was a minister of the gospel (v. 23). Now he says that he is a minister of the church. The word for "minister" is the one from which we derive our word "deacon," and it simply means "a servant." It occurs about thirty times in the New Testament, eight times in the Gospels and twenty-two times in Paul's writings.

The Lord Jesus illustrates the scope of the word in His statement that "the Son of man is come not to be *ministered* unto, but to minister, and to give his life a ransom for many" (Matt. 20:28). Paul saw the Christian ministry as one of service. He understood that a special "dispensation" of service had been entrusted to him. He had been commissioned for a special purpose, to declare fully God's Word. The *ministry* of the church, then, as exemplified by Paul, is to preach God's Word.

(2) Its mystery (1:26)

Even the mystery which hath been hid from ages and from generations, but now is made manifest to his saints.

"The holy secret!" That is one rendering of the word *mystery*. In the New Testament, the word denotes a truth that cannot be discovered by human reasoning but only by divine revelation, regardless of whether it is hard to understand.

The word, as employed by Paul, is borrowed from the ancient mystery religions, including Gnostic systems the rites and initiation of which were kept secret and were the prerogative of a chosen few. Paul takes the word away from them. The Christian faith incudes secrets great and glorious, but they are open secrets. They are available to everyone, not just to a special class of initiates.

The church itself is a prime example of a New Testament mystery. Old Testament believers had no concept of it whatsoever. Truth concerning the church was *concealed* in the Old Testament, but it has been *revealed* only in the New Testament. There are numerous word pictures of the church to be found in the types of the Old Testament. Many of the brides of the Old Testament are types of the church. Eve, for example, depicts the *formation* of the church, Rebekah displays the *faith* of the church, Asenath portrays the *future* of the church, and so on.

The finding of a bride for Isaac (Gen. 24) is a richly illustrative type of Christ and His church. The father, Abraham, sent an unnamed servant (a type of the Holy Spirit) into the world to seek a bride for Isaac, the father's well-beloved son (a type of Christ). The servant did not talk about himself. He talked about the father and the son. He brought rich gifts with him for the bride-to-be. Rebekah responded to the invitation to come to Isaac and give herself to him to be his very own.

The journey to Isaac was undertaken step by step under the guidance and under the protection of the servant. We can envision Rebekah's *learning* of Isaac, asking the servant a thousand questions about him and learning ever more about the father's house and of the symbolic "death" and "resurrection" of Isaac on Mount Moriah. We can envision Rebekah's *longing* for Isaac. The farther behind she leaves her old life and the more she thinks of Isaac himself, as revealed to her by the servant, the more he extols and exalts him, the more her affections become engaged to him. Finally, we can envision her *looking* for Isaac, anticipating his coming to meet her.[12]

And so on with many other Old Testament types. Although we can see the church thus concealed in the Old Testament, the believers of that era saw no such thing. Truth concerning the church was not revealed until the New Testament. In Matthew 16:16–19, the Lord foretells the coming of the *universal* church, and in Mathew 18:1–20, He depicts the coming of the *local* church. The full revelation concerning the church, however, awaited the writing of the New Testament epistles, especially those of the apostle Paul and particularly his epistle to the Ephesians.

(3) Its message (1:27)

> *To whom God would make known what is the riches of the glory*
> *of this mystery among the Gentiles; which is Christ in you, the*
> *hope of glory.*

The "mystery" truths of the New Testament are many and varied. We have, for instance, *the mystery of the kingdom of heaven* (Matt. 13:11), as set forth in the mystery parables designed to conceal truth even while revealing it.

There is *the mystery of the fulness of the Gentiles* (Rom. 11:25). The "fulness" of the Gentiles refers to the time of Gentile *spiritual* preeminence over Israel, beginning at Pentecost and ending with the Rapture. The expression stands alongside the period known as the "times of the Gentiles," an expression that refers to the period of Gentile political dominance over Israel, beginning with Nebuchadnezzar and ending with the Antichrist.

---

12. See John Phillips, *Exploring Genesis* (Grand Rapids: Kregel, 2001).

Paul mentions *the mystery of the gospel* (Rom. 16:25–26; Eph. 6:19–20), God's marvelous plan for saving sinners. He mentions *the mystery of the Cross* (1 Cor. 2:7–16), the preaching of which was so much foolishness to the intellectual Greek and such a stumbling block to the religious Jew.

There is also *the mystery of the Rapture* (1 Cor. 15:51–55; 1 Thess. 4:15–5:11), including the wonders that lie ahead for us when we receive our resurrection bodies.

There is *the mystery of this age of grace* (Eph. 3:1–12) and *the mystery of the church,* the bride of Christ (Eph. 5:25–33), truths undreamed of by the Old Testament prophets. Along with this is the awesome *mystery of godliness* (1 Tim. 3:16), God's wondrous purpose in the incarnation of His Son.

Two other great mysteries have been revealed, but they anticipate end-time events after the rapture of the church. There is *the mystery of iniquity* (2 Thess. 2:7), the coming of the man of sin to usurp total rule over this planet, and *the mystery of Babylon,* the harlot church (Rev. 17:1–18).

A separate book would be necessary to expound all of these hidden truths now revealed. Here in Colossians, however, Paul seizes on what perhaps has to be the greatest of them all—"Christ in you, the hope of glory." Who can hope to grasp the dimensions of a truth like that?

Here we touch the very heart of the matter, the mystery of mysteries. The Lord Jesus not only incarnated Himself in human flesh, but He has chosen to take up residence in each of His own! Here is the very genius of Christianity—"Christ in you!" Christianity is not a religion, it is not a code of laws or a set of creeds. It is Christ! A real living Person. One who came to this planet in space, who chose to live among us, who was willing to die for us, who is now ascended on high, and who yet lives in us. He who once gave His life *for* us now abides in us to give His life *to* us. He who once died *as* me now lives *in* me. What an astounding truth!

How glorious a truth this is can be gathered from the way Paul piles up words to describe it.

For instance, he speaks of "the riches of the glory of this mystery." This is no ordinary truth. It is a rich truth, a glorious truth. There was a *Judaistic* flavor to the heresy at Colosse, an insistence on rules, rituals, and regulations. Striking at this Jewish feature, Paul declares that the glory of this mystery lies in its application to *Gentiles.* Judaism was miserly and beggarly in its narrow nationalism, but the gospel changed all of that. The church is not just another Jewish sect. Jewish religious thought, even in its noblest and most generous mood, conceived no such truth as this. Moreover, Jews disliked Gentiles. They avoided them, would not consider eating with them, thought of them as unclean, and likened them to dogs. In their most magnanimous moments they would concede that their religion could be offered to Gentiles—but only if they became Jews. Their coming messiah would bless Gentiles, but they would be subservient to Jews in an empire over which Jews ruled. That the Christ of God would not only love Gentiles as much as He loved Jews but also make them coheirs of all of the vast spiritual blessing that He had to bestow, breaking down "the middle wall of partition" (Eph. 2:14) between Jews and Gentiles, making of them "one new man, one glorious church," and that He would indwell regenerated Jews and Gentiles alike—such concepts were totally foreign to Jewish thought. More! Because Gentiles outnumber Jews in the church by an overwhelming preponderance, this truth—"Christ in you, the hope of glory"—has become a predominantly Gentile truth.

"The hope of glory!" For the ultimate goal is glory! The Lord put it like this when He spoke from heaven: "Behold, I stand at the door and knock: if any man hear my voice, and open the door, I will come in to him, and will sup with him, and he with me" (Rev. 3:20). The hope of glory! Christ comes to live in us, poor lost sinners of the Gentiles though we be, that we might go to live forever with Him.

(4) Its mission (1:28–29)
    (a) Reaching men for Christ (1:28)

Christ . . . whom we preach, warning every man, and teaching
every man in all wisdom; that we may present every man perfect
in Christ Jesus.

Every man! Every man! Every man! Paul uses the expression three times. We are to *evangelize* "every man," preaching Christ with a warning not to reject Him. We are to *educate* "every man," with all wisdom making known the whole counsel of God. We are to *edify* "every man," so that they might be presented fully matured to Christ. The word for "perfect" is *teleios,* signifying something that has revealed its end. It comes from the word *telos,* "the end." The equivalent Latin word would be *finis,* that is, "finished," or "nothing beyond." This is the first part of the church's mission: to reach people *for* Christ and to bring them to spiritual maturity in Christ. The three great church gifts are involved in this process—the gifts of the evangelist, the teacher, and the pastor.

(b) Reaching men through Christ (1:29)

Whereunto I also labour, striving according to his working,
which worketh in me mightily.

It is the indwelling Christ who does the work. If we are doing the work, nothing will be achieved. As Jesus Himself said, "Without me ye can do nothing" (John 15:5). The statement occurs in the Lord's teaching concerning the vine and the branches. The branches are wholly dependent on the vine for life and growth and fruit.

When Moses first cast in his lot with the people of God and made his decision for Christ, he set out to strike a blow for God and to win the freedom of the enslaved people. But that blow was struck in the energy of the flesh. As a result, Moses the missionary became Moses the murderer. It took forty years for God to get Moses to the place where he could be used as Israel's kinsman-redeemer. Even in Old Testament times, a man could not do God's work man's way and with man's means. It is even more so now in New Testament times.

Paul's testimony sums it up: "I labour, striving according to his working, which worketh in me mightily." We are to reach men through Christ. It is the only way we can reach them.

PART 3

The Truth About the Cult

Colossians 2:1–23

III. THE TRUTH ABOUT THE CULT (2:1–23)
  A. Experiencing the truth (2:1–7)
    1. About Christians (2:1–2a)
       a. We are engaged in a common battle (2:1)
       b. We are encircled in a common bond (2:2a)
    2. About Christ (2:2b–4)
       a. In an increasing way (2:2b)
       b. In an inexhaustible way (2:3)
       c. In an invincible way (2:4)
    3. About Christianity (2:5–7)
       a. Life in a new dimension (2:5)
       b. Life under a new direction (2:6)
       c. Life with a new distinction (2:7)
          (1) Abiding in Christ (2:7a)
          (2) Abounding in Christ (2:7b)
  B. Exposing the lie (2:8–23)
    1. Secular reasoning and the gospel (intellectualism) (2:8–10)
       a. Its menace (2:8a)
       b. Its method (2:8b)
       c. Its mistake (2:9–10)
          It ignores:
          (1) The meaning of Christ's birth (2:9)
          (2) The mystery of Christ's body (2:10a)
          (3) The majesty of Christ's being (2:10b)
    2. Sundry rituals and the gospel (ceremonialism) (2:11–17)
       a. That which has been shed through Christ (2:11)
       b. That which has been shared with Christ (2:12–13)
          (1) The divine operation (2:12)
          (2) The divine opportunity (2:13)
       c. That which has been shown by Christ (2:14–15)
          (1) The question of sin (2:14)
          (2) The question of Satan (2:15)
       d. That which has been shattered by Christ (2:16–17)
    3. Special revelations and the gospel (mysticism) (2:18–19)
       a. The false modesty of the cult (2:18a)

      b. The false mediators of the cult (2:18b)

      c. The false mentality of the cult (2:18c–19)

         (1) It inflates man's pride (2:18c)

         (2) It infringes Christ's place (2:19)

    4. Stricter rules and the gospel (legalism) (2:20–23)

      a. How man-made rules chain us (2:20–21)

         (1) Blinding us to the teaching of God (2:20a–b)

            (a) Our status as Christians (2:20a)

            (b) Our stature as Christians (2:20b)

         (2) Binding us to the teachings of men (2:20c–21)

            (a) How they are imposed on us (2:20c)

            (b) How they are impressed on us (2:21)

      b. How man-made rules cheat us (2:22–23)

         (1) Where they collapse (2:22a)

         (2) Whence they come (2:22b)

         (3) Why they convince (2:23a)

         (4) What they cause (2:23b)

III. THE TRUTH ABOUT THE CULT (2:1–23)

   A. Experiencing the truth (2:1–7)

     1. About Christians (2:1–2a)

       a. We are engaged in a common battle (2:1)

For I would that ye knew what great conflict I have for you,
and for them at Laodicea.

Paul is about to open up a full-scale assault on the cult that was imposing itself on the church at Colosse. But first he nails his colors to the mast. He displays the banner of truth. Soon his readers will have to choose sides. How they choose will reveal a great deal about them. It is imperative that they know and recognize the flag of divine truth. There could be no compromise between truth as represented by Paul's banner and error as represented by the flag of the cult.

Paul has a twofold approach to the problem of false teaching at Colosse. He calls upon the believers to *experience the truth* and then to *expose the lie.* For there was a battle raging at Colosse. The enemy had to be stopped there or not only the Colossian church but also all of the Christian world would be imperiled. It was not just a local matter. That is why Paul, although he had never been to Colosse so far as we know, made the battle of the Colossian church his own.

One would have thought that Paul had enough troubles as it was. He was in prison, accused both of propagating an illegal religion and high treason. His final judge was Nero, and that fact in itself was disquieting. And Paul was not a well man. With all of these pressures to contend with, Paul, nevertheless, did not hesitate. It made little difference what happened to him, and he told the Philippians so in a letter written to them about this same time (Phil. 1:12–30). It was not that important what happened to him, but it was critically important what happened at Colosse.

A common battle was going on. Paul was in the thick of it at Rome. They were in the thick of it at Colosse and at Laodicea. The battle lines were drawn all across the world. They have been drawn down all of the ages of time. Wherever a gathering of Christians occurs, whether in a cottage or a cathedral, there runs the front line. The enemy is everywhere. That was how Paul saw the battle. He girded on his armor and sallied forth to war. His invincible weapon—a pen!

Against Laodicea, the enemy's tactic was *luxury*. Satan let the Laodiceans grow rich so that they thought that they had need of nothing, not even of Christ, who is depicted as outside their church altogether (Rev. 3:14–22). The tactic against Colosse was *lies*. Satan sought to entangle the Colossians with false teaching.

As soon as Epaphras began to unfold to Paul the characteristics of the cult, Paul recognized the danger. This was to be a fight to the finish. This was crucial. This did not just concern a handful of believers in a backwoods town in a remote corner of the world. This concerned the church universal. It was Paul's battle, too. He could not stand aloof.

Can we stand aloof, when we have brethren right now face-to-face with the foe? Some time ago, for instance, a Wycliffe missionary was taken hostage by guerillas in Colombia. The ultimatum: "All Wycliffe people out of the country in ten days or we kill the hostage." Wycliffe's answer: We do not bargain with terrorists, and we do not pay ransom for hostages. We stay. Our missionary's life is expendable for the cause of Christ. He knows it; we all know it. This is part of our commitment.

How many who heard that story stopped to pray for the missionary? Surely, if we could do nothing else, we could pray. It is a common battle. At this very moment, we know of Christians facing fierce temptation, heartache, trouble, even loss of faith. The enemy has them on the run. Their battle must be our battle, too.

b. We are encircled in a common bond (2:2a)

That their hearts might be comforted, being knit together in love.

We think at once of David and Jonathan and how their hearts were knit together after David took Jonathan's place in the valley and slew the great giant from Gath. The same thing happens to us when we become believers in the Lord Jesus. Our souls are not only knit to Him but knit also to all of those who own and love His Name.

We cannot unravel our lives from those of other believers. We come from different social backgrounds. We have different levels of education. Often we have been raised in different countries and cultures. But we are knit together. A woman like Mary Magdalene is made one with a woman like Mary, the mother of Jesus. A man like Simon the Zealot is made one with Matthew the publican. Peter the doer is made one with John the dreamer. We share a common bond.

2. About Christ (2:2b–4)
    a. Know Him in an increasing way (2:2b)

Unto all riches of the full assurance of understanding, to the acknowledgement of the mystery of God, and of the Father, and of Christ.

When we know the Lord Jesus Christ as we ought to know Him, we are protected against the subtle sophistries of clever but deluded men.

Go back and read this verse again: "Unto all the riches of the full assurance of understanding, to the acknowledgement of the mystery of God, and of the Father, and of Christ." That is a Pauline skyscraper of a sentence. Statement is piled on statement. Such Pauline statements are sometimes hard to unravel, so let us break this verse down into its component parts and see what we have.

First, a proper knowledge of Christ *enriches* us. All riches are ours in Him. The word used here is *ploutos*, which means to be rich, to be abounding in riches, to be wealthy. The noun is used of the rich man whose prosperity was such that he contemplated building bigger barns to contain all of his goods (Luke 12:16–20). It is used of the rich man who let poor Lazarus starve at his gate (Luke 16:19–31).

The Greek word is also used of spiritual riches because all of our riches are of a different kind. They are centered in Christ. Paul says here that we need to realize what spiritual riches are ours in Christ. That will keep us from showing interest in the beggarly, worthless trifles offered by the cult.

Then, too, a proper knowledge of Christ *enlightens* us. It enlightens us in terms of *the mind*. We can have "full assurance of understanding." All of the doubts and difficulties raised by the cult are swept away when we understand fully all that we have in Christ. It is the Devil's trick to sow doubts in our minds. When he tempted Eve (Gen. 3:1–5) he began with a *doubt* ("Yea, hath God said"), continued with a *denial* ("Ye shalt not surely die"), and finished with a *delusion* ("ye shall be as gods"). Satan always goes after the mind (2 Cor. 4:3–4). God offers us in Christ "full assurance of understanding." He wants to set our mind at rest.

A proper knowledge of Christ enlightens us not only in terms of the mind but also in terms of *the mystery:* "acknowledgement of the mystery of God." "The mystery of God" is Christ. He is the One who incarnates the fulness of the Godhead. There's enough mystery in that one thought alone to keep our minds and hearts occupied for all eternity.

Finally, a proper knowledge of Christ *enthralls* us. The way the verse reads in the Authorized Version, the wonder of it all, includes not only God (the word used is *theos,* which corresponds with the Elohim of the Old Testament, that is, the Creator) but also the "Father" and "Christ." Both are God. The thrill of that thought alone would be enough to keep us occupied, too, for eternal ages of time.

The fact of the matter was that the cultists at Colosse said that they had a secret. Paul scoffs at that claim. The truth was that *God* had a secret. That secret was Christ, Christ incarnate, Christ in whom dwelt all of the fulness of God. The embattled Colossians needed to know more and more of this wondrous Person so that their spiritual experience might grow richer and richer.

Recently, I saw a stage magician perform a very elaborate and mystifying illusion on television. He had onstage two large, colorful boxes. He opened them up, back and front, to show that they were empty. He then closed the boxes and lifted one box and put it inside the other box. Then the lid flew off and out stepped a full-grown woman—from an empty box inside an empty box! The two boxes were then placed side by side. This time, the cameras were placed at the back of the boxes so that the television audience could watch the boxes from the back while a live, theatre audience could watch them from the front. Again we were shown that the boxes were empty, and again he lifted one and placed it inside the other box. Again the lid burst open—and out came the show host!

Someone from the audience wanted to know if the magician would show how it was done. He made a comment that struck me at once. "Oh no!" he said, "You see, a stage magician knows that it is all-important that he keep the secret—that's our line."

In stage magic, it is always important to keep the secret. Now listen to God. We are invited (as someone has put it) "to become richer and richer by learning more and more of God's great secret." That secret is Christ! God sees a watching, mystified world out there, a prey to countless tricks and deceptions of the Evil One. God says to us as we exhibit the miracle of new life in Christ, "You see, in redemption it is always important that we give away the secret—that's our line."

b. Know Him in an inexhaustible way (2:3)

In whom are hid all the treasures of wisdom and knowledge.

I read somewhere recently that every hour scientists are publishing enough new information to fill a thousand-page volume of the *Encyclopedia Britannica.* Think of it—enough information every day to fill an entire edition of an encyclopedia!

We are living in what has been called "the information society." Nowadays it takes more time to find out if a particular experiment has been done than it does to carry it out again from the beginning. Those today who are ignorant of computer skills are said to be "computer illiterates." They have been compared to a person in the eighteen million-volume Library of Congress but with no card catalogs, no Dewey decimal system, no alphabetical arrangement of books, and no way to recover the enormous amount of information available.

The modern technological miracles continue. We have megachips able to store more than a million bits of information and capable of pouring out 1,048,576 bits of information before we can say "Hi!" Moreover, the megachip containing all of this information is smaller than a fingernail. But all of that is obsolete! Technology is now contemplating chips containing one hundred million components. The lines on these chips will be only four hundred atoms wide. They will be able to give information at the speed of trillionths of a second. And, doubtless, by the time this book is published, all of this information will be out of date.

Knowledge! Jesus has it all. "In [Him] are hid all the treasures of wisdom and knowledge." The cult at Colosse claimed to have special knowledge. Nonsense!

Jesus has it all. The humblest believer who knows the Lord Jesus has access to more essential knowledge and wisdom than any unsaved person, no matter how brilliant that person might be.

"In [Him] are hid all the treasures of wisdom and knowledge." We have plenty of knowledge. But we do not have much wisdom. Just before He went to Calvary, the Lord said that in the last days just before His return, there would be perplexity of nations (Luke 21:25). W. E. Vine suggests various ways of rendering this phrase. He says that it can be translated "at a loss for a way," or "no solution to their embarrassments," or "at their wit's end," or "without resources."[1] Can we think of a collection of phrases that more aptly express the modern dilemma of the nations? Nobody seems to know what to do about militant Islamic fundamentalism, about terrorism, about the spread of weapons of mass destruction, about the threat of AIDS and the EBOLA virus, about the inability of the United Nations to keep the peace, and so on.

Knowledge indeed! Plenty of knowledge but no wisdom. When the Lord Jesus lived on earth, He was forever opening His treasure chest to show men examples of His wisdom. He spoke with authority, not as the scribes (Mark 1:22). They said, "Never man spake like this man" (John 7:46). They said, "How knoweth this man letters, having never learned?" (v. 15). And He, Himself, with that characteristic honesty of His, going back to the days when men marveled at the wisdom of Solomon, declared, "A greater than Solomon is here" (Matt. 12:42).

In one brief day toward the end of His life, the Lord displayed His peerless wisdom four times. Three times He spoke to *answer* His enemies. A fourth time He spoke to *annihilate* His enemies. Three times they questioned him about *the Law.* Once He questioned them about *the Lord* (Mark 12).

First, the Herodians and the Pharisees, who hated each other, teamed up to ask Him a catch question. Was it lawful to pay taxes to Caesar? Were they not under *God's* law? Did God's law condone paying taxes to a foreign power, one that oppressed them and curtailed their liberty? The Herodians compromised on the issue; the Pharisees castigated it. If the Lord advocated not paying taxes, the Herodians would denounce Him to the Procurator. If the Lord advocated paying taxes, the Pharisees would denounce Him to the people. The Herodians would say, "This Messiah wants to end Roman rule." The Pharisees would say, "This Messiah wants to endorse Roman rule." They were sure that they had Him.

---

1. W. E. Vine, *An Expository Dictionary of New Testament Words* (Old Tappan, N.J.: Revell, 1966), section 3, "Perplexity," 177.

Whose law took precedence—the law of the government as represented by Rome or the law of God?

The Lord cleverly sidestepped the trap. Let them show Him a coin of the realm. Whose picture was on the coin? Whose inscription—Caesar's? Very well, then, let them give Caesar what was due to him and let them give to God what was due to Him! "They marveled at him," Mark says. The word he used was *ekthaumazō*. They wondered beyond measure.

Now it was the turn of the skeptics—the Sadducees. These men were the aristocratic conservatives politically but outright liberals doctrinally. They denied the existence of angels and scoffed at the doctrine of the resurrection. They, too, piously appealed to the Mosaic Law. They cited Deuteronomy 25:5–10, the law that made provision for a widow in Old Testament times. Under that law, if a man died without children, his brother was required to marry his widow. The firstborn of the marriage was to bear the name of the deceased former husband. This law ensured that the deceased's name was not blotted out and that his property remained in the family.

The Sadducees concocted a story to ridicule the doctrine of resurrection. They told the Lord about a widow and seven brothers. The first of the brothers married a wife and died without children. The widow was married to the next bother in line. He died, too, without children. The widow was married then to the next brother. He died without children as well. In the end, the widow outlived all seven brothers to each of whom she was married and by each of which she was left childless. Finally, the poor woman herself died. We can picture the relish with which the Sadducees told this old favorite of theirs and the eagerness with which they arrived at the punch line: "In the resurrection therefore, when they shall rise, whose wife shall she be of them? for the seven had her to wife" (Mark 12:18–27).

In His reply, the Lord exposed the three basic inadequacies of rationalism and of liberal theology. They were self-deceived. They were ignorant of the clear teaching of the Bible. They knew nothing at all about an omnipotent and omniscient God who has the power to intervene in the affairs of the universe at will. *Of course,* God can raise the dead! The God who made us can certainly remake us. The trouble with the Sadducees and with modern liberal theologians is that their god (if they have one) is too small.

Having exposed the ignorance of the proud Sadducees, Jesus took up the evidence for resurrection using the very Scriptures of which they were so ignorant. First, He pointed out that, in heaven, marital relationships are dissolved because the reproductive cycle is no longer relevant. As for the resurrection, when God spoke to Moses at the burning bush (Exod. 3:2–6), He referred to Himself as "the God of Abraham, the God of Isaac, and the God of Jacob." At the time He spoke to Moses, Jacob had been dead for about two hundred years. Isaac had been dead for 225 years, and Abraham had been dead for 330 years. Dead? No! Very much alive indeed and in the presence of God. "God," Jesus said, "is not the God of dead people." Those living beyond the grave will assuredly rise again; the Scriptures said so (Job 19:23–27; Dan. 12:2). But more than that, death involves a change of condition, not an end to being. The dead are very much alive. There was no excuse for Sadducean skepticism.

A scribe stood up next. He approached the Lord with greater caution and courtesy than the others. He had a legal question. Could the Lord state which commandment of all the 613 commandments in the Mosaic Law ranked first? Perhaps he thought that because the Lord was not the product of the rabbinical schools, He might stumble over a question like that. It was a typical lawyer's question. The Lord, however, knew His Bible better than to be caught by such a question. He at once quoted Deuteronomy 6:4–5. The first and greatest commandment calls upon us to love God with all of our heart, mind, soul, and strength—something that the scribe did not do. For good measure, the Lord set before His questioner the second greatest commandment, this time quoting from Leviticus 19:18—"Thou shalt love thy neighbour as thyself"—something else that the scribe did not do. The exchange ended. The lawyer admitted that the Lord spoke the truth. The Lord told the lawyer that he was not far from the kingdom of God (Mark 12:34).

That put an end to all further challenging of the Lord. He was too wise to be taken in. "No man after that durst ask him any question," Mark says (12:34).

But now it was His turn. "The Messiah!" He said. "The scribes say He is the Son of David." That, of course, was true. It was written into the Davidic covenant (2 Sam. 7:8–16). The Lord quoted from Psalm 110: "The LORD [Jehovah] said unto my [David's] Lord [Adonai], Sit thou at my right hand, until I make thine enemies thy footstool" (v. 1). Adonai, here, was to be both David's Lord and David's Son. In the East (v. 1) no man would acknowledge his son to be his lord. The Messiah, then, was to be David's Son. At the same time, David owned that Son to be his Lord—to be his Adonai. And David speaks in Psalm 110 of that One being equal with the Lord (Jehovah). The Lord's questioners did not answer Him. The psalm, clearly messianic, proves the Messiah to be not merely David's Son but God's Son, and that was the last thing that the Lord's enemies wanted to admit—that Jesus was David's Son and David's Lord.

Such was the wisdom of the Lord Jesus in applying the Scriptures. He knew His Bible as no man ever knew it. It was a sharp, two-edged sword in His hand (Heb. 4:12). "In [Him] are hid all the treasures of wisdom and knowledge," both sacred and secular.

c. Know Him in an invincible way (2:4)

*And this I say, lest any man should beguile you with
enticing words.*

The word for "beguile" is *paralogizomai.* It means to deceive by false reasoning. It occurs only here and in James 1:22 where we are warned against deceiving ourselves. The expression "enticing words" comes from the word *pithanologia,* which occurs only here. It refers to persuasive speech and plausible arguments. The Gnostic cultists were glib talkers. They marketed clever philosophical clichés and were able to make their arguments sound logical but they did not deceive Paul. He saw right through them.

Just the same, they were making an impact on the unwary believers at Colosse who, until they received this epistle, were ill equipped to deal with them. Such glib talkers occupy the seat of the learned in our high schools, colleges, and universities and, often enough, in our seminaries and pulpits. Our young people are often poorly armed to refute their scornful tirades against Christianity and the great doctrines of the faith.

Paul is about to begin a masterly dissection of the cult. But first he brings his readers back to Christ one more time, for all truth is centered in Him. He is the truth (John 14:6). It is worth remembering that by the time Christ came, all major world religions except for Islam had already been founded. Buddha and Confucius had come and gone. The great thinkers of the Greek and Roman worlds had seen their day. Socrates, Plato, Aristotle, Diogenes, and Pythagoras had each held the stage and then retired. The worlds of man-made religion and human philosophy had shown themselves to be bankrupt. Paul puts forth Christ with whom no one can be compared for He stands alone. His words and wisdom are as high above the musings of men as the heavens are high above the earth. "Don't let any man beguile you with enticing words," Paul warns. Christ has totally eclipsed all others. Know Christ! That is Paul's advice. "Know Him," and you will be invincible. All of this world's clever ideas stand exposed in their moral and spiritual bankruptcy when made to put their balance sheets alongside Christ's.

3. About Christianity (2:5–7)
   a. Life in a new dimension (2:5)

For though I be absent in the flesh, yet am I with you in the
Spirit, joying and beholding your order, and the stedfastness of
your faith in Christ.

Paul was immobilized, a prisoner in Rome, under house arrest, chained to a soldier, and under constant surveillance. There was no way he could be in Colosse. He could, of course, be with the Colossian Christians in imagination, just as we can imagine ourselves to be here or there. Paul could picture the Colossian congregation in his mind's eye. He could conjure up from his memory a mental picture of his dear friends, Philemon and Archippus. He could sketch in from information given to him by Epaphras what the church looked like, where it met, who came, how the services were conducted, and who took the lead. But that wasn't the same as being there.

And that is not what Paul meant either when he wrote of being with them "in the Spirit." He meant something far greater than imagining himself sitting down at the Lord's table with the Colossians. Even unsaved people can imagine themselves to be somewhere where they aren't.

Paul has already reminded the believers at Colosse that the Christian life is lived in at least two dimensions at the same time. They were "in Christ . . . at Colosse" (1:2). He himself was "in Christ" at Rome. Later, John would tell us how he was "in the isle" and also "in the Spirit" (Rev. 1:9–10). John was describing a very real, two-dimensional mode of living. His physical conditions were harsh, but in the Spirit he was up among the angels and on down the distant ages. Paul reminds the Ephesians that they, too, were not only at Ephesus but also seated with Christ in heavenly places (Eph. 2:6). Indeed, all of our blessings and all of our battles are in the heavenlies (Eph. 1:3; 6:11–13). It is a very real place.

While Paul was *in Christ at Rome,* he was also *in Christ at Colosse.* In the *Spirit* he could be really and truly there with the believers, beholding their order and steadfastness "in Christ." He was in Christ. They were in Christ. Where two or three are gathered in His Name, there the Lord is present "in the midst" (Matt. 18:20). So "in the Spirit" and "in Christ" the ordinary laws of time and space no longer bind us. We can be anywhere Christ is.

This is what helps make prayer so potent. We can be inside the veil (Heb.

10:19–23), in the presence of God, and we can be right there and at the same time in our prayer room at home and also right there in the midst of that needy situation that has so stirred us to pray. We can be with that missionary in a canoe on the Amazon or in a lonely prison with a suffering national believer in China. We can be in the White House helping to influence the affairs of state. We can pray for those who have the rule over us and help defeat "the counsel of Ahithophel," and help hinder Satan's secret plans for this age. We can do these things in the Spirit while remaining very much in the body. In the same way, we can travel in time and relive the past or anticipate the future.

So "in the Spirit" Paul was able to take his place with his brothers and sisters in Christ at Colosse. He could rejoice as he beheld their order and steadfastness for it would seem the cultists had not made much progress as yet.

Paul's words have a military ring to them. Indeed, the word for "order" is a military word. It denotes an "orderly array" of disciplined soldiers. The word for "stedfastness" occurs only here. It paints a picture of solidity. The idea conveyed by the word is that of "a solid front." When Roman soldiers confronted the charge of the enemy, they took their great rectangular shields and locked them together to form a solid wall of steel against which the enemy hurled its spears and arrows in vain. It seems the Colossians were putting up just such a solid resistance against the cult.

b. Life under a new direction (2:6)

> *As ye have therefore received Christ Jesus the Lord,*
> *so walk ye in him.*

The order of the words is deliberate, not arbitrary. When the Lord is referred to as "Jesus Christ," the name "Jesus" is emphatic by reason of its position, and the title "Christ" is subsidiary and descriptive. In the Gospels, the words *Jesus Christ* refer to Jesus as Israel's Messiah. In the Epistles, it goes beyond that. It denotes Jesus as the One who humbled Himself but who is now exalted on high, the glorified One.

When the order is reversed, "Christ Jesus," as here, the opposite emphasis prevails. The title "Christ" is emphatic by its position, and the name "Jesus" is subsidiary and descriptive. When this order of the words appears, the truth conveyed is that the One who is now exalted and glorified once humbled Himself. The Colossians had received this One in all of His preeminence and magnificence.

It was this glorious One whom the cultists were trying to demean and whose deity and humanity they were attacking. Let the Colossians remember that they had received this One into their hearts and homes and that He was in their midst when they met.

But there was more to it even than that. They had received "Christ Jesus the *Lord.*" The Greek word is *kurios.* It speaks of authority and lordship, especially lordship connected with ownership. The Christian life is life under a new direction, not just a lifestyle that we choose for ourselves. It is a life in which "we walk in Him." In other words, every step is directed by the Lord who has the authority by right of ownership to tell us what to do and where to go.

Paul's statement here in Colossians 2:6 was not only a statement of fact but also another blow struck at the cult. The Gnostics, toward the end of the first century, made a distinct difference between the *man* Jesus and "the Christ." They declared "the Christ" to be one of the intermediary spirits, or "aeons," as they called them. They taught that this aeon ("the Christ") came upon Jesus at His baptism and left Him at Calvary. Paul anticipates and repudiates this kind of heretical teaching. The now-exalted One, who once humbled Himself (Christ Jesus), the One who became obedient to death, even the death of the Cross, is and was "the Lord," the absolute Master and Owner of all things.

> c. Life with a new distinction (2:7)
> (1) Abiding in Christ (2:7a)
> (2) Abounding in Christ (2:7b)

Rooted and built up in him, and stablished in the faith, as ye
have been taught, abounding therein with thanksgiving.

Abiding in Him! *Abounding* in Him! Paul piles up the words. Rooted! Built up! Established! Taught! Thanksgiving! All great words to arm us against heresy. The weird, fanciful notions of the cults, their clumsy attacks upon the Lord Jesus Christ, and their distorted notions of what Christianity is all about must wither when confronted by such a dynamic, Christ-related life as Paul proclaims to be the normal Christian life.

Paul often mixes his metaphors, and he does so here, talking in one sentence of being "rooted" and of being "built up." Paul begins with an *agricultural* metaphor. We are "rooted"—past tense. At once, he switches over to an *architectural* metaphor. We are "built up"—present tense. The Lord Jesus is the deep, congenial soil in which we have been "rooted." He is also the solid, unshakable Rock on which we are being built.

We are to think of ourselves first as a great tree. A tree is a marvel of nature. On a mountain in California just north of Death Valley grows a gnarled and weather-beaten bristlecone pine. It is known as "Methuselah," and it is well named for it is estimated to be forty-six hundred years old. When David was writing his psalms, old Methuselah had been growing and growing for some sixteen hundred years. When Abraham was born in Ur of the Chaldees, old Methuselah had been growing for hundreds of years and was already a hardy veteran on earth. In fact, if its age is correctly estimated, Old Methuselah has been here since the days of the Flood.

Trees live so long because of their unique structure. Active life resides in the root tips, in the outer layer of wood, and in the one-cell-thick living sheath that envelops the trunk. This sheath is continually renewed as new layers of sapwood are formed and the old ones cease to function and become the annual rings. Except for fire, loggers, parasites, and destructive winds, trees are practically ageless. Year by year, they send their roots deeper into the soil. They are rooted indeed.

A mighty oak, for instance, with its great branches spreading in all directions, has a root system commensurate to the amplitude of its branches. As the branches reach out higher and higher and farther and farther, so the roots go down deeper and deeper and spread out wider and wider.

Thus, we are rooted in Christ. The hidden life of the believer is to be developed in equal proportion with the outward life seen by those around him or her. A believer with roots like that is indestructible. He is not going to be overthrown by some light, passing breeze of a phony cult.

We think next of a great building. In Paul's day, the Jews would think of their temple. Today, we would think of some great cathedral. It is impossible to visit a cathedral and not be awed by its majesty.

Those old cathedrals that grace so many European cities were "built up." *Up* is the word. Up and up they went until they towered over farm and countryside like enormous cliffs. Their creators had three things in mind—height, space, and light.

One's first impression when entering a cathedral is that of space, plenty of space, space that makes room for people to move about, space that dwarfs the worshiper, and makes him realize how small and insignificant he is. That vastness of space makes the visitor feel that mere talk is irreverent and that he ought not to speak above a whisper. This sense of space reminds us that nothing about the Christian life is narrow or bigoted.

The unsaved view the Christian life as a long list of negatives. In fact, it is as wide as the universe and as vast as eternity, designed to give the widest possible scope to the development of natural talent and spiritual gift. After all, in the church God is training us for eternity.

The second impression we receive when we enter a cathedral is that of sheer height. Massive verticals of granite or marble seem to leap from the ground to climb skyward. These soaring perpendiculars automatically catch one's eye and it follows the upward sweep of the colonnades. It finds itself caught, lifted up higher and higher, by ribbed and sculptured arches. Those old masons cut marble as though it were lace. The eye wanders from one marvel of stone tracery to another, each a wonder of fernlike fronds wrought in stone.

Again, the unsaved think that Christianity stunts growth. They think that it is for small people, not for educated, sophisticated people on their way up, on the cutting edge of scientific thought. Christians, they believe, think only in terms of a flat earth—or more popular today, of a young earth. Those soaring cathedral arches tell a different tale. The Christian faith is for people truly on the way up, all the way up. God has already seated us in the heavenlies. He intends us to reign with Christ far, far above this little world below.

The third impression that we receive when we enter a cathedral is that of light. Stained glass windows tower fifty feet into the air. These windows are full of symbols, colorful scenes, and dancing mosaics. As the sun streams in through these windows, all is a blaze of color and splendor.

The unsaved think of Christianity as dull and drab. On the contrary, it is a life ablaze with the light of the knowledge of the glory of God as seen in the face of Jesus Christ (2 Cor. 4:6). Paul knew whereof he was talking. He had seen the face of the martyr Stephen (Acts 6:15). It was like that of an angel. That face haunted him in his unconverted days until he saw the face of Jesus on the Damascus Road. Thereafter, that was the face that filled his vision. It was the face that Peter, James, and John had seen on the holy mount, a face that shone like the sun (Matt. 17:2). *Light* and *glory* are the distinctive words of our faith.

"Built up!" That was what Paul was stressing. We are to be built up. Someone has called the sum total of a cathedral's magnificence "frozen music"! Indeed, those old-time builders sometimes spent all of their lives creating these masterpieces and achieving the impossible. They thought of Christianity in terms of space, height, and light. They expressed their thoughts in timber, glass, and stone.

We still wonder at what they wrought. Likewise, God thinks of Christianity in terms of space, height, and light. But when God builds, He expresses His thought in the body, soul, and spirit of a person born again.

"Built up in Him." Our lives are to become cathedrals of praise, bringing glory to God and blessing to men.

B.   Exposing the lie (2:8–23)

Paul now brings up his heavy artillery and trains it on the Colossian cult. But before we explore his brilliant exposure of the cult, it will be helpful to take a general look at the high-sounding nonsense being put forward by the cultists as an "improvement" on Christianity. The cult at Colosse was propagating five major errors. Paul unravels them. They were advocating *intellectualism* (2:8–10), *ritualism* (2:11–13), *legalism* (2:14–17), *mysticism* (2:18–19), and *asceticism* (2:20–23).

The Gnostic heresy was in its beginning stages. It did not come to full flower and fruit until the second century, when it was professed in every part of the civilized world. Its schools were as numerous and as zealously attended as any of the great academies of Greece or Asia, even in their brightest days.

D. M. Panton has well outlined the main features of full-grown Gnosticism as follows.

1.   Historically, it absorbed non-Christian thought into the Christian faith.
2.   Philosophically, it lodged sin in matter and, therefore, repudiated the Creator as either impotent or evil.
3.   Practically, numerous Gnostic schools prohibited marriage as multiplying incurable matter.
4.   Similarly, numerous Gnostics prohibited the eating of certain foods, such as wine and meat, as being inherently evil.
5.   Theologically, the Jehovah of the Old Testament was portrayed as the tribal God of Israel. He was denounced as an alien and hostile deity.
6.   Christologically, it separated Jesus from the Christ, denying both the deity and the humanity of the Lord.
7.   Inevitably, it sank finally into irreparable apostasy. Apostasy is not merely corruption of the truth; it is a total change of the truth or a complete abandonment of the faith previously held.[2]

---

2. D. M. Panton, *Present Day Pamphlets: "Gnosticism: The Coming Apostasy"* (London: Thynne & Jarvis, 1925), 3–5.

The word *Gnostic* comes from the Greek word *gnōsis,* which simply means "to know." The Gnostics thought that they had special knowledge that could be revealed only to those who were initiated into their secrets. The common people could think whatever they wished; only those who had been initiated could find the real truth. This use of the word *gnōsis* inspired T. H. Huxley to coin the word *agnostic.* A Gnostic is a man who says that he knows; an agnostic is a man who says that he doesn't know.

We do not have to look far for modern Gnostic cults. Theosophy is unblushingly Gnostic. In Theosophy, Jehovah is the creating Aeon, the Demiurge. He is charged with "all the attributes of arrogance, jealousy, hatred and revenge which exist in the unregenerate and sinful human heart." Madame Blavatsky, founder of Theosophy, said, "Jehovah is Cain."[3]

Christian Science is equally Gnostic. Mary Baker Eddy taught that Jehovah was a tribal god idolatrously worshiped by Israel, ranking with Baal, Moloch, Vishnu, and Aphrodite. She declared, "Jesus was born of Mary, Christ was born of God," a doctrine characteristic of Gnosticism. The bottom line in Christian Science is the Gnostic belief that all evil is lodged in matter. Christian Science uses Christian words and terms but empties them of all Christian meaning and redefines them in Gnostic terms.[4]

Swedenborgianism is the same. Swedenborg said that "a spirit purporting to be the Virgin Mary informed Swedenborg that 'she had been the mother of the Lord, for He was born of her; but that when He was made God, He put off all the humanity which He had from her.'"[5]

On such dubious communications Swedenborg based his creed, closely related to the Gnostic belief that "the body from Mary was gradually dispersed," a body that, it was declared, "was in affiliation with every hell; it was a field to which all the forces of evil had access; its lusts were an open circle to pandemonium."[6] Swedenborg, a vegetarian, stands self-betrayed by life and doctrine as a Gnostic antichrist.[7]

Such is modern Gnosticism. One of its advocates declares, "Gnosticism was the voice of an older cult growing more audible in its protest against a superstition [Christianity] as degrading and debasing now as when it was [then] denounced."[8]

3. Ibid., 22.
4. Ibid., 24–25.
5. Panton, *Present Day Pamphlets: "Gnosticism: The Coming Apostasy,"* 21, n. 3.
6. Emanuel Swedenborg, *True Christian Religion* (1781), 125.
7. Panton, *Present Day Pamphlets: "Gnosticism: The Coming Apostasy,"* 212.
8. Ibid., 21.

No wonder Paul seized his pen so promptly when he heard from Epaphras the sort of thing being taught by the Colossian cultists!

The Gnostics were divided when it came to the person of Christ. Some of them embraced a philosophy known as *Docetism.* The name is derived from the Greek word meaning "to seem." The teaching was that because matter was evil, Christ could not possibly be associated with a human body—despite the clear teaching of the New Testament. The man, Jesus, only *seemed* to have a human body. He was not born, He did not die, His body was an illusion. This form of Gnosticism denied the *humanity* of Jesus.

There was another form of Gnosticism known as *Cerenthianism,* so called after its author, Cerinthis, an Egyptian Jew who studied philosophy in Alexandria, possibly in the school of Philo. As is noted elsewhere, these Gnostics taught that "the Christ" came upon the human body of Jesus in the form of a dove at His baptism and that it left Him at the beginning of His sufferings at Calvary. According to them, this explains why Jesus cried, "My God, my God, why hast thou forsaken me?" This form of Gnosticism denied the *deity* of Jesus.

Gnostic ideas regarding the evil nature of matter gave rise to divergent forms of Gnostic teaching regarding the human body. One school of Gnostic thought advocated *asceticism.* The thing to do was stringently deny the body its desires. The body needed to be starved and scourged and made to suffer. Getting married was forbidden. Eating meat was forbidden. This kind of teaching has always appealed to certain individuals. Among the Jews, the Essenes taught it; among the Greeks, the Stoics were its great advocates. Among Christians, monks who took vows of poverty and the flagellants who wore hair shirts and who scourged themselves are prime examples. Simon Stylites, for instance, who lived in the fourth century, was renowned for his incredible feats of asceticism. He ended up perched on a pillar said to be sixty feet high, where he endured the scorching Syrian suns and bitter winter winds for some thirty years. His disciples brought him such scraps of food as he would condescend to eat.

A different school of Gnostic thought went off in the opposite direction. This Gnostic brand embraced what came to be known as *antinomianism.* Those who espoused this path believed that the best thing to do with the body was to indulge its appetites to the point where they were saturated and satiated to the point of exhaustion. The Epicureans and Nicolaitans took this road.

This kind of thing in its earliest stages was being circulated at Colosse. This religious brew was made even more potent by the addition of some Jewish ingredients and some toxic flavoring of mysticism.

1. Secular reasoning and the gospel (intellectualism) (2:8–10)
   a. Its menace (2:8a)

> *Beware lest any man spoil you.*

The verb for "spoil" means "booty." It occurs only here. The sentence could be rendered, "Look out lest anyone carry you off as booty" or "look out lest someone rob you." The word is used in classical Greek as "carrying off a man's daughter." It is used of kidnapping. It is used of the plundering of a house and of the seduction of a young woman.

Such is the menace of false teaching. Those who persuade people to abandon truth for error are seducers and robbers. Paul begins by alerting the Colossians. They were to recognize that far from their gaining anything by following the cultists, they would be tragic losers. They would be giving up the truth as it is in Christ Jesus the Lord for a pack of lies. Let them remember Esau who traded his birthright, something of incredible worth, for a mess of pottage (Heb. 12:15–17). Let them think of Ahithophel, who traded David for Absalom and honor for treachery, and all for the sake of revenge (2 Sam. 15:21–31; 17:23). Let them think, too, of Achan, who traded the esteem of his fellows for a fistful of money and a robe, and at the cost of his life (Josh. 7). Let them think of Judas (Matt. 27:5) and of Ananias and Sapphira (Acts 5) and before long of Demas, who traded the mantle of an apostle for this present evil world (2 Tim. 4:10). To trade truth for error is apostasy, the highest and most expensive form of treachery of all.

   b. Its method (2:8b)

> *Through philosophy and vain deceit [or to use J. B. Phillips's*
> *famous rendering, "intellectualism and high-sounding nonsense"],*
> *after the tradition of men, after the rudiments of the world.*

The key here is the word *deceit.* It occurs nineteen times in the New Testament and is always used of Satan and his works.

Human reasoning, philosophy ("intellectualism"), has its limitations. Some truths are, by the very nature of things, beyond the scope of human reasoning. We cannot know by reasoning how the universe began. We cannot know what another person is thinking unless he speaks and reveals himself. The truth that we have in the Bible stems not from the unaided human intellect. It is the result of divine revelation as to its substance and to divine inspiration as to its source. In the Bible, God tells us about things that we could never know apart from divine revelation—what God is like, His attributes, His character, His will, His attitude toward us, and His redemptive purpose. All of these things are known to us not because we have figured them out but because He has revealed them.

In the actual process of committing to writing the things that He has revealed, God chose to use human instruments. We see a blending of the human and the divine in their writings. Holy men of God put pen to paper. They were men of assorted character ability, background, age, and century; so it is not surprising that we detect differences in personality, style, and approach. At the same time, God saw to it that every single word they wrote, even down to the very "jot and tittle" (Matt. 5:18), was exactly, infallibly, inerrantly what He wanted to say, put the way He wanted it said, and in the words that He Himself chose. As a result, the whole Bible in its originally autographed documents is uniquely the Word of God.

Satan has always tried to imitate God. We should not be surprised then that he has inspired the writing of false bibles. He, too, overshadowed various individuals and energized them to write books that have deceived millions. Behind every cult is the energizing, inspiring, directing, and deluding driving force of "the rulers of the darkness of this world" (Eph. 6:12). This explains why cults and false religions are so successful and why they take such rapid root and have such a tenacious hold upon people. People will believe the most outrageous absurdities. They always have and they always will. Satan seems to delight in manufacturing nonsense for people to believe He is very clever at inventing religions and philosophies of all sorts. He sows his counterfeit tares into the world alongside God's wheat.

The word *philosophy* occurs only here. It is not a popular word with divine authors. To the Greeks it "denoted the highest effort of the intellect." Paul picks up the word, uses it here, and then discards it forever. It was a word totally inadequate to be the vehicle to convey divinely revealed truth. The believer, by contrast, has a higher plane of knowledge, understanding, and wisdom than anything that can be offered by mere human philosophy. "Vain deceit" is Paul's label here for human philosophy. It was human philosophy that the Gnostics were marketing at Colosse.

In Paul's day, Greek philosophy was becoming popular with the Hellenist

Jews. Its great advocate was Philo of Alexandria. Philo was at home in the Greek Septuagint version of the Old Testament. He was also an ardent admirer and disciple of the philosopher, Plato. Philo became obsessed with the idea of synthesizing Jewish religion and Greek philosophy. To make the Septuagint more palatable to Greek intellectuals, he tried to clothe Jewish religion in Greek ways of thought. He employed allegory and platonic philosophy in his exegesis of the Scriptures. Whether he greatly impressed the Greeks is questionable. He certainly caught on with the Hellenist Jews, who warmly embraced Philo's teachings and used them as a means of deriving all sorts of fanciful "interpretations" from the biblical text. It was this kind of "philosophy and vain deceit" that was being propagated at Colosse. It has plagued the church ever since.

The cult, moreover, bolstered its phony intellectualism with "the tradition of men." The word used is *paradosis,* a word used in both a good sense and a bad sense in the New Testament. It is used of the handed-down teaching of the rabbis whose traditions negated the plain statements of the Mosaic Law. By contrast, the word is used of apostolic teaching (1 Cor. 11:2) and of Christian doctrine in general (2 Thess. 2:15).

Here, in Colossians, it apparently refers to the cult's claim to be able to transmit secret Gnostic "mysteries" to its initiates. As Handley Moule says, "Great is the charm of secrecy, of the mysterious." The "mystery" religions of antiquity ensnared millions, just as Masonic orders do today, by offering secret knowledge to its adherents. The Devil from the beginning has found this kind of thing to be a very successful bait. He said to Eve, "If you eat of this tree, the tree of knowledge of good and evil, you will be as gods" (see Gen. 3:5).

The expression "rudiments of the world" would seem to refer to the elementary lessons in divine truth that make up so much of the Old Testament. The Jewish religion, although divinely ordered and arranged, was designed for a biblically illiterate people. It belonged to the kindergarten stage of divine revelation. It was taken up with tangibles, with such things as tabernacles and temples; rites, rules, and regulations; feast days and fast days; codes and commandments; and sacrifices and services. The whole system was suited to the picture-book stage of revelation. These elementary lessons had their place and time, but they have all been replaced now by the gospel. They belonged to the Old Testament period of the infancy of the faith, to a time when God's people could handle only milk. This age is for grown-ups who can now handle the meat of the Word. Any attempt to take people back to "the rudiments of the world" represents retrogression, not advancement.

Note carefully what Paul does here. He picks up two words—*philosophia* ("philosophy") and *stoicheion* ("elements") and puts them side by side. The one word stood for all of the thinking of the Greek, Roman, and Jewish-Hellenist worlds, as represented by the philosophers of Athens, Rome, and Alexandria. The other word signifies that which is elementary. The word *stoicheion*, for example, was used of the letters of the alphabet, the very first thing we learn, the basic elements of speech. A touch of sarcasm and irony appears in Paul's deliberate marrying of *philosophia* to *stoicheion!* It was Paul's way of ridiculing the false teachers. They were boasting of their superior knowledge, but what they had to offer was childish.

The idea that any kind of philosophy, any kind of human tradition, could enhance Christianity is nonsense. What was being offered was not worthy of serious consideration by a believer. Why? Because it was "not after Christ." It either left Him out altogether or misrepresented Him totally. Consequently, what the Gnostics were offering in terms of human reasoning was "high-sounding nonsense." Paul elaborates on this fact.

    c. Its mistake (2:9–10)
       (1) It ignores the meaning of Christ's birth (2:9)

For in him dwelleth all the fulness of the Godhead bodily.

That is God's answer to whatever weird "mysteries" the Gnostics might have been promoting. The antidote to cultic "mysteries" is the "mystery of godliness," as Paul calls it elsewhere, the mystery of "God . . . manifest in the flesh" (1 Tim. 3:16). This great revealed truth cuts the ground from under all Gnostic speculation. A phantom body indeed! High-sounding nonsense! Jesus had a very real human body.

Human reasoning always errs concerning the person of Christ. Panton cites the views of several apostate church leaders of his day who boldly voiced their reprobate view of Christ. One said, "Buddha, Confucius and Mohammed are saints." Another declared, "We utter their names with reverence as great souls who have received God's message for their contemporaries and all after time"— this despite the fact that Confucius was a necromancer who sacrificed to the dead and that Buddha was a false god who declared, "No one is like me; in the world of men and of gods, no one is like me," and that Muhammad was a false prophet (Deut. 18:12; Ezek. 28:2, 8; 1 John 2:22).[9] There is no comparison between

---

9. Ibid., 32.

Christ, in whom dwells all the fulness of the Godhead bodily, and these human religious leaders.

What happened at Bethlehem sets Jesus apart from all other men. "The Word was made flesh," John says (John 1:14). Deity was clothed in humanity. God came down to "pitch His tent" among us, to dwell among us bodily filled with all of the fulness of God. That can be said of no one but Jesus. No room for error can exist here. The Holy Spirit uses the most definite language to tell us the truth about the Lord Jesus Christ.

In Him *resides* all the fulness of the Godhead bodily. The same word, *dwelleth*, is used in the most prosaic sense in Acts 2:5, where we read that "there were dwelling [*katoikeō*] at Jerusalem Jews, devout men, out of every nation under heaven." The same word is used here in Colossians to tell us that the totality of the attributes and powers of the Godhead took up their abode in the Lord Jesus. The Greek word carries the idea of settling down in a dwelling or of living permanently in a certain place. The Godhead, in other words, has taken up permanent residence in the body of Jesus. So much for all of the Gnostic speculations about matter and aeons and the like. The body of Jesus was fashioned by the Holy Spirit in the virgin's womb. In that body, Jesus lived and displayed His essential deity. In that body, He died. In that same body, He rose from the dead. In that body, He ascended into heaven. And in that body, He is now seated on the throne of God, serving as our great High Priest. In that body, He is to come again to sit upon the throne of David and rule over the empires of earth. That body is now His forevermore.

In Him resides *all the fulness* of the Godhead. Could words be more plain? The word for "fulness" is *plentitude (plerōma),* a word already used in this epistle by the Holy Spirit (1:19). It is used elsewhere of the church (Eph. 1:23) and also of the believer (Eph. 3:19). The word speaks of all of the glorious totality of what God is in His nature, person, and personality and in His character, attributes, and essence.

In Him dwells all the fulness of the godhead *bodily.* The word here is *sōmatikōs.* It is used in its most ordinary and prosaic sense in its adjective form of bodily exercise (1 Tim. 4:8). It is used, also, of the Holy Spirit's coming down from heaven "in a bodily shape" at the Lord's baptism (Luke 3:22). In every sense the Lord Jesus was "God . . . manifest in the flesh" (1 Tim. 3:16). He was man inhabited by God. He was "the Word . . . made flesh" (John 1:14). The Holy Spirit reminds us of it time and again.

(2) It ignores the mystery of Christ's body (2:10a)

And ye are complete in him.

Paul now refers to the believer as being a member of the Lord's mystical body, the church. Human philosophy and the world's religions know nothing of that. The word for "complete" is *plēroō*. It means "to be made full." We are filled full in Him. Our fulness comes from His fulness. We are mystically so united to Him that we, as members of His body, share His life to the full. This truth is developed more fully in Paul's companion letter to the Ephesians. In Colossians, the emphasis is on the Lord Jesus as the Head of the body of which we are the members; in Ephesians, the emphasis is on the church as the body of which Christ is the Head.

The truth of all of this we can grasp only falteringly. It is beyond all finite thought. Gnostic notions and supposed secrets are trash and tinsel in contrast to the vast gold mine of truth that we have here. In a coming eternity, all of that fulness and completeness that is ours in God's Beloved will be displayed, "worlds without end," to all of the awe-struck created beings in the universe and to the utmost bounds of the everlasting hills throughout all of the ages yet to be.

The cult at Colosse was offering to "complete" the Christian believers by initiating them into their secrets. "Nonsense!" says Paul. We are already complete in Him. At most, what the Gnostics had to offer was some worthless trivia. At worst, it offered access to the deep things of Satan and to forbidden secrets that are dark, dreadful, and damning in nature, effect, and consequence.

(3) It ignores the majesty of Christ's being (2:10b)

And ye are complete in him, which is the head of all principality
and power.

Paul does not deny the Gnostic claim that ranks exist among the angels. He simply declares that the Lord Jesus is the head of all such beings, be they good or bad, fallen or loyal to God's throne. Paul refers to these beings again (v. 15) and shows us elsewhere what resolute enemies they are to the human race (Eph. 6:10–13). These principalities and powers rule over the nations of earth as Satan's viceroys (Dan. 10:11–13, 20–21). They wield vast power. They dwell on high. They preside over this world's spiritual darkness. They are "wicked spirits." We engage them in battle when we pray and must be arrayed in full spiritual armor when we do so.

Little do most people realize that our planet has been invaded from outer space. Evil spirits, some of them of vast power and great dignity (Jude 9), roam our world. They are invisible and keep the human race in perpetual bondage, ignorance, and strife. They hate us with a malignity that beggars description. But we can overcome them, break through their hostile ranks, and come boldly into the very presence of God. They are no match for the Holy Spirit. And they are desperately afraid of the Lord Jesus for He was "manifested, that he might destroy the works of the devil" (1 John 3:8). The word for "destroy" that John uses, interestingly enough, is *luō,* which literally means to loose, to dissolve, to sever, to break, to demolish. The Lord Jesus has already played havoc with Satan's unseen empire, but He is by no means through. At His second coming, He will dissolve it forever.

Isaiah tells us that when the Lord Jesus returns to reign, He is going to overthrow the Gentile world empire on earth and Satan's global rule in the heavens. He says, "And it shall come to pass in that day, that the LORD shall punish the host of the high ones that are on high [i.e., Satan's spirit overlords], and the kings of the earth upon the earth [the Gentile world powers headed by the Antichrist]" (Isa. 24:21).

Such, then, is Paul's exposure of the boasted intellectualism of the Gnostics. Paul, himself one of the greatest intellectuals of all time and with a mind open to the Spirit's revelation and inspiration, was not impressed by the claims of the cult. Human reasoning might sound very clever, but when it ignores God, His Word, His Holy Spirit, and His Son, then it is all so much folly.

> 2. Sundry rituals and the gospel (ceremonialism) (2:11–17)
> a. That which has been shed through Christ (2:11)

In whom also ye are circumcised with the circumcision made
without hands, in putting off the body of the sins of the flesh by
the circumcision of Christ.

Some people love ritual; others cannot stand it. In the Old Testament, a strong emphasis was placed on it. The Old Testament believer had his faith supported and sustained by ritual, indeed by a whole catalog of rituals. The ritual revolved around a magnificent temple in Jerusalem. A hereditary priesthood was clothed in rich vestments and ordained to an elaborate ministry. Endless sacrifices of various kinds occurred. They had special days, annual feasts, rules for deciding what could and could not be eaten, and initiation ceremonies such as circumcision and ordination. All of this was divinely inspired, and it all had a deeper, spiritual, and typological meaning, most of which escaped the majority of the people. Moreover, it all pointed to Christ. The typology was hidden to the Old Testament believers, but it is an open book to those who understand the New Testament and who have learned how to crack the typological code.

The death of Christ rendered all of this Old Testament ritual obsolete. When Jesus died, the veil of the temple was supernaturally rent in two (Matt. 27:51; Heb. 10:19–23), symbolizing and heralding an end to all of this round of ritual. The elementary school was closed. The Old Testament picture book would now be significant only as a source of illustration for New Testament truth. We are now no longer occupied with types and shadows. A new day has dawned. Believers in Christ are regenerated by the Holy Spirit, indwelt by the Spirit, and baptized by the Spirit into the mystical body of Christ. No need exists for the religious props and crutches that are provided for Old Testament believers by the endless round of Old Testament rituals.

But for all of that, ritualism dies hard. As more and more Jewish priests became Christians, so the tendency to graft Jewish rituals onto Christianity grew. Jewish converts had a great deal of difficulty understanding that such things as circumcision, keeping the Sabbath, observing strict dietary laws, living by the Jewish religious calendar, and making the requisite sacrifices and offerings to cover offenses were of the past and totally voided by the death, burial, and resurrection of Christ and the coming of the Holy Spirit.

What the Jewish believers wanted to do was graft Christianity onto Judaism. The apostle Paul fought many a battle royal to counter this seductive desire. The Jerusalem conference (Acts 15), the epistle to the Galatians, and the book of Hebrews reflect the fact that Judaism is now over and done with. The Old Testament shadows have been replaced by the New Testament substance.

In Colossians, Paul comes to grip with one aspect of the issue—circumcision. Paul had already fought and won the battle over circumcision at Jerusalem and in Galatia. But here it was again.

Circumcision was a minor but painful surgical operation administered to infant Jewish boys when they were eight days old. It was the sign and seal of the Abrahamic covenant (Gen. 17). An uncircumcised Jew was excommunicated from the covenant. Gentile proselytes to Judaism were required to be circumcised. It was a major stumbling block to conversion to Judaism among Gentile males. Jewish Christians had to give up the idea that Gentiles had to become Jews to become Christians. If the Jews had been allowed to have their way over this issue, they would have driven Gentiles away from the church in droves. They would have stunted Christianity at its birth and made it just another Jewish sect. Their error lay in failing to recognize that the church is not founded on the Abrahamic covenant but upon the new covenant (Jer. 31:31; Matt. 26:28).

The cultists at Colosse were trying to resurrect this dead issue. They were demanding that Gentile converts be circumcised to be saved. They seemed to imagine that circumcision was an initiatory ceremony of some sort and that it was necessary for salvation or at least for fellowship in the church. Churches that advocate the baptism of infants perpetuate a similar error.

Christianity, however, is not some kind of extension of Judaism. The church is not "spiritual Israel," as some people imagine. It is a new entity entirely. Everything about it is supernatural. It was supernaturally injected into history in the Upper Room on the day of Pentecost when the Holy Spirit came down to baptize people into the mystical body of Christ. Members are added to it supernaturally by means of the new birth. It will be supernaturally ejected out of history at the Rapture, when the Lord Jesus comes down to take it to be with Him on high.

In view of these things, the notion that some kind of a ritual can have any saving or sanctifying value, whether it be the Jewish rite of circumcision or the church ordinance of baptism, is patently false.

It will be helpful to review when and why God instituted circumcision as the seal of the Abrahamic covenant.

In Genesis 12, God promised Abraham a seed. He would make Abraham great and create a new nation out of his descendants.

In Genesis 15, the promise was repeated. Abraham would have a son. He would be given a land that would stretch from the Nile to the Euphrates.

In Genesis 16, Abraham came to grips with the fact that he was already an old man and that Sarah, his wife, was an old woman beyond childbearing age. He discussed the matter with Sarah. They decided to help God out. Abraham would marry Hagar, Sarah's Egyptian maid, and would beget a son by her. In adopting this plan, Abraham acted in the energy of the flesh, and that which was born of the flesh was flesh—Ishmael! God did not speak to Abraham again for thirteen years (Gen. 16:16; 17:1).

In Genesis 17, God appeared to Abraham again. He amplified the original promise, endorsed His own covenant with Abraham, repudiated Ishmael as

Abraham's heir, rejected him out of hand as being the promised seed, declared that His promise of a son still stood and that a child would be born to Sarah within the year and who was to be called Isaac. At this point, God instituted the covenant seal of circumcision. There was to be no more unbelief, no more acting in the flesh, no more "Egyptian" expedients, and no more Ishmaels.

Circumcision stamped with death the organ of man's highest physical power. Circumcision was God's answer to the flesh. It underlined our ruin in Adam and our total incapacity to produce the kind of life that God expects. Abraham had to take the knife to the flesh.

This time, Abraham acted by faith. He took to heart the painful lesson, a lesson reinforced by the enactment of the rite of circumcision. Isaac was born, and Abraham circumcised the boy when he was just eight days old. In Scripture, the number eight is associated with resurrection and a new beginning. Ishmael was also circumcised, but he was circumcised when he was thirteen years old. In Scripture, the number thirteen is associated with rebellion and apostasy. The circumcision of Ishmael shows that circumcision without faith accomplished nothing. Rituals, however biblical, never can accomplish anything.

Thus, circumcision was instituted by God to be the seal of the Abrahamic covenant. It was simply and solely a Jewish affair.

Paul's argument in Colossians is that we no longer need circumcision under any circumstance because in Christ the physical is replaced by the spiritual. The ritual is replaced by the reality. The pictorial is replaced by the actual. In Christ, the believer sheds the whole body of carnal affection, lust, self-effort, and reliance on the flesh. The whole corpus of these things, not just part of it, is cut off. A Jewish boy was made a partaker of the Abrahamic covenant by the rite of circumcision. We are made partakers of the new covenant by means of the Cross. No religious rite (baptism administered to an infant, for instance) can bring a person into the good of the new covenant. The blood of Christ does that.

Paul's expression here, "putting off" the body (of the sins) of the flesh, is most expressive. The Greek word is *apekdusis*. It is used only here. It comes from a word used of the stripping off of one's clothes, but it involves more than that. The word conveys the idea not only of getting out of one's old clothes but also of leaving them behind forever. One translator says that the word is a very strong one, adding the word *quite* to his rendering: "putting quite off the body of the flesh."

Paul is here emphasizing the fact that *our* circumcision is a spiritual one that enables us to get quite away from what we are by nature. The "body of the flesh" is the body as conditioned and controlled by the flesh. What the knife did in ritualistic, Old Testament circumcision and in picture form, the Cross of Christ now does for us in New Testament reality. The "body of the flesh," the body as controlled by the flesh, is "put off," divested. In Christ, we can experience a glorious deliverance from the assaults of evil that come through it.

The rite of circumcision, therefore, is no longer valid. The outward, ceremonial act has been replaced by the inner spiritual *fact*.

The same principle applies to all Old Testament rituals. They are foreign to the church age. They emphasize the outward, the material, and the temporary. The New Testament, however, emphasizes the inner, the spiritual, and the eternal. The church, down through the ages, has greatly erred in adding sundry rituals to its modes of worship. It has added a priestly cast in imitation of Israel's Aaronic priesthood. It has dressed its man-made priests in distinctive, religious garbs and miters and intruded its priests between man and God. It has vested its priests with the supposed right to forgive sins. It has introduced the burning of candles and incense. It has put distance between priest and people. It has introduced altars, special days to be observed, and special fasts to be kept, all such things that belonged to the Old Testament Jewish religion. They have been transplanted by well-meaning men into the professing church, where they have flourished as an exotic growth. Although they are undoubtedly dear to many people, they are quite alien to the simple Christianity of the apostles.

b. That which has been shared with Christ (2:12–13)
   (1) The divine operation (2:12)

Buried with him in baptism, wherein also ye are risen with him
through the faith of the operation of God, who hath raised him
from the dead.

Paul moves on to the question of baptism. In no way is baptism related to circumcision. The one is a Christian ordinance whereas the other is Jewish rite. The one is strictly for believers who are able to testify personally and publicly to new life in Christ whereas the other is for eight-day-old Jewish infants. The one is associated with water whereas the other is associated with blood.

The Lord Jesus left His church with just two ordinances—no more, no less—baptism and breaking of bread, both of which speak of Christ and His Cross. In baptism, the believer bears witness to *his death with Christ*. In breaking of bread, he bears witness to *Christ's death for him*. Both ordinances have been grossly distorted by the church.

No elaborate detailed instructions are given in the New Testament for the administering of these ordinances. The actual ceremony is played down in both cases, and emphasis is placed on their significance.

Peter says that baptism is "the answer of a good conscience toward God" (1 Peter 3:21). The evangelist Philip baptized an adult convert by immersion (Acts 8:35–38). Paul baptized adult believers of the house of the Philippian jailer (Acts 16:30–34). Paul tells us here in Colossians the significance of believer's baptism as he does elsewhere (Rom. 6:1–4). In baptism, a believer proclaims his death, burial, and resurrection with Christ. The idea of baptizing infants is foreign to the New Testament.

Some people have tried to make infant baptism a New Testament equivalent of Old Testament circumcision. It is supposed to bring infants into a covenant relationship with God. The error is bolstered by the notion, foreign to the New Testament, that the church is "spiritual Israel." Infant baptism has its roots in Romanism. The New Testament knows no more about infant baptism than it does about a Roman priest's being able to consecrate wafers and turn them into the body, blood, soul, and divinity of Christ.

Having dealt with what has been *shed* through Christ (the encumbrance of Old Testament rituals) as exemplified by circumcision, Paul now turns to two things that have been *shared* with Christ, one setting before us a divine *operation* and the other a divine *opportunity*.

The divine operation is baptism. In the New Testament, this ordinance is intended to be the outward expression of an inward experience.

When a person is baptized scripturally, he first takes his stand in the water (Acts 8:38–39). Water is an element that spells death to us. We cannot live in water. (We are reminded of the person who wished that an acquaintance of his whom he greatly disliked would apply to his Baptist brethren for baptism and that they would hold him under the water—"for ten minutes or so!") The candidate for baptism, then, takes his stand in the water, an element that spells death to all that he is by natural birth. He is immersed, but under the water, symbolically buried. He is then raised up by the power of another's arm to stand on resurrection ground and to walk henceforth in newness of life.

Baptism, then, is a graphic illustration, a one-time ordinance, that symbolizes to a watching world the believer's identification with Christ in death, burial, and resurrection because this is what we share with Christ. He not only died *for* me but also *as* me. Because I am a believer, when He died, I died; when He was buried, I was buried; when He arose, I arose. That is the divine operation. This is no mere ritual; it is the glorious reality. The ordinance simply but graphically portrays it.

(2) The divine opportunity (2:13)

And you, being dead in your sins and the uncircumcision of your
flesh, hath he quickened together with him, having forgiven you
all trespasses.

The Cross has thus become God's instrument for dealing effectively with all that we are by natural birth. We who were dead spiritually by reason of our sins are now alive! We have been "quickened" (made alive) together with Him. Our "uncircumcision" was witness to our lost estate. We had no covenant relation with God, no Abraham to stand astride our genealogical path. Our pedigree went straight back to fallen Adam. Circumcision gave the Jew the potential of becoming a beneficiary of the Abrahamic covenant. We Gentiles had no such hope. Many Gentiles in Paul's day, sickened by paganism, looked longingly at Judaism. Some of them went so far as to become "God-fearers," but most of them balked at circumcision. It was much easier for a Gentile woman to become a Jewish proselyte than for a man to do so. The continuing "uncircumcision" of the God-fearing Gentile technically barred him from participation in the Abrahamic covenant.

Calvary has changed all of that. Christ's death, burial, and resurrection has opened up "a new and living way" to God (John 14:6; Heb. 10:20). What the knife did to the flesh by way of circumcision, the Cross does to the heart by way of crucifixion. Circumcision sealed the Abrahamic covenant; Calvary seals the new covenant. We are made alive in Christ, and all of our trespasses are forgiven. Circumcision is no longer relevant. What an opportunity God now extends to all people, Jews and Gentiles alike, to lay aside the dead ritual for the living reality of being taken "together with Him" to resurrection ground.

c. That which has been shown by Christ (2:14–15)
(1) The question of sin (2:14)

Blotting out the handwriting of ordinances that was against us,
which was contrary to us, and took it out of the way, nailing it
to his cross.

The Cross effectively deals with not only the question of "self" (v. 13) but also the question of sin (v. 14) and the question of Satan (v. 15). Paul has just raised the matter of forgiveness. Now he shows us why we need forgiveness and where to find forgiveness.

Our problem is "the handwriting of ordinances." God has a case against us. Far from being a help, Paul says that "ordinances" are a hindrance. They are not for us but against us. All of the vast machinery of sacrifices and offerings that were such an integral part of the Mosaic Law did not really cancel sin. All it did was cover sin—sweep it under the rug, so to speak (Heb. 10:1–4). Nowhere was this fact more evident than in the elaborate ritual of the Day of Atonement (Lev. 16). Following is a summary of the "ordinance" of that day of days in the Jewish religious calendar.

A. ORDINANCES DEALING WITH PERSONAL SIN (LEV. 16:1–14)
1. The high priest selected a young bullock for a sin offering.
2. He also took a ram for a burnt offering.
3. He washed himself.
4. He put on his holy linen garments.
5. He took two kids of the goats for a sin offering for the congregation.
6. He took a ram for a burnt offering for the congregation.
7. He presented the goats.
8. He cast lots for the goats.
9. He sacrificed his bullock as a sin offering for his personal sin.
10. He took a censer of burning coals.
11. He filled his hands with incense and brought it inside the veil.
12. He took a censer and filled it with live coals off the golden altar.
13. He put the incense on the fire so that the cloud of incense might cover the mercy seat so that he not be killed.
14. He brought the blood of his bullock and sprinkled it before and on the mercy seat.

B. ORDINANCES DEALING WITH PUBLIC SIN (LEV. 16:15–26)
15. He killed the goat for the people.
16. He went in alone with the blood into the Holy of Holies.
17. He came out and sprinkled the blood on the golden altar in the Holy Place.
18. He took the live goat and laid his hands upon it.

19. He confessed over it all of the sins of the people.
20. He handed the goat over to a "fit" man.
21. The fit man led the goat away into the wilderness.
22. The high priest went back into the tabernacle.
23. He took off his holy linen garments.
24. He washed himself.
25. He put on his garments of glory.
26. He offered his ram as a burnt offering.
27. He offered the people's ram as a burnt offering.
28. He burnt the fat of the sin offering on the altar.
29. The fit man returned from the wilderness.
30. The fit man washed his clothes.
31. The fit man bathed his flesh.
32. The fit man came into the camp.

C. Ordinances Dealing with Persisting Sin (Lev. 16:27–31)

33. An unknown man took the carcass of the bullock (the high priest's sin offering) and the carcass of the goat (the people's sin offering) outside the camp.
34. The unknown man burned the remains of the bullock and the goat, including their skin, flesh, and dung.
35. The unknown man washed his clothes.
36. The unknown man washed his flesh.
37. The unknown man came back into the camp.
38. The people afflicted their souls.
39. The people totally abstained from work.
40. The people were made to recognize that all of this was an unending process—a statute forever.

Such was "the handwriting of ordinances," elaborate and detailed but most unsatisfactory because it had to be repeated year after year. It was an annual interminable raking up of the sin question. No ordinance could "once and for all" (once for all sin, once for all people, once for all time) take away sin.

It was the same with the daily offerings. Five major offerings were required to be offered under the terms of the Mosaic Law (Lev. 1:1–7:38). These five offerings were brought continuously and offered endlessly. The *burnt offering* was the highest and greatest of all of them. This was the *Olah*, so called from the verb *alah*, "to cause to ascend," as the flame and smoke ascend when something is burned. The Greek equivalent word means to be wholly burned.

Then came the *meal offering*, the *Minchah*, "a present." Its purpose was to secure favor. The word is used of both Cain's offering and Abel's offering (Gen. 4:3–5). It is also used of the present that Jacob gave to Esau to secure his favor. (Gen. 32:13–21).

Next was the *peace offering*, the *Shelem*, from the root *Shalam*. It conveys the idea of peace based on perfect compensation or recompense. It was more eucharistic than propitiatory.

Then there was the *sin offering*, the *Chattath*, from *chat'a*, to sin by falling short or by missing the mark in sins of commission.

Finally, there was the *trespass offering*, the *'Asham*. This offering took in sins of omission, and it had to do with sin in relation to the Mosaic Law and to sins of error arising from ignorance or negligence.[10]

None of these sacrifices had any value or significance apart from Christ. The first three offerings, called "sweet savor offerings," had to do with the Godward side of Calvary. In the *burnt offering* we see the Lord Jesus offering Himself wholly and unreservedly to God. All but the skin of the offering was consumed on the altar. The skin was given to the officiating priest as a reminder of his total inability, trained and consecrated professional though he was, to comprehend anything beyond the surface of things when it came to the burnt offering aspect of Christ's death.

The *meal offering* consisted of fine flour mingled with oil and salt. It put the emphasis on Christ's flawless life, His anointing with the Spirit, and His utter sinlessness and freedom from corruption. Only such a life could be offered to God from whose blazing holiness even the sinless seraphim hide (Isa. 6:1–3).

The *peace offering* was "eucharistic" in that the sacrifice consummated in priest and offerer feasting together upon the offering in the presence of God. It pictures the wondrous fellowship into which Christ's death has brought us.

The remaining two offerings were known collectively as "sin" offerings: the sin offering and the trespass offering. The *sin offering* had to do with the principle of sin; the trespass offering had to do with the practice of sin. The sin offering was concerned with what we *are*—sinners; the trespass offering was concerned with what we *do*—sin. We do what we do because we are what we are. That is the principle behind the sin offering. An apple tree is not an apple tree because it

---

10. E. W. Bullinger, *The Companion Bible*, (Grand Rapids: Kregel, 1990), app. 43.

bears apples; it bears apples because it is an apple tree. Similarly, we are not sinners because we sin; we sin because we are sinners. The sin offering related particularly to this aspect of our sinfulness.

The *trespass offering* took cognizance of a sinful act. It demanded that restoration be made to the injured party along with the addition of a 20 percent penalty. On the Cross, the Lord Jesus, by identifying with us, made atonement for what we are as well as for what we *do*.

All of this "handwriting" in the Mosaic Law has been "blotted out" by Christ. His death for us on the Cross renders all of the Old Testament types and pictures obsolete. The shadows of the Cross have been swallowed up by the Cross itself.

The word for "handwriting" is *cheirographon*. It occurs only here. It signifies an autograph, a note of hand, a bond, a promissory note, a promise to pay. At Sinai, God handed to the Hebrew people the Mosaic Covenant, what we commonly refer to as "the Law." That Law represented heaven's irreducible minimum. It tells us what God expects of us. It embodies His rules and requirements, His commands and ordinances. The Hebrews put their hand to it. "All that the Lord hath spoken we will do," they declared. It was their "handwriting," so to speak, their unconditional (and totally irresponsible) promise to pay. They defaulted. The history of the Hebrew people throughout the entire Old Testament period was one long failure to keep their promise.

They could not keep these ordinances and neither can anyone else. So Christ came. He fulfilled to the letter all of the requirements of the moral law in His sinless life, and then He fulfilled all of the requirements of the ritual law in His atoning death. He, thus, took "the handwriting" of ordinances away, nailing it to His Cross.

What folly then for the cultists at Colosse to try to bring believers in the Lord Jesus back under the bondage of Hebrew ordinances! The Cross is God's answer to all such notions. The Cross says it all.

At one stage in my banking days, I served in the loan department of a large Canadian bank. When a customer wished to borrow money, the agreed-upon terms were spelled out in what was called a promissory note. It stated the amount borrowed, the interest rate to be charged, and the terms of repayment along with the borrower's signature. When the loan was repaid, the bank canceled the promissory note by recording the payment received and by drawing two diagonal lines across the front of the note. One line ran from the top left corner to the bottom right corner; the other line ran from the top right corner to the bottom left corner. The two lines, drawn through the face of the note, were penned in red ink and the words "paid in full" were added. The note was canceled by a cross.

That is what Jesus has done for the believer. He has canceled our foolish handwritten promise to pay by means of His Cross. The Cross cancels it all. God is satisfied when He sees the Cross!

(2) The question of Satan (2:15)

And having spoiled principalities and powers, he made a shew of
them openly, triumphing over them in it [i.e., the cross].

Paul's keen eye sees here a Roman triumph. He sees the conquering general approach the capital as the cheering crowds line the streets. Chained to his chariot wheels and adding luster to his triumph are the warriors whom he has taken captive in war. They have been spared only to add to his triumph—then away with them to the arena, the executioner, or the slave block.

Thus has Christ triumphed over Satan and all of his principalities and powers. They were drawn to Calvary. There, they added to His torments on the tree, gloating for a brief moment in His death. But it was all premature. When His sufferings were over, the Lord of Glory bowed his head and dismissed His Spirit. Down He went to the underworld, and the foundations of Hades shook to the tread of His feet. There, He preached to the spirits in prison. There, Satan and his minions learned the full extent of their defeat and doom. The keys of death and of Hades were wrenched from the hand of Satan, who until then had held in his hands the power of death. The tidings ran back and forth across the underworld. His body was asleep in a virgin tomb, untouched by taint or decay, awaiting resurrection, ascension, and enthronement at the right hand of the Majesty on high! He Himself was Lord of these "things under the earth" as well as everywhere else. Ahead for Him was more! The Holy Spirit was coming! The church was coming! Eternity was coming! The lake of fire was coming!

Yes, those evil spirits who had taunted him would be spared for a millennium or so. But they would be chained to His chariot wheels. Spoiled! A public spectacle to all of the heavenly hosts—and all because of His Cross. The Cross was their greatest mistake! They had hounded him to His Cross. Little did the scornful emissaries of the Abyss know that the Cross was the power of God and the wisdom of God (1 Cor. 1:19–24; 2:6–8)

"Made a show of them openly," Paul says. So much for those so-called "aeons" of the Gnostics, those principalities and powers of Scripture. The word he uses for "show" is *deigmatizō*. It means "to expose to public infamy." The word is used of Joseph's hesitation to "make a publick example" of Mary (Matt. 1:19). It is used of apostates who "crucify to themselves the Son of God afresh" and "put him to an open shame" (Heb. 6:6).

Well, these dark satanic powers sought indeed to put the Lord of Glory to an open shame by so working on the thoughts and emotions of wicked men that they ended up nailing Him to a cross. Now that Cross has triumphed! Satan and his hosts fiercely attacked the Lord Jesus as He hung on the tree, as well He knew they would. "This is your hour, and the power of darkness," He told His enemies (Luke 22:53). They pressed Him sorely. Now He has "spoiled" them. The word used suggests the thought that He flung them off. More, He has them on a chain. He allows them some length of chain to go about their nefarious business because that is part of the unfinished mystery of iniquity. But they are chained just the same and to *His* chariot wheels. It galls and terrifies them. The preaching of the Cross chills their innermost beings. It spells their doom.

d. That which has been shattered by Christ (2:16–17)

Let no man therefore judge you in meat, or in drink, or in respect
of a holyday, or of the new moon, or of the sabbath days: Which
are a shadow of things to come; but the body is of Christ.

From the beginning, the church has had to contend with those who would shackle it with Jewish ideas about diets and days and all of the other rules and regulations that made up the Jewish religion. If it wasn't someone wanting to impose circumcision, it was someone wanting to force the Sabbath on the church. The Law had become an intolerable burden to the Jews, a fact that made it all the more senseless for Jewish Christians to try to force it on a church comprised mostly of Gentiles (Acts 15:6–12).

Much confusion has arisen in the church from the failure to distinguish between the Mosaic Law as a *standard* and the Mosaic Law as a *system*. As a standard, the Law proclaims binding and deathless rules of conduct (Rom. 13:8–10), although even at that, all can be summed up in the commandment to love one's neighbor as oneself. As a system, the Law represents and upholds a vast system of God-ordained religion distorted by the rabbis and their traditions. This system, which we meet constantly in the four gospels and the book of Acts, was abolished at Calvary. Then, on the Day of Pentecost, Judaism itself was replaced by the church.

At the end of the first century, Judaizers and their Gentile proselytes were still trying to pour the church into the narrow Jewish mold. Thus, we read in the letter to Smyrna of "them which say they are Jews and are not, but are the synagogue of Satan" (Rev. 2:9).

Historically, the Roman church has always been infatuated by the rules and rituals of mere religion, some Jewish in character, others of her own invention, and many of them completely pagan. Moreover, the papacy has always confused the church with the kingdom. It has always failed, too, to distinguish between the kingdom of God and the kingdom of heaven. As a result, over the centuries it has arrogated secular power to itself and has sought to subjugate the nations of the earth by diplomacy and force.

The Reformers, as great as were some of the changes they wrought, never did throw off some of Rome's inventions. Martin Luther, for instance, was infatuated by the Mass. The state churches that took the place of Roman churches retained such errors as infant baptism, a priestly cast, prayers to the Virgin Mary, the burning of candles, and the like. These Romish errors have frequently wormed their way into Protestant religion. To this day, countless Christians still imagine that the church is "spiritual Israel," that it, the church, is now heir to all of God's Old Testament promises to His earthly people and that it, the church, has permanently replaced the nation of Israel in the plans and purposes of God. To maintain this position, covenant theologians are forced to spiritualize much of the Old Testament. They have to explain away many clear distinctions between the nation of Israel and its destiny as an *earthly* people and the church and its members as God's *heavenly* people. In the process of "Christianizing" Judaism, many churches have espoused infant baptism and denied the truth concerning the Lord's coming millennial kingdom.

The Colossian error contained Jewish elements. Paul has already dealt with the matters of circumcision (v. 11) and ordinances (v. 14). Now he comes to the matters of diets and days, a feature of mere "religion" so beloved to this day in segments of Christendom.

Christianity is not a matter of diet. "Let no man judge you," the Holy Spirit says, "in meat or in drink."

Some years ago, I was ministering in a town in northern Canada. A number of people were saved and added to the church, including a young man who said that he had been greatly helped by a special diet. He had suffered with a crippling form of arthritis until he met a doctor who put him on this particular diet. The basic philosophy behind the diet was simple—never mix proteins and carbohydrates in the same meal. There were some other oddities about this diet, too, as I recall. It included eating wheat-germ muffins and large quantities of canned tomatoes. Our friend declared that he had been healed by this diet, and he certainly seemed to be the picture of health although his body bore evidence of his past affliction.

Well, he accepted Christ and came into the fellowship of the church. He remained, however, a strong advocate of his diet. He canvassed all of us. A few people were persuaded to try it. Our own experiment with it did not last long. The meals were too boring. Before long, he approached the rest of us with his great idea. We should incorporate his diet into our doctrine. His argument went something like this:

"God wants the best for us, right?"
"That's right, Don."
"That would include good health, right?"
"Possibly, although not necessarily."
"And good health can be affected by what we eat, right?"
"That sounds reasonable up to a point."
"Well, look at me! I'm a living testimony to the health-giving power of Dr. Wonder's diet, right?"
"You certainly do seem to be the picture of health, Don."
"Well, I'm healthy because I never mix proteins and carbohydrates at a meal. This diet made a new man out of me. Everybody ought to be on this diet. We ought to teach people how to care for their bodies as well as their souls. So we ought to teach Dr. Wonder's diet along with teaching the Bible. Right?"

We did not want to discourage this young new believer, but we had no intention of adding diet to doctrine. What should we say to him? To gain some time we asked if anyone had anything to say in response to this proposal. The perfect answer came from another young Christian. He had been saved about the same time as Don. He said,

"You believe that the Lord Jesus is God, Don. Is that right?"
"Yes."
"Would you agree, Don, that the Lord Jesus, since He is our Creator

and the One who made our bodies, would know what was best for them? Right?"

"Right!"

"Then how come, if Dr. Wonder's diet is right, the Lord fed loaves and fishes to the five thousand? He gave them both proteins and carbohydrates at the same meal."

That was the end of it! We heard no more about adding that diet to our doctrine.

"Let no man therefore judge you." The word used denotes a legal decision or other decision. Plain common sense tells us that some diets are better for us than other diets. We know a great deal more about vitamins, calories, and nutrition and things like that than we used to. Still, we need to be on our guard against fads, especially against New Age and occult diets that decry eating meat and promote a vegetarian diet conducive to spiritism, witchcraft, and occult religion.

Paul here declares that diet has nothing to do with New Testament doctrine. The Old Testament mandated a strict adherence to abstinence from "unclean" meats (Lev. 11). This rule no longer applies (Mark 7:18–23; Acts 10:10–16). Indeed, Jewish dietary laws, strictly observed, were one of the instruments that effectively kept Jews and Gentiles apart (Acts 10:24–29). This division is abolished in Christ and indeed is foreign to the spirit of oneness in the church (Eph. 2:11–15). The church settled the issue at its first general conference (Acts 15:1–29).

Similar freedom is extended to us regarding what we drink. We are not to drink to excess (Eph. 5:18), and we are not to indulge in anything that might occasion the fall of a weaker believer (Rom. 14:1–4). Paul deals with broad principles, not with legalistic rules and regulations. At times, we might voluntarily abstain from certain foods and drinks on medical grounds (1 Tim. 5:23), but that is not the issue here. Here, Paul scorns the idea that there is any virtue in adding lists of dietary do's and don'ts to Christian doctrine.

The same freedoms are extended to us regarding feast days and fast days, holy days and holidays. The Gnostic teachers at Colosse were seeking to reimpose upon Christian believers the worn-out Jewish religious calendar. The Jewish year moved from feast to feast (Lev. 23) and from Sabbath to Sabbath (Lev. 23) and from new moon to new moon (1 Chron. 23:31). The "holy days" to which Paul refers are doubtless the annual Jewish religious feasts (Lev. 23). The "new moons" would refer to monthly celebrations. The Jews had added special features in the liturgy of the synagogue to go along with the observance of the first day of the month, the new moon time. The Hebrew year was one of 360 days based on the waxing and waning of the moon. The first day of the month coincided with the new moon and was a regular feast day (Num. 10:10; 28:11–14). The Passover coincided with the full moon. The "Sabbaths" would be the weekly Sabbaths (Exod. 20:8–11), the *simple Sabbath* whereby the seventh day of the week was set apart for rest and worship.

In addition, there was the *special Sabbath,* a Sabbath of years (Lev. 25:1–7). The seventh year was to be set apart for the land to lie fallow. No pruning of trees was allowed and no produce was to be harvested. One reason for the seventy-year Babylonian captivity was so that the land might enjoy its accumulated Sabbaths of which the people had robbed it (2 Chron. 36:21).

Moreover, there was a *super-Sabbath* (seven times seven years), a period that ushered in the Year of Jubilee, a period when all debts were canceled, all slaves were set free, and all land was restored to its original owners. It was because of the jubilation associated with that fiftieth year of release that the year was known as the Year of Jubilee (Lev. 25:8–55).

All of these special days were related primarily to the nation of Israel and its tenure of the Promised Land. They are not relevant to the church age. Paul writes them off here with a stroke of his pen. The elaborate rituals associated with some of these special days have typological and illustrative value, but the days themselves belonged to Israel.

The cultists at Colosse wanted to set up a religious calendar for the church—although every day ought to be a holy day for a child of God. So now we have Christmas Day, New Year's Day, Lent, Shrove Tuesday, Ash Wednesday, Whit Sunday, and so on throughout the whole year. This "saint" has to be honored on this day, and that saint has to be honored on that day. Nor are we satisfied yet. The secular world has seen its opportunity to capitalize on all of this. So we have to honor St. Valentine's Day, Mother's Day, Father's Day, Secretary's Day, and as many more special days as the card business can dream up.

Paul turns his back here on all such innovations. He does not give an out-and-out command to abolish all of this day keeping. He satisfies himself by telling us not to allow ourselves to be brought into bondage by those who advocate them. We should be impervious to their judgment. He shows a surprising measure of tolerance in writing on the same subject to the Roman church (Rom. 14:5–6). He makes clear, however, that all such reverence for this day or that day is of marginal value at best. That is not what Christianity is all about.

Historically, the Sabbath question is what has most plagued the church. The concept of setting aside one day in seven for rest is rooted in God's activities in Creation (Gen. 2:3). Nothing was said about the Sabbath thereafter for twenty-five hundred years of human history. It was institutionalized in the Mosaic Law (Exod. 20:8–11) and was incorporated into the Mosaic covenant as a sign between Jehovah and Israel of Israel's separation to God (Exod. 31:13–17). It was observed by complete rest (Exod. 35:2–3), and it was a capital offence to violate it (Num. 15:32–36). It was "made for man" (Mark 2:27), a benevolent and beneficial gift from God.

The Jews found themselves unable to leave it alone. They had to tinker with it and add a thousand rules and regulations of their own to it until they succeeded in making the keeping of it an intolerable burden.

The early church soon distinguished between the Jewish Sabbath (a day when the Lord Jesus lay in Joseph's tomb) and the first day of the week (the day Christ arose from the dead) (Matt. 28:1). Christians honored *that* day from the first. It became a day of remembrance and worship to Christians (Acts 20:7; 1 Cor. 16:1–2). The Sabbath is mentioned in Acts only in connection with the Jews. Elsewhere, it is mentioned only twice—Colossians 2:16, where Paul downplays it, and Hebrews 4:4, where it is used as a type. Christians have their rest in a Person, not in a day.

The Holy Spirit built the significance of the first day of the week being distinct from the seventh-day Sabbath into the typology of the Old Testament. It was on the first day of the week that the Jews were to offer the wave sheaf ("the morrow after the Sabbath") in anticipation of Christ's resurrection (1 Cor. 15:23). The annual Day of Pentecost took place, likewise, on the first day of the week (Exod. 34:22; Deut. 16:10–16; 2 Chron. 8:13; compare Luke 24:1; Matt. 28:1). These Scriptures show that Pentecost had its *roots* in the first day of the week (the feast of firstfruits) and had its *fruit* on the first day of the week as well:

SUN (firstfruits)—Mon—Tues—Wed—Thurs—Fri—*SAT*

Sun—Mon—Tues—Wed—Thurs—Fri—*SAT*—Sun—Mon

Tues—Wed—Thurs—Fri—*SAT*—Sun—Mon—Tues—Wed—Thurs

Fri—*SAT*—Sun—Mon—Tues—Wed—Thurs—Fri—*SAT*

Sun—Mon—Tues—Wed—Thurs—Fri—*SAT*—Sun—Mon

Tues—Wed—Thurs—Fri—SAT—SUN *(Pentecost)*

Similarly, the joyous annual feast of tabernacles placed the emphasis through-out on "the first day" and "the eighth day" (i.e., the first day of the next week). Both of these days were especially significant (Lev. 23:34–35, 39). All of this Old Testament emphasis on the first day of the week anticipated the end of the old Jewish Sabbath and the dawn of a new and better day and a greater and more glorious dispensation in God's dealings with men.

Paul has a ready reason for discarding days and diets as having anything to do with vital Christianity. They are only "a shadow of things to come," he says, "but the body is of Christ." There is all of the difference in the world between a man and his shadow! Judaism was a religion of shadows. The substance of those *shadows* is Christ. How silly to go back to the shadows of Christ revealed in the Old Testament types and rituals when we now have Him! So much then for the cultic idea that secular reasoning and sundry rituals can add anything to Christianity. If God-ordained rituals, the rituals of Old Testament Judaism, could add nothing to Christianity, how much less do the man-made rituals of Christendom help!

   3. Special revelations and the gospel (mysticism) (2:18–19)
       a. The cult's false modesty (2:18a)

Let no man beguile you of your reward in a voluntary humility.

The multifaceted cult at Colosse had woven into its fabric the same strands that appear so often in modern cults. They claim not only superior reasoning but also special revelations. It is amazing how easily some people can be persuaded to give up the seamless robe of divine revelation for some ideological garment woven of inferior fabric on the looms of human imagination and speculation. The cults have five favorite colors for the threads with which they weave their wares. These colors are intellectualism, ritualism, legalism, mysticism, and asceticism. In this passage, Paul deals with mysticism, the idea that we can have extrabiblical revelations from God. This strand shows up in Romanism with its emphasis on traditions, in Mormonism with its Book of Mormon, in Spiritism with its claims to be able to communicate with the dead in occultism and its intercourse with demonic powers, and in the so-called charismatic movement with its tongues and prophecies of dubious origin.

The believers at Colosse were in danger of being led astray by other people's dreams and visions and by their claims to have had ecstatic experiences and extrabiblical revelations.

Some years ago, a friend of mine was approached by a woman who claimed to have seen Christ. She described to him this wonderful vision that had been given to her. She sensed his impatience. "You don't believe me, do you?" she asked. "No, I don't," he answered bluntly enough. "That is to say, I don't deny you had some kind of vision, but I don't believe that you met Christ. If you are going to meet Christ anywhere today, it will be within the covers of your Bible. It is a very unwise thing to do, to pin your faith on some filmy vision, some extrabiblical experience when God has already given you a full and adequate revelation of the Lord Jesus in His Word." The woman was not too happy, but the preacher was right.

That is not to say that God cannot and does not reveal Himself at times by dreams and visions to those who have never had the opportunity of reading about Him in His Word. Dan Crawford, an early pioneer missionary in central Africa, had an extraordinary encounter with some natives who had been entrusted with a remarkably accurate divine revelation. He records the incident in his fascinating book *Thinking Black*. He concluded from this incident, "God can still speak to those to whom He does not write." But that is an altogether differing thing from the semioccult and outright occult "revelations" being touted by the Gnostic cultists and similar such "prophecies" being accepted so uncritically by many people today.

Christianity is supernatural and makes no bones about it. It is concerned with a supernatural person, Jesus, who is the Son of the living God. He entered into time by means of a supernatural birth. He lived a supernatural life bending the forces of the natural world to His will. He died amid a display of supernatural events. He rose supernaturally from the dead and ascended supernaturally into heaven.

He was followed on earth by another supernatural person, the Holy Spirit. He supernaturally brought the church into being, endowed its apostles with supernatural powers and supernaturally seated it in the heavenlies. To become Christians, we need a supernatural new birth. We become members of the church by means of a supernatural baptism of the Holy Spirit. The Christian life itself is a supernatural life made possible by only the supernatural indwelling of the believer by the Holy Spirit. As for the church itself, its great hope is a future supernatural event, the Rapture, which will remove it from earth to heaven. Everything about Christianity is supernatural. The Book on which all is based is a supernatural Book, God-breathed, authoritative, and inerrant.

So why does Paul attack the supernatural element in the cult at Colosse? For the simple reason that there is *another* supernatural dimension in the universe. It is headed by Satan, a supernatural being, aided by vast hordes of evil spirits, motivated by a hatred of Christ and His people, and determined to deceive by all means, if possible, God's very elect. It is possible for us to make one of two mistakes. We can pooh-pooh the whole supernatural side of Christianity, as so-called liberals do, or we can promiscuously embrace the supernatural, naively believing that if it is supernatural it has to be of God, as the charismatics do.

At Colosse, some people were deliberately embarking on the risky venture of sailing into uncharted occult seas (v. 18). The south wind might blow softly at first but Euroclydon lay ahead. The ship would be caught, and those aboard would find themselves unable to bear up into the wind. Ahead, too, were the quicksands, darkness, and shipwreck (Acts 27:13–20). Paul knew it well. He had been up against the occult before (Acts 13:8–12; 16:16–24). He knew all about Satan's devices (2 Cor. 2:11). As for "charismatic" gifts, he had run into the wild excesses of that kind of thing before (1 Cor. 12, 14).

Already the Colossian cultists were advocating the worship of angels. Those practicing this forbidden activity (Rev. 22:8–9) were pretending to be very humble about it. They were exhibiting what has been described as "the artificial humility of a trained devotee."

The word for "beguile" here means "to defraud." One use of the word by the Greeks was to denote an umpire's decision against a competitor. The statement could read, "Let no one umpire against you." Many are the occasions when an umpire makes a wrong call, and the athlete loses the prize that is rightfully his. The word for "humility" is sometimes rendered "lowliness of mind," but here it is used to describe a false humility. The cultists were pretending to be very humble about what they were doing, perhaps declaring themselves unworthy to approach God directly. The Romanists do this. They ignore that One Mediator between God and man, given to us by God (1 Tim. 2:5), and seek other "mediators" such as the saints, the angels, and the Virgin Mary. It might be, on the other hand, that the cultists had made contact with evil spirits and, although pretending to be humble about the revelations coming to them from this tainted source, were actually very proud of their achievement.

Many religious systems produce this kind of false humility, a kind of inverted pride. Paul warns against it. Monastic life tended to produce a form of carnal humility. In fiction, Dicken's famous villain, Uriah Heep, oozes the most nause-ating "humility." Pride is never more ugly than when it is pretending to be humble. Of course, cultists have no monopoly on this kind of thing.

True humility is a rare exotic plant seldom found on earth. Jesus displayed it (Phil. 2:8). The word used to describe His true humbleness primarily signifies "low-lying." It is used of low-lying hills (Luke 3:5) and of mountains made low. Paul displayed true humility. He reminded the Ephesians that his ministry among them had been "with all humility of mind" (Acts 20:19).

> b. The cult's false mediators (2:18b)

Let no man beguile you . . . in . . . worshipping of angels.

Good angels always indignantly refuse to accept worship (Rev. 19:10; 22:9). Evil angels, as illustrated by Satan their fallen master, solicit the worship of men (Matt. 4:8–10). Satan tried to bribe the Lord into worshiping him. The Lord, in refusing to do any such thing, thrust the Evil One through with a verse of Scripture: "It is written, Thou shalt worship the Lord thy God, and him only shalt thou serve" (Luke 4:8). The Devil fled. The very first commandment sums up the rule: "I am the LORD thy God. . . . Thou shalt have no other gods before me" (Exod. 20:2–3).

The Roman church has erred greatly in this direction. It actually teaches its people to worship angelic beings. It justifies this clear violation of Scripture by pretending that there are different levels and kinds of devotion.

Catholics claim to worship God with a higher kind of devotion *(latria)*. They worship the Virgin Mary, they say, with a different kind of adoration *(hyperdulia)*, the same kind of worship that they allegedly accord to the human nature of the Lord Jesus. When it comes to saints and angels, they declare that they worship them with only the lowest kind of adoration *(dulia)*.

The division is quite artificial in practice. In any case, the lowest form of worship postulated by Rome *(dulia)* includes not only praying to saints and angels but also bowing down to their images and burning candles to them—all of which is expressly forbidden (Exod. 20:4–5).

Some years ago, I was in the Basilica of Mary, Queen of the World, in Montreal. It is patterned after Saint Peter's Cathedral in Rome. I watched a well-dressed businessman pursue his devotions. He crawled on his hands and knees from one shrine to another, pausing at each to pour out his prayers and "Hail Mary's" in passionate appeal and adoration. There was not one iota of difference in either his attitude or his emotion whether he was bowing down to a graven image of the Virgin Mary or the image of a saint.

The Colossian cultists had fallen prey to their own propaganda. They had postulated all of these "emanations" between God and man (angel beings that were either the figments of their own imagination or else actual fallen angels of Satan actively soliciting worship) and were now not only worshiping them themselves but also trying to persuade the Christian believers to do the same.

"Don't let anyone defraud you!" Paul declares to the people of God. The Colossians were in danger of being victimized by frauds.

c. The cult's false mentality (2:18c–19)
(1) How it inflates man's pride (2:18c)

Intruding into those things which he hath not seen, vainly puffed up by his fleshly mind.

The first clause of this sentence seems to have caused the translators considerable difficulty. As the clause reads in the Authorized Version, the cultist is said to be poking his nose into occult mysteries about which he really knows nothing. Other translators, relying on what they consider to be adequate textual evidence, omit the negative. This view would make the verse say the very opposite, that the cultists were intruding into areas where they had seen things, things which made them cocksure of themselves.

The word for "intrude" occurs only here and can be rendered "investigating." W. E. Vine mentions an alternative reading, "treading on air." The word is believed to have been used of an initiate being inducted into the mysteries of a pagan god. If the alternate reading (without the negative) is adopted, then the cultists were boasting of things that they claimed to have seen. Indeed, they might have seen them, but they saw them under the spell of seducing spirits.

One way or the other, dabbling in occult mysteries made these cultists "vainly puffed up." The phrase comes from the word for a bellows. It literally means "to inflate." These dabblers in spiritism, witchcraft, and the occult likely enough had experienced weird things because Satan and evil spirits lurk in these things. They could, therefore, boast of experiences not granted to others. Consequently, they became inflated with pride.

Many today have a craving for the supernatural and the sensational. Sometimes this craving is a reaction against the coldness and the formality of many modern churches, even some that still hold to fundamental truth. A reaction against formalism and deadness is one thing, but to seek an answer in extrabiblical experiences is to go from one extreme to another. No one would deny that ec-static experiences are to be had because the Devil counterfeits the work of the Holy Spirit and is willing enough to give supernatural thrills and chills to those whom he wishes to deceive and enslave. The issue today with those who cross over to the charismatic movement is that charismatics are all too willing to exalt experiences and devaluate doctrine. Those who go further and dabble with spiritism, witchcraft, astrology, and eastern occult religions place themselves in even greater peril.

No one has any right to say that some supernatural experience he has had or that some special revelation he has received is of God unless that experience or revelation has been tested in the way the Holy Spirit demands (1 John 4:1–3). Believers themselves can be deceived. Then, too, people often accept error simply because an esteemed brother or Bible teacher promotes it. He has had the super-natural experience, he has had the extrabiblical revelation, he is such a gifted teacher and such a godly man so people blindly follow him. But good men can be deceived and godly men can be in error. Satan rejoices when he can ensnare someone who has a reputation and a following because so many thoughtless people will follow him into error.

Countless deceiving spirits are abroad in the unseen world. Again, D. M. Panton sounds the alarm. He quotes an ex-medium, Rev. W. H. Clagett, who says, "I have yet to meet the first Spiritist of whom I did not find one of two things to be true—either they were renegade church members or they were persons who at one time had been under deep conviction from the Holy Spirit and had driven away their convictions. I do not say it is true of all Spiritists but I have never met one (and I have met a great many) of whom it was not true."[11]

Panton also quotes Stainton Moses, a leading Spiritist of his day, "The central dogmas of the Christian faith seemed especially attacked; and it was this that startled me. 'It has been one of our chiefest difficulties,' the spirits said, 'to up-root false dogmas from your mind; so long as you reply to our arguments with a text we cannot teach you.'"[12]

The charismatic movement's careless if not hostile attitude toward sound doctrine, especially regarding the person and work of the Holy Spirit, ought to alarm those people who are drawn into its orbit. Error cannot flourish where sound doctrine holds sway.

---

11. Panton, *Present Day Pamphlets: "Gnosticism: The Coming Apostasy,"* 14.
12. Ibid., 20.

The attack on the Bible comes from many sources. The "higher criticism" of the ancient Gnostic heretic Marcion has been revived in our own age. It has reduced the Bible in the thinking of many people to the level of the Rig Veda or the Koran. Marcion accepted no gospel except Luke. All of the Gnostics rejected the Old Testament.

GRS Mead, called "the greatest of modern Gnostics" by D. M. Panton, declared, "The older deposits of the Bible draw largely from the mythology of other nations and falsify history to an incredible extent; are in their oldest deposits profuse in immoral doctrine and patent absurdities and paint the picture of God that revolts all thinking minds: and the books of the Christian portion are equally called in question on numerous points."[13]

Whenever the Bible in whole or in part is dethroned and its doctrines despised and set aside, it leads to the enthronement of error and in the end leads to the triumphs of pagan religious thought or a mixture of false beliefs.

"Doctrine is divisive!" That is the answer that charismatics give for their attitude toward the great doctrines of the faith. They would unite people across the wide spectrum of Christendom on the basis of a "charismatic" experience. No matter if a person is a liberal theologian or a Catholic devotee of the Virgin Mary. If they have spoken in tongues, given a trance-induced prophetic utterance, had some kind of a vision, profess to be able to heal people, or have been "slain in the Spirit" (whatever that means), then all is well. They are embraced on the basis of their experience or their desire to have the experience. Never mind doctrine—doctrine divides.

Those who espouse such causes and adopt such positions are in peril of "intruding" into places where fallen angels and evil spirits prowl, looking for those whom they may devour (1 Peter 5:8).

(2) How it infringes Christ's place (2:19)

And not holding the Head, from which all the body by joints and bands having nourishment ministered, and knit together, increaseth with the increase of God.

The unity so many would like to see in the church is not the ecumenical unity that the apostate church would like to forge. That unity is based on a total com-

---

13. Ibid., 30–31.

promise of doctrine, and it espouses the concept of a global worldly church dedicated to political action and humanitarian causes.

Nor is it the unity that Rome would like to impose upon the church universal. The world has had a taste of Romish rule in times past. It gave the church the Inquisition and papal arrogance. Rome dreams of regaining her lost power. One day, she will join forces with the Antichrist in one final fearful fling to regain global power. It has been well said that when in the minority, Rome is a lamb; when in equality, Rome is a fox; when in power, Rome is a tiger. May we be long preserved from unity, Roman style.

Nor is it the unity of which charismatics dream—everyone united in wonderful experiences, everyone "naming it and claiming it" and on the road to health and wealth, and Christians outvoting non-Christians to bring in the kingdom.

The unity that God has in mind for the church is an organic unity. Paul envisions believers baptized by the Spirit into the mystical body of Christ (1 Cor. 12:13–27), joined together under the control of the Head and mutually growing in the life of that body.

The cult at Colosse was doing something a cult always does. It was putting something in the place of Christ. The cultists were putting their imagined aeons in His place. Rome puts the pope in His place as the Head of the church and Mary in His place as the one Mediator between God and man. A cult insists that we sign on its particular dotted line or jump through its particular hoop. We must join its particular group, read its particular books, submit to its particular authority, obey its particular rulers, give to its particular causes, submit to its particular rituals, and have its particular hallmarks. Paul brings the Colossians back to Christ. Anything that intrudes between the Head and the members of the body cannot be of God.

He calls upon believers to "hold" the Head. Christ is the Head of the church. Believers are to get a firm, unshakable grip upon that great truth. Paul elaborates by describing the unity of a body. For instance, he speaks of its "joints" or ligaments as the way by which its parts fit and fasten together. In the body, ligament is fibrous tissue gathered together as cords, bands, or sheets. Ligaments hold organs in place or fasten bones together. They are as strong as rope. A sprain is an injury to ligaments caused by tearing or twisting forces across a joint. Ligaments heal slowly, sometimes not at all if they are torn completely apart.

Paul speaks also of the body's "bands." The word here is the usual word for a fetter or anything used for tying. It comes from a word meaning "to bind, to fasten with chains." The word was used by Peter when he exposed the hypocrisy and wickedness of Simon Magus: "I perceive that thou art . . . in the *bond* of iniquity" (Acts 8:23). It is a medical word for a ligature. A ligature is a thread used in surgery to tie a bleeding blood vessel.

A healthy body is not only securely fastened together but also has to be "nourished." The word that Paul used here carries the thought of abundance. Paul uses the word to describe the abundant way in which the Lord Jesus, as the Head of the church, ministers to each individual member of His body.

Paul adds that the whole body is "knit together." The Greek word is used of the apostle Paul's activities in Damascus right after his conversion. He had gone there to make havoc of the church. Instead, he threw himself into the work of evangelism. He confounded the Jews, "*proving* that this is very Christ." As used here, the word shows us Paul "bringing together" unanswerable arguments for the gospel.

All of these words paint a picture of the true oneness and unity of the mystical body of Christ. The cultists at Colosse were trying to tear it apart. Time, however, was not on their side, no matter what seeming success might attend their subversive activities. The very gates of hell cannot ultimately prevail against the true church (Matt. 16:18).

Paul adds boldly that the church, despite all its inward and outward foes, "increaseth with the increase of God." All of the power of the Godhead is behind the growth of the church. Sometimes, the growth seems to be very slow indeed. Few people seem to be getting saved. Many people show an interest but then fall by the wayside. Even those who go on often never seem to grow up. All of that is taken into account already (Matt. 13). We see only bits and pieces of the whole. God's work is vast. It is growing. Nothing can stop it—not even a Satan-energized cult.

4. Stricter rules and the gospel (legalism) (2:20–23)
   a. How man-made rules chain us (2:20–21)
      (1) Blinding us to the teaching of God (2:20a–b)

Wherefore, if ye be dead with Christ from the rudiments of the world, why . . . are ye subject to ordinances.

Paul takes one last look at the cult. Not least among its snares was its attempt to tie the believers up with the cords of legalism and asceticism, to reduce Christianity to a list of rules. This smorgasbord cult had something for everyone's tastes. Man is a religious creature. Satan, the Master Chef, cooks up a variety of tempting morsels to pander to everyone's religious tastes. Does a man incline toward a spicy sauce? Satan has some exotic experiences for him to sample. Would he prefer a more conventional dish, something from an old and proven recipe? Satan has some very old concoctions indeed. So be it pomp and circumstance, ritual and ceremony, rules and regulations, thrills and chills, or even high-sounding nonsense, Satan has it all—and it is all deadly.

Many people like to have it spelled out for them. They like to be given a list of do's and don'ts. But that is not what Christianity is all about. Christianity is very simple. Christianity is Christ. Judaism went in for rules and regulations, hundreds of them. It ended up crucifying Christ because He did not conform to their ideas of what was permissible under the Law and what was prohibited. In Christianity, legalism is replaced by love, precepts are replaced by principles, and codes are replaced by Christ. Paul writes off as childish the attempt at Colosse to go back to checklists of things to do and avoid.

We have probably all watched someone doodling on a notepad while talking on the phone. He jots down a note or two and then begins to draw. He draws a circle, adds two dots and a line, and has begun on a face. The two dots are the eyes. The line is the nose. A curve is added to make a mouth. Some glasses are added and a mustache. A hat is put in next with a big feather. The mouth needs some attention. It is enlarged to a grin. Teeth appear, a pipe, smoke. . . . It is almost impossible to leave things alone. The simple lines of the original have to be embellished until at last they are buried under a mass of detail.

That is what people have done with the simple truth of the New Testament. It has been so embellished with rules that it is often hard to find the original.

These rules blind us to the teaching of God. They blind us first to *our status as believers*, "wherefore, if [i.e., "since"] ye be dead with Christ . . . why . . . are ye subject to ordinances" (2:20).

The supreme practical problem that any cult has to face is what the Bible calls "the flesh," that is, our old Adamic nature. That nature finds sin attractive. Our natural inclination is to indulge the dictates of our own unregenerate desires. The cultists at Colosse had a threefold answer, an answer that crops up repeatedly in the world's false religions and in the various cults of Christendom. They advocated (1) the performance of supposedly helpful rituals, (2) the adherence to a strict regime of self-imposed and cult-oriented religious devotional exercises, and (3) the imposition of severe privations and punishments on the body, seen as the source of all of the trouble. Fasts and flagellations and wearing hair shirts next to the skin, self-mutilation and self-immolation all have their place in this scheme of things. Thousands of people have fled to monasteries and convents seeking refuge from the world only to find that they have brought the flesh with them.

It doesn't work! None of it works. You cannot use the flesh to eradicate the flesh. Paul has the biblical answer—the Cross (Rom. 6:6–7). God has dealt with the problem of the flesh by means of our identification with Christ in His death, burial, and resurrection. The believer is not to endorse the laws of a cult but to embrace the Lordship of Christ. He has to recognize his status. He is "dead with Christ" (v. 8), as Paul puts it here. He must take his stand on that.

The rules invented by religious people blind us not only to our status as believers but also to *our stature as believers:* "Wherefore, if ye be dead from the rudiments of the world . . . are ye subject to ordinances" (2:20). We are supposed to grow up and put on some stature and maturity. The word *rudiments* has already appeared in this discussion (v. 8). It suggests "elementary rules." Trying to live according to a given set of rules is pretty childish stuff. The inability of lists of rules to produce a genuinely holy life has been demonstrated once and for all in the Old Testament. It was tried in the elementary school of God's dealings with men for fifteen hundred years. It is nonsense to go back to it. A grown-up believer ought to have enough spiritual stature to see through this cultic trick. Christianity is not a matter of our keeping kindergarten rules. It is a matter of being indwelt by the living Christ who, having given His life for us, now gives His life to us.

(2) Binding us to the teachings of men (2:20c–21)
(a) How they are imposed on us (2:20c)

Why, as though living in the world, are ye subject to ordinances . . . ?

The world has its religions—hundreds of them. They are all varieties of Cain's religion (Gen. 4:1–5). That religion was fathered by Satan, founded on self-effort, and furthered by violence. It was very attractive to the carnal mind. Cain decked his altar with boughs of holly and loaded it with fruit and flowers. It was fragrant, beautiful, and the work of his own hands. It ignored Calvary, set at naught the Word of God, offended God, and was pointedly rejected by God. Far from that bringing about Cain's repentance, it made him only more determined to propagate his own ideas. His religion is bluntly branded "the way of Cain" (Jude 11). It still flourishes in all of the world's religions. It has its countless followers. It has, too, its many "ordinances."

It seemed incredible to Paul that the Colossians would allow people to come into their church and saddle them with all kinds of legalistic rules. The Greek word for "subject" here literally means "to impose dogmas on someone." We have been delivered from all of that kind of thing. We enthrone doctrine, and we depose dogma and man-made rules of religion.

All religions try to fasten dogmas and rules on people. Resurgent fanatical Islamic "holy" men, for instance, overthrew the Shah of Iran and returned the country to the Middle Ages to the beat of a religious drum that we had thought had long since lost its power to charm. All across the Middle East, Moslem countries are listening to that drum. Moderate regimes live in fear that fundamentalism will sweep them away, too.

What happened to Judaism is another example of what happens when men get their hands on religious rules. As though the Mosaic Law was not extensive enough and thorough enough, the Jewish scribes kept on enlarging it and extending it. They added to it the *Halachoth* (rabbinical decisions on all questions of ceremony and ritual). They added the *Mishna,* the legal code that resulted from those rabbinical decisions. Then they added all kinds of sacred legends, the *Gemara.* Then came the *Midrashim,* commentaries on the Old Testament, and the *Hagada,* reasonings based on these commentaries, and finally the *kabbala,* full of mystical teachings and far-fetched allegories, similar to Origen's methods of interpretation and to the "spiritualizing" of some who equate the Church with Israel.

The lengths to which the Jews went in embellishing the Law are almost unbelievable. They multiplied rules, many of them petty to the point of puerility, to safeguard the Sabbath until they made Sabbath-keeping a nightmare. They debated the commandment against seething a kid in its mother's milk for years and came up with a list of rules that plague orthodox Jewish housekeepers to this day. By the time of Christ, one had to accept this mass of traditional teaching as truth to be orthodox. The Lord rejected it out of hand, and they killed Him for it.

Nor was that the end. After the destruction of the Jewish temple, the Jews sought refuge in all of this so-called "Oral Law." It became their spiritual home. It became known as the Talmud, and it completely overshadowed the Scriptures. It became as voluminous as the *Encyclopedia Britannica.* For many centuries, it was forbidden to write it down. Rabbinic prodigies carried the whole thing around in their memories.[14]

---

14. See John Phillips, *Exploring the World of the Jew.*

All of this was so much religious doodling on the pad of the Mosaic Law. That Law had said all that needed to be stated in 613 simple commandments. Even that modest code was reduced to ten commandments in the Decalogue (Exod. 20:1–17) and reduced still further to two commandments by the Lord Himself (Mark 12:28–31).

At Colosse, the cultists wanted to introduce similar doodling on the page of New Testament truth. Paul, who was a trained rabbi and who had long since seen through the folly of it all, challenges the Colossian Christians not to be so foolish as to fall for all of these "ordinances."

(b) How they are impressed on us (2:21)

(Touch not; taste not; handle not. . . .)

Once we start along the road of rules and regulations, everything has to be spelled out in ever greater detail. The Law itself took this road. It poked and pried into every nook and cranny of life. It spelled out the rules for personal hygiene. It listed what animals could or could not be eaten. It specified what clothes a priest should wear and the exact number of years he could serve. It laid down laws for bird nesting, when a fire could and could not be kindled, under what conditions a man could wear long hair, what kind of fabric could be used for clothing, under what conditions a man could be exempt from military service, under what terms a loan could be made, where the lines were to be drawn in getting married, under what terms servants could be indentured, what to do about a rebellious son—and so on and on. Everything had to be spelled out.

The Gnostic teachers had already revealed their agenda for the church. "Touch not!" they said. Beware of ceremonial defilement. "Taste not!" Beware of forbidden foods! "Handle not!" Beware of getting a feel for that which is forbidden.

Paul chants out the chorus, "Touch not; taste not; handle not!" Then he abruptly breaks off. What was the use of adding to the liturgy. There was no end of it. We stand on higher ground. We do not need endless lists of rules hammered into our memories by constant repetition.

The New Testament deals in principles, not lists of rules. For instance, some things we might be well-advised not to touch—alcoholic beverages, for example. The New Testament lays down a general, guiding principle—do not do anything that might cause a weaker brother to stumble. Many a person has fallen into immorality by not keeping his hands to himself. We do not need someone to provide us with a long list of things that we mustn't touch—as though we were four-year-olds.

The Christian has been set free. He is not, therefore, free *to* sin; he is free *from* sin (Rom. 6:1–2). We who once were dead *in* sin are now dead *to* sin. So away with chains forged for us in the workshops of those who would make themselves the arbiter of our conscience! That is the work of the Holy Spirit (John 16:7–11).

> b. How man-made rules cheat us (2:22–23)
> (1) Where the system collapses (2:22a)

Which all are to perish with the using.

Paul has almost finished with the cult. He concludes by leveling four final telling blows against the idea that stricter regulations have anything to do with vital New Testament Christianity.

He tells us, for instance, where the system collapses. These man-made rules (touch not, taste not, handle not, and the like) are all destined to "perish with the using." We might just as well try to play a game of tennis with a bubble as live by these artificial rules. As soon as you think they are beginning to work, they burst.

Take Martin Luther for instance. He had swallowed "hook, line, and sinker," as we say, Rome's rules for holy living. He fasted. He flogged himself. He said long prayers. He did penance. He went to fanatical extremes. His life became a painful agony. His privations reduced him to a skeleton. He went on a pilgrimage to Rome, begging for a crust of bread here and for a copper coin there. He came to Pilate's staircase. He began the long, painful ascent on his knees, pleading with the Virgin Mary at every step.

It did no good. He persisted—one more step—another. Then the light dawned. The voice of God rang in his soul, "The just shall live by faith!" He stood up. He turned around. He marched boldly back down the stairs, careless of the coveted indulgence that awaited the persevering penitent at the top. He marched on out of the Roman church and took half of Christendom with him. The bubble burst about halfway up the stairs. Nor could all of Rome's horsemen and all of Rome's men ever put that bubble together again!

Martin Luther had seen the truth. It was not by fear, not by fasting, not by flogging, not by formula. It was by faith. One verse of Scripture is worth more than ten thousand books of man-made rules. The system collapses because rules do not and cannot change human nature. They sound like a good idea, but they cheat us because they promise what they cannot deliver.

(2) Whence the system comes (2:22b)

. . . after the commandments and doctrines of men?

The words *commandments* and *doctrines* are both plural. By contrast, the early church was safeguarded by the apostles' doctrine (singular) (Acts 2:42). We have the same thing in Paul's first letter to Timothy—three times in one chapter—doctrine! doctrine! doctrine! (1 Tim. 4:6, 13, 16). The lesson is obvious. The plural is used of the doctrines of men because they are various, differing, numerous, and contradictory. God's teaching is one superb, organic whole.

The system of rules and regulations breaks down because of where it comes from—men! At best, they are the uninspired inventions of men, often well-meaning men. At their worst, they reflect "the doctrines of devils" (1 Tim. 4:1).

(3) Why the system convinces (2:23a)

Which things have indeed a shew of wisdom in will worship, and humility, and neglecting of the body.

The bottom line here is "neglecting of the body." The Greek word occurs only here and means "not sparing the body." And what is behind that is what Paul calls "a show" of wisdom. The word for "show" is *logos*, sometimes used of mere talk. Behind all of this talk is the desire to have a reputation. The Colossian heretics were cultivating a reputation—a reputation for wisdom; for being initiates into the hidden secrets of the unseen world; for being holy men, observers of appropriate rites and guardians of truth and tradition. They were setting themselves up as great teachers, as outstanding saints of God whose teachings should be received and whose reputations should be revered. To enhance their reputation for holiness, they neglected their bodies. They beat them and branded them. They were prodigies of the faith.

Paul scoffs at the whole thing. It was all simply "will worship." The word used occurs only here and means self-imposed or self-inspired worship. It suggests devoteeism, invented and elaborated by human personal choice. It tends to fanaticism. It is not of God. The cultists wanted the Colossians voluntarily to adopt the system of worship that they had invented.

(4) What the system causes (2:23b)

. . . not in any honour to the satisfying of the flesh.

The whole cultic system with its boasted secret knowledge, its abuse of the body, its "will worship," its imposition of iron discipline, its strict adherence to rules and regulations, and its fascination with religious codes, whether those of the eastern guru or those of the western monk, does no good. God rejects it. And, in the end, the flesh is still there as fierce, as strong, and as wicked as ever.[15]

So Paul exposes the cult. It has no leg left upon which to stand. The Holy Spirit repudiates the whole system of secular reasoning, special revelations, sundry rituals, and stricter regulations. Intellectualism, mysticism, ritualism, legalism, and asceticism are all inadequate, and they cover the entire spectrum of cultic dogma. All such things end up ministering to human pride.

So much for the cult. Paul now turns his attention to practical Christianity.

---

15. See the appendix "The Gnostic Heresy."

PART 4

The Truth About the Christian

Colossians 3:1–4:6

IV. THE TRUTH ABOUT THE CHRISTIAN (3:1–4:6)
   A. The statement of what is expected (3:1–4)
      1. The reality of Christ's resurrection (3:1a)
      2. The reality of Christ's rapture (3:1b–3)
         a. What we are to seek (3:1b)
         b. What we are to set (3:2)
         c. What we are to see (3:3)
      3. The reality of Christ's return (3:4)
         a. Sharing in His life now (3:4a)
         b. Sharing in His lordship then (3:4b)
   B. The steps to what is expected (3:5–4:6)
      1. In our personal life (3:5–14)
         a. The old man (3:5–9)
            (1) The old man's ruin (3:5–7)
               (a) The reality of this ruin (3:5)
               (b) The roots of this ruin (3:6–7)
                   i. The attitude of man: racial disobedience (3:6a)
                  ii. The attitude of God: righteous displeasure (3:6b)
                 iii. The attitude of believers: real discernment (3:7)
            (2) The old man's rags (3:8–9)
               (a) His evil whims (3:8a–c)
                   i. The feeling of ill will (3:8a)
                  ii. The flash of ill will (3:8b)
                 iii. The fostering of ill will (3:8c)
               (b) His evil words (3:8d–9a)
                   i. Speaking to defame (3:8e)
                  ii. Speaking to defile (3:8f)
                 iii. Speaking to defraud (3:9a)
               (c) His evil ways (3:9b)
         b. The new man (3:10–14)
            (1) The new man's righteousness (3:10–11)
               (a) The creation of the new man (3:10)
               (b) The character of the new man (3:11)
                   In Christ, God has abolished
                   i. All differences of country (3:11a)

         ii. All differences of creed (3:11b)

        iii. All differences of culture (3:11c)

        iv. All differences of class (3:11d)

    (2) The new man's robes (3:12–14)

      (a) Goodness (3:12)

        i. We receive a holy character (3:12a)

        ii. We reveal a holy character (3:12b)

      (b) Graciousness (3:13)

      (c) Godlikeness (3:14)

2. In our church life (3:15–17)

  a. The principal element (3:15)

    (1) The enthronement of Christ's peace (3:15a)

    (2) The enlargement of Christ's peace (3:15b)

    (3) The enjoyment of Christ's peace (3:15c)

  b. The parallel element (3:16)

    (1) The Word abiding in us (3:16a)

    (2) The Word abounding in us (3:16b)

  c. The practical element (3:17)

    (1) Doing things proportionately (3:17a)

    (2) Doing things properly (3:17b)

    (3) Doing things prayerfully (3:17c)

3. In our domestic life (3:18–21)

  a. Our role as partners (3:18–19)

    (1) God's order in the home (3:18)

    (2) God's orders to the husband (3:19)

  b. Our role as parents (3:20–21)

    (1) The principle of parental rule (3:20)

    (2) The principle of parental responsibility (3:21)

4. In our business life (3:22–4:1)

  a. Men and their tasks (3:22–25)

    (1) The measure of their service (3:22a)

    (2) The manner of their service (3:22b–23)

    (3) The motive of their service (3:24–25)

  b. Masters and their trusts (4:1)

    (1) As a man in authority (4:1a)

    (2) As a man under authority (4:1b)

5. In our secular life (4:2–6)

    a. We must be prayerful in character (4:2–4)
       (1) Prayer: the great habit of life (4:2a)
       (2) Prayer: the guarded habit of life (4:2b)
       (3) Prayer: the grateful habit of life (4:2c)
       (4) Prayer: the grandest habit of life (4:2d)
    b. We must be prudent in conduct (4:5)
       (1) Guarding our testimony (4:5a)
       (2) Guarding our time (4:5b)
    c. We must be pungent in conversation (4:6)
       (1) Adding sweetness to our conversation (4:6a)
       (2) Adding seasoning to our conversation (4:6b)
       (3) Adding spirit to our conversation (4:6c)

IV. THE TRUTH ABOUT THE CHRISTIAN (3:1–4:6)
    A. The statement of what is expected (3:1–4)
       1. The reality of Christ's resurrection (3:1a)

If ye then be risen with Christ. . . .

The resurrection of Christ has changed everything for both the world and the Christian. The cult has nothing to compare with that.

Paul has been dealing with the cult in verse after verse. It is almost with an audible sigh of relief that he turns back to the Christ. Having spelled out what Christianity is *not*—intellectualism, high-sounding nonsense, worshiping angels, keeping all kinds of man-made rules, or performing prodigious feats of self-denial—Paul now shows us what Christianity *is*. The Christian life is a shared life. The life of the all-victorious, risen, ascended Christ is shared with each believer by means of the indwelling Spirit of God.

The paragraph now opening up before us is one of the superlative paragraphs of Scripture. Paul takes us into the bank of heaven. He shows us the illimitable resources of the living God that fill the vaults and every available nook and cranny of space. "Help yourself," He tells us. "It's all yours." This is better than anything to be found on some fabled treasure isle.

Paul begins by pointing out to us the true mysteries, not the counterfeit mysteries or the satanic mysteries, offered by the cult, but the true mysteries of a life hidden with Christ in God. He sets before us truth so mystical that we have to keep on reminding ourselves that it is also real and genuine and intensely practical. We may indeed be "in Christ" but Paul does not forget for a moment that we are also "at Colosse" (1:2). Paul might have his head in the clouds, but his feet are very much on the ground. He might be dwelling in the heavenlies, but he was constantly reminded of the earthlies by the dismal rattling of his chain and the restless movements and, perhaps, exasperated curses of the soldier to whom he was chained.

The soaring sentences that begin this new section of the Colossian masterpiece are sublime beyond all merely human thought. They are written, however, in a very specific context. They are designed to direct us away, once and for all, from all cultic solutions to the problem of ingrained sin. Paul wants us to live above the world. We are in the world, but we are not of the world. Sin's temptations assail us from without. Our sinful temperament attacks us from within. The answer to it all is Christ.

"The verses," says Handley Moule, "are a chain of God's indissoluble facts for the Christian's use amidst the formidable facts of the devil, the world, and the flesh."[1]

They *are* facts. The truth that Paul sets forth here and elsewhere (Rom. 6, for instance) may indeed be mystical, but it is certainly not mythical. These are real, concrete facts for us to count on in the rough-and-tumble circumstances of life. They are as much facts of life for the believer as birth and death, health and sickness, wealth and poverty, and freedom and imprisonment. The only difference is that those are physical facts, and the facts with which Paul is dealing here are spiritual facts. They are nonetheless real on that account. They can be relied on, translated into experience, and made part of the warp and woof of life.

What made the Colosse conspiracy so dangerous was that it came close at times to the truth. Circumcision *was* required—in Old Testament times. Rules and regulations *were* commanded—under the Mosaic Law. Principalities and powers, beings of great might and fearful malice, do exist, but they serve Satan. Angels, myriads of them, do exist, and they are sent forth to minister to those who are heirs of salvation (Heb. 1:14)—both Peter and Paul met their guardian angels—but no invocation of angels is allowed. An angel escort accompanied Jacob from Padan-aram to Peniel. He even wrestled with an angel there. Tongues and prophecies and gifts of healing and performing of miracles *did* accompany the creation of the church, but all of these things belonged to the church's infancy

---

1. Handley Moule, *Colossians and Philemon Studies* (Westwood, N.J.: Revell, 1897), 192.

and soon became a distraction rather than a means of spiritual growth, so they were discarded. Fasting *does* have its place; but it, too, can become a snare, as real a snare as gluttony.

All of these things miss the mark. "Risen with Christ!"—that is Paul's great secret. That is the supreme fact, the great liberating truth before the blazing light of which all cultic teaching dissolves like shadows before the rising sun.

Paul begins this new section then with the reality of Christ's resurrection. The resurrection of Christ is *a fact of sacred history*—just as much a fact of history as the conquest of Britain by Julius Caesar. When Christ's body lay there in Joseph's tomb, Christianity seemed very dead indeed. The disciples crept around in fear for their lives. One of them was dead, a self-confessed traitor and a suicide. Peter, one of the leaders, was totally discredited by his denials and curses. John had been given the Lord's own mother to take care of by the dying Lord, and he had taken her home. The two disciples on the way home to Emmaus were convinced that the dream was over. The tomb itself was sealed and guarded, and His lifeless body slept within.

But the Lord had foretold His resurrection just as He had foretold his crucifixion. So it was that when the foretold three days and three nights had run their course, He came back from the dead right on time. Today, the whole world rings with the news—"He is risen!" It is a fact of history. Although secular historians would like to ignore it, it is the bedrock on which two thousand years of history rest.

Then, too, the Resurrection is *a fact of sound theology.* Paul puts it thus: "If Christ be not raised, your faith is vain; ye are yet in your sins" (1 Cor. 15:17). "He was seen!" Paul says it half a dozen times. He was seen by His followers, seen by His family, and seen by His foe (1 Cor. 15:5–8).

Moreover it is *a fact of spiritual victory.* "If ye then be risen with Christ. . . ." The glorious irrepressible fact is that Christ is raised from the dead, and our identification with Him is so complete that we actually stand with Him on the resurrection side of the grave. Regardless of whether we *feel* this to be so is immaterial; God declares it to be a fact.

Nowhere is this fact better illustrated than in the Bethany home of Martha, Mary, and Lazarus—after the resurrection of Lazarus.

We see *Martha working,* but it is a different Martha. "Martha served," John says. The critical spirit that she had displayed before has gone. Preoccupation with self has gone. Martha is quietly going about her business ministering to Jesus and His disciples and no longer comparing Mary's role with hers. What has made the difference? Martha has entered into the truth that the Lord is the resurrection and the life. She is living in the joy of that fact.

We see *Mary worshiping*, but she is a nobler Mary now, no longer the victim of uncontrollable grief. She brings ointment of spikenard, "very costly," and uses it to anoint the feet of Jesus so that the whole house is filled with the fragrance of her act. There is a calm acceptance of the truth of resurrection. None of the others understood what the Lord was talking about when He foretold His resurrection. The Lord's disciples utterly failed to grasp it, although the Lord told them of it again and again. Mary did not go to the Cross or to the tomb. She had progressed beyond that. She had grasped the great truth of resurrection, both His and hers. In her innermost soul, she was "risen with Christ."

Finally, we see *Lazarus witnessing*. Nobody in that home that day had entered into the truth of resurrection quite the way Lazarus did. "Much people," we read, "knew that Jesus was there and they came not for Jesus' sake only but that they might see Lazarus also, whom He had raised from the dead."

People did not come all the way from Jerusalem to Bethany just because Lazarus was a fine man, a known friend of Jesus, or one who loved the Lord and His people. Those facts impressed very few people. But multitudes came to see a man living in the power of resurrection. Those who hated the Lord noted this new Lazarus and saw him as a threat. Many Jews came, saw, and went away believers. What made the difference? He was risen! The world beat a path to his door.

"If [the word can be rendered 'since'] ye then be risen with Christ. . . ." There is no "if" about it if we are truly saved. God has put us where Jesus put Lazarus—on the resurrection side of death. Only in our case it is even more wonderful than that. Lazarus was put on the resurrection side of his own death; so, doubtless, he died again. We are put on the resurrection side of Christ's death, beyond the reach of sin and death forever. The home where we live, the place where we work, and the church where we worship should be places where spiritually dead people meet people living on resurrection ground.

What a tragedy it is that we fail to count on it—*reckon* is Paul's word elsewhere (Rom. 6:11). What would happen to our land if lost people could see resurrected people living in homes across America; resurrected people driving the expressways; resurrected people working in the factories, shops, and businesses of the American workaday world; and resurrected people filling the pulpits and the pews of the land? We *are* risen with Christ. The world naturally enough would like to see that it is so. How much better way to express the Christian life than by trying to adhere to the notions of the cult!

2. The reality of Christ's rapture (3:1b–3)
   a. What we are to seek (3:1b)

. . . seek those things which are above, where Christ sitteth on the
right hand of God.

The Lord Jesus not only is risen but also has ascended on high. Paul now draws our attention to the throne where the Lord sits in heaven. He is enthroned in the seat of absolute power so that He is well able to make good to us the fruits of his victory.

Think again of the stupendous thing it was that happened just ten days before Pentecost. The Lord, risen from the dead, walked publicly through the streets of Jerusalem accompanied by more than a hundred people. He passed through the city gate, crossed the Kidron, walked past the Garden of Gethsemane, and headed for the brow of Olivet. The disciples had a thousand questions to ask Him. He had one last instruction for them—wait!

At the top of the mountain, the Lord paused. He raised his hands in parting benediction and stepped into the sky. Up, up He went, soon out of their sight and heading for home. He arrived at the pearly gates of the Celestial City. In He went, heading now for His Father's Great White Throne. Then, in a nail-scarred but resurrected human body, He sat down at God's right hand in heaven.

That is where He is today! And *that* is where the Holy Spirit would have us live! We are to "seek those things which are above, where Christ sitteth on the right hand of God."

John Bunyan, in his usual vivid, picturesque way, shows us the dismal failure of so many people to enter into all that is theirs on high. He pictures for us the man with the muck rake in his hand. Illustrated editions of *Pilgrim's Progress* make the picture even more vivid. They show us an old man, bent, careworn, and gray. His back is stooped, and he has a rake in his hand. He is wholly occupied both with the rake and the muck about his feet, which he is patiently turning over and over in the vain hope of finding something worthwhile. Meanwhile, over his head stands a shining angel, offering him a golden crown. But all the man can see is muck.

John Bunyan captured the spirit of that poor man and the spirit of many another. He wrote his epitaph:

Could'st thou in vision see
The man God meant:

> Thou never more could'st be
> The man thou art, content.

And so it is with many people. The psychologist says to all such, "Look within." The opportunist says, "Look around." The optimist says, "Look ahead." The pessimist says, "Look out!" God says, "Look up!" We are to set our affections on things above. We are to "seek those things which are above." The cultist's advice was to look down—to pick up a new set of chains, to put on a new straitjacket, to bow down before a new guru tyrant. No! Look *up!*" See Him! As J. Denham Smith put it more than a hundred years ago,

> Rise my soul, behold 'tis Jesus!
> Jesus fills thy wondering eyes:
> See him now in glory seated,
> Where thy sins no more can rise.

b. What we are to set (3:2)

Set your affection on things above, not on things on the earth.

"Change your point of view!" That is Paul's advice.

In Genesis 4, we have a list of names, the names of this world's worthies, proud, successful, and brazen sons of Cain. What a godless crowd they were! They were inventors, pioneers, and Prometheans. They had power. They loved the world and its pleasures. They promoted its philosophies and endorsed its perspectives. For their generation, they were shrewder than the children of light. The produced a virile culture but one that was also utterly vile. They set their affections on things below, lived for what this world had to offer, and perished in the Flood.

In Genesis 5, we have another list of names, the names of the descendants of Seth. And what dull reading it makes to most people! This one lived so many years, begat sons and daughters, lived on so many years, and died. That one lived so many years, begat sons and daughters, lived on so many years, and died. They did nothing spectacular. They produced no great scientists, philosophers, or entertainers. They made no front-page news. Of course not! They were not living for this world; they were living for the world to come. They set their affections on things above, not on things on the earth. That is the whole point of Genesis 5.

The people in the godly line of Seth were *in* the world, but they were not *of* the world. They had learned how to work down here while they lived up there. They lived by faith and, consequently, they were not shackled with all of the trappings of Cainite religion. And death, when it came, simply lifted them up to that other world that they had loved so long.

    c. What we are to see (3:3)

For ye are dead, and your life is hid with Christ in God.

    What a revolutionary concept! Where in all of the world's literature can we find the like? You are *dead!* Your life is *hid!* It is hid *with Christ!* It is hid with Christ *in God!* You are beyond the reach of sin, self, and Satan!

    Union with Christ produces a moral and spiritual change in the believer that can be likened only to death, burial, and resurrection. We have already passed over to the other side of death. Physically, we are still here; spiritually, we are already over there. Paul keeps on saying it. Perhaps by repeating it he will get it to sink in.

    There is a safe, still point of color and repose within the center of the flame. There is a place where a child could rest in the utter calm of the hurricane's eye. It was in the center of raging fire that Meshach, Shadrach, and Abednego strolled with the Son of God. Their lives were hid with Christ in God beyond the reach of this world's rage. It was in the center of such a whirlwind that Elijah reposed. The mighty arms of the tempest wrapped him around, whirling and thundering all about him; but in its secret place he was as safe as though he was at home in bed. His life was hid in Christ in God (1 Kings 19:10–12)—and so is ours.

    3. The reality of Christ's return (3:4)
      a. Sharing in His life now (3:4a)

When Christ, who is our life, shall appear. . . .

    Paul has been telling us of what is expected of us as Christians. The cult offered fasts, floggings, endless rules, and rituals. The Holy Spirit offers a share in the Resurrection, the Rapture, and the return of the Lord Jesus, life in a new dimension, set free from the bondage of sin and death and the Law. Moreover, He wants us to share in this new dimension of life *now.* "Christ," he says, *"is* our life."

The life we are invited to share is the very life that the Lord Jesus lived when He was on earth—the life that He lived as a boy and as a young teen in that Nazareth home; the life that He lived as a Man, as the village carpenter of Nazareth; the life that He lived with His fishermen friends beside the Galilean lake; and the life that He lived as a traveling Prophet, going about doing good, a Friend to one and all. We are to share that same life of perfection, peace, and power; the life of Man inhabited by God; the life that took Gethsemane, Gabbatha, and Golgotha in its stride; and the life that carried Him in triumph to His home beyond the stars and on to the seat of power at the very throne of God.

That is the life that the Holy Spirit brought down with Him at Pentecost to bestow as the birthright on all of those who put their trust in Him. That is the life that He breathed into those who were present in the Upper Room and that He now imparts to all of His own. "Christ is our life," says Paul; conversely, our life is His life.

In Christ we have all that we need for life and godliness (2 Peter 1:3). That is the pragmatic and open secret of victorious Christian living. Philosophical speculations are not our life. Burdensome ceremonies are not our life. The straitjacket of religious rules is not our life. Whips and hair shirts and prolonged fasts are not our life. Christ is our life! We bring the little teacups of our puny lives to that vast ocean of His boundless life, and we let the Holy Spirit fill us and fill us over and over and over again (Eph. 5:18) until we are "filled with all the fulness of God" (Eph. 3:19). What more could we want than that?

b. Sharing His lordship then (3:4b)

Then shall ye also appear with him in glory.

"The glorious appearing of the great God and our Saviour Jesus Christ" (Titus 2:13) is the ultimate goal of history. He came once in grace; He is coming back in glory. He came once to redeem; He is coming back to reign. He came once as Savior; He is coming back as Sovereign. As we have shared in the benefits of His first coming, so we shall share in the bliss of His coming gain.

The Greek word for "appear" that Paul uses here means "to make visible" or "to manifest," to "uncover," "lay bare," "reveal."

The world in which we live, generally speaking, has a poor opinion of God's people. In all honesty, we often give them cause enough for scorning us. We forget that we are in Christ and therefore enthroned with Him on high, His own joint-heirs. All too often, we are so taken up with the problems of life—trying to make a living, trying to bring up children in a godless world, and trying to keep up with endless demands upon us—that we forget the limitless resources that we have in Christ. As a result, we act like the world, talk like the world, and have the same goals as the world. The children of Israel were willing to settle for the wilderness when they could have crossed Jordan and entered into Canaan. We, too, fail to appropriate all that we have in Christ and settle for the world and a life of discouragement and defeat (Heb. 3:7–4:10).

The Holy Spirit is not content to leave it at that. He never gives up. He forgives us, cleanses us, and fills us once more.

The day is coming, however, when "He shall appear," John says with joyful anticipation and irrepressible optimism that "we shall be like him; for we shall see him as he is" (1 John 3:2). When Christ comes back, bringing us with Him, a startled world will fall back, blinded by the brightness of His glory—and blinded equally by His glory in us!

The hymn writer has caught the picture:

> Our Lord is now rejected
> And by the world disowned,
> By the many still neglected
> And by the few enthroned;
> But soon He'll come in glory,
> The hour is drawing nigh
> For the crowning day that's coming
> Bye and bye.
>
> The heavens shall glow with splendor,
> But brighter far than they
> The saints shall shine in glory
> As Christ shall them array.
> The beauty of the Savior
> Will dazzle every eye
> In the crowning day that's coming
> Bye and bye.[2]

---

2. E. L. Nathan, "The Crowning Day Is Coming," in *Sacred Songs and Solos,* by Ira D. Sankey (London: Marshall, Morgan and Scott, n.d.).

That day has not yet dawned, but it is on the way. Meanwhile, these great truths are introduced to put the paltriness of the cult in proper perspective and to show us how to live the Christian life.

Having taken us into the heavenlies, Paul now brings us back down to earth again. He spells out the practical application and implication of the truth that "Christ is our life."

    B. The steps to what is expected (3:5–4:6)
        1. Our personal life (3:5–14)
          a. The old man (3:5–9)
            (1) The old man's ruin (3:5–7)
              (a) The reality of this ruin (3:5)

> *Mortify therefore your members which are upon the earth;*
> *fornication, uncleanness, inordinate affection, evil concupiscence,*
> *and covetousness, which is idolatry.*

What a contrast! What a catalog! What a bundle of contradictions we are! It is all well and good for us to know theologically and theoretically that we are dead to sin and alive to God. But how does that translate into everyday living?

Paul illustrates the transition by bringing two men before us, the old man and the new. The "old man" is the man of old, the man we used to be. The "new man" is what we are in Christ, the man we are now to be because Christ is our life.

The "old man" is what we are by natural birth. Adam passed on a fallen nature, the Adamic nature, to all of his posterity. When we are born again, the Lord gives us a new nature, His own sinless nature, brought into our lives by the regenerating work of the Holy Spirit. The old nature remains, however. God does not convert it or condone it; He crucifies it (Rom. 6:6). Still, it remains lodged in our innermost being, and we triumph over it only so long as we "reckon" it dead. So far as God is concerned, the "old man" is already dead although we are all too sadly aware that it is still there, warring against the new nature. Paul states the fact—"Ye are dead" (Col. 3:3). This is the critical fact. It does not depend on whether the old nature *feels* dead. God says it *is* dead.

The *critical fact,* however, to do us any practical good, must be accompanied by the *corresponding act,* "Mortify therefore your members which are upon the earth." We are still on earth in our mortal bodies. We have not yet received our perfect, undying, and sinless spiritual bodies (1 Cor. 15:39–58). The old Adamic nature seizes every opportunity to express itself, taking advantage of those moments when we fail to reckon it dead. All too often, it gets its chance to express its sinful disposition, desires, and deeds. So God calls upon us to act upon the fact, to mortify our members so that the "old man" might be proved to be dead.

"Mortify!" The force of this peremptory command is, "Give to death, therefore." It is a strong and startling word. The cult had its formula for dealing with the sins of the body. None of them could do any lasting good. God has His formula—"Mortify!" Reckon the old nature to be dead. Although we cannot deal with it, God can and has. The word *mortify* comes from *nekroō*, literally "to make dead." It is related to the word *nekros,* the usual word for the death of the body. The Holy Spirit demands that we actively appropriate the fact that we died with Christ to deprive the old nature of its efforts to use our living bodies as the instrument of its own expression.

We will be eager to comply with this command once we look at the "old man's" portrait. Paul now shows us the old man's ruin and invites us to take a good look at him. He paints for us a picture of fornication, uncleanness, inordinate affection (i.e., impurity, lust, and passion), evil concupiscence (evil desire), and an overpowering covetousness that can be likened to idolatry.

This sordid list resolves itself into impurity and covetousness. These two sins, it is said, make up nearly the whole sphere of human selfishness and vice. Lust and greed account for the majority of human sins, the sins which hold the human race in an iron grip. Even in the light of the *gospel* and with centuries of Judeo-Christian ethic as a base, our legislators dare not punish these things as crimes. We make thieves pay when they are caught, but fornicators, adulterers, wife stealers, and the like often get off scot-free. The law takes no cognizance of these things.

All of these lusts and all of this lawlessness we carry around with us in our hearts. The "old man" watches sleeplessly for an opportunity to seize control of the body that it once owned for yet another fling. He is like some sleeping vampire of a horror story. He lies there in his grave, a denizen of the darkness, waiting his chance to seize us by the throat and slake his horrid appetites and thirsts. We must drive the mighty stake of the Cross of Christ through his hellish heart. We must deny him access to our members. We must reckon him dead and remember Calvary. The body is the key to all of this, as we learn from Romans 12:1. Both the ruined life of the "old man" and the regenerate life of the "new man" are expressed through the body. By means of the Cross, God has cut off, positionally, the "old man's" access to the body. Now we, practically, must reckon this to be indeed so (Rom. 6:11–13).

(b) The roots of this ruin (3:6–7)

i. The attitude of man: racial disobedience (3:6a)

For which things' sake the wrath of God cometh on the children
of disobedience.

The kind of behavior that Paul has just described—illicit sex, lustful living, depraved passion, and wicked desires, and the worship of money—are what one would expect from the unregenerate. The unsaved person succumbs to these things or, as often happens, he struggles against them, using the kind of weapons advocated by the Colossian cultists. We have been delivered from this kind of behavior positionally by the Cross, and we are delivered from it practically when we claim our birthright as believers to live on resurrection ground.

At this point, Paul goes back to the roots. The attitude of the old nature is one of racial disobedience. It was "by one man's disobedience" (Rom. 5:19) that sin entered. "For which things' sake" (i.e., fornication, uncleanness, and the like along with covetousness to the point of idolatry) that "the wrath of God cometh on the children of disobedience." Adam's sin was one of flagrant disobedience. His children are "the children of disobedience" (Eph. 2:2).

Every child of Adam is born with disobedience at the very core of his being. Nobody has to teach a child to be disobedient. He is born self-willed. Rebellion against authority is expressed by the smallest child before he can walk or talk. Unless it is curbed, that disobedience will express itself at all levels of life. The child will begin by defying parental authority, then school authority, then civil authority and, at all levels, divine authority. There's the root.

ii. The attitude of God: righteous displeasure (3:6b)

For which things' . . . the wrath of God cometh. . . .

The human race is exposed to the wrath of God. The word used means "hot anger," anger as the strongest of all of the passions. It refers also to God's purposes in judgment. People take a tolerant attitude toward sin in our permissive society. God does no such thing. Sin causes His anger to burn.

God has His own ways of dealing with sin. He deals with it in this life often by sovereignly overruling a person's circumstances. From time to time, He acts against whole nations, bringing about their overthrow. Now and then He acts in catastrophic judgment, bringing about a holocaust as when He overthrew the antediluvian world and when He overthrew Sodom and Gomorrah. He will act in judgment in the terrible events described in the Apocalypse. And He will act in judgment in eternity. Those who die unrepentant and unregenerate will face his wrath at the Great White Throne.

We hear very little preaching on the subject of hell. That does not alter the fact that teaching about it is woven into the very fabric of Scripture. Jesus spoke more about hell than He did about heaven. It was because He knew the full horrors of that place of anguish that He came to earth to offer Himself as an atonement for sin. Thus, God demonstrated His love. Those who will not have His love as offered in the redemption that is in Christ Jesus must have His wrath.

iii. The attitude of believers: real discernment (3:7)

In which ye also walked some time, when ye lived in them.

As the verbs indicate, however, all if that is in the past. "You had your life in these things" is one way of putting it. No more! True, a believer can fall, he can even wander in the wilderness for many years, but he can never again feel at home living in sinful disobedience to God. Never again can he find in the polluted environment of this world a congenial atmosphere, a native habitat. He can no longer have his life in these things. Once he did, but now he cannot.

Thus, Paul deals with the "old man's" ruin. Before following the apostle into the next phase of his discussion, let us review God's part and ours in the new life of faith, obedience, and holiness. *God's part*—"ye are dead." *Our part*—"mortify, therefore, your members." *God's part—an accomplishment*—"Ye are dead." *Our part—an acceptance*—"mortify, therefore, your members." *God's part—truth revealed*—"ye are dead." *Our part—truth realized*—"mortify therefore." *God's part—the eternal fact*—"ye are dead." *Our part—the daily act*—"mortify therefore."

It is this deliberate response to revealed truth that makes the Christian life possible. It is this that makes our practice conform to our position and our state to conform to our standing. It is this—not the effort of self to conform to creeds, codes, and rituals—that is ours in Christ. It is this that brings heaven down to earth where we live. We respond to what God has done. God says that the "old man" is dead. We say, "If God says so, it is so." We reckon it to be true. We "trust and obey." And as we appropriate the truth, we prove it true. The same Holy

Spirit who reveals the truth objectively in the realm of Scripture lives within us to activate that truth subjectively in the realm of our bodies.

(2) The old man's rags (3:8–9)
(a) His evil whims (3:8a–c)

But now ye also put off all these; anger, wrath, malice, blasphemy,
filthy communication.

The "old man's" rags, his stained and tattered clothing, are his habits. The dictionary defines the word *habit* as *(a)* "a behavior pattern acquired by frequent repetition" and as *(b)* "clothing, particularly a costume characteristic of a calling, rank or function—for instance a riding habit is a costume sometimes worn when horseback riding."

So we can legitimately think of the "old man's" habits, his habitual bad behavior, as his clothes. He wears these evil habits as the characteristic clothing of his evil calling. What a vile wardrobe he has! Paul tells us that we are not to be seen wearing any of the "old man's" rags (the habits characteristic of him). We are to put them off. In the Greek, this statement is quite clearly a command, an imperative, something required of us and something that we can do if we determine to do so. The indwelling Holy Spirit is the One who guarantees that. We must deliberately divest ourselves of the evil habits acquired from our Adamic nature. *Not one of us was born with any evil habits.* We have put on every evil habit we have. We have put them on, so we must put them off. The Holy Spirit provides the power that we need to do so.

Paul now invites us to come and take a closer look at the "old man's" wardrobe, at his evil habits. He has something for every occasion.

We begin the tour of inspection with the "old man's" evil whims. The first of these is anger. Anger here is habitual anger, the settled, habitual anger that makes some people so difficult to live with and work with and makes them lash out at all who offend them. It includes within its scope the deliberate planning of revenge. It is the *feeling* of ill will that some people cherish toward others.

There is also the *flash* of ill will that blazes out all of a sudden. The Holy Spirit uses the word *wrath*. The word suggests the boiling up of hot temper in sudden, violent rage. It happens to all of us. Suddenly we explode. Sometimes we surprise even ourselves. We didn't know that we had it in us to say or do such things. Moses exhibited this flash of temper when he smote the rock after God had told him to speak to it. At the time, he was utterly exasperated with the constant nagging and bickering of the Israelites. He exploded. Normally the meekest of men, he spoke angrily and struck out with his rod. That flash of temper cost him dearly. It kept him out of the Promised Land.

Then, too, there is the *fostering* of ill will. The word *malice* suggests malignity, the desire to injure. The person who wears this habit nurses grudges against other people, as Shimei nursed a grudge against David (2 Sam. 16:5–11) and as Ziba nursed a grudge against Mephibosheth (2 Sam. 9:9–10; 16:1–4; 19:24–30).

These are the "old man's" whims. Off they go! We say, "I can't divest myself of these evil desires." God says, "You can and you must."

(b) His evil words (3:8b–9a)

Put off . . . blasphemy, filthy communication out of your mouth.
Lie not one to another.

We can speak, for instance, to *defame*. That is the thought behind the word *blasphemy*. It carries the idea of slander, of speaking to detract from another's reputation, something that injures another person's good name.

Anyone who excels at his job or profession or who has a well-developed skill for which he is frequently in demand or applauded is particularly prone to wear this piece of clothing. Just let someone come along who is better than he is, who receives greater applause, or who is more successful and in greater demand—then let him look out. His evil heart will begin to eye that rival. He will watch for every opportunity to cut down the other person.

It was this spirit that motivated the rabbis, the scribes, and the Pharisees to be ever on the lookout for an opportunity to say something derogatory about the Lord. In the end, when they could find nothing against Him but saw rather that the Lord's popularity was growing, they had Him arrested and then sought for false witnesses to lie about Him.

We can also speak to *defile*. The word for "filthy communication" means just that, foul speaking and obscene speech. A believer should never be guilty of telling smutty stories. He should never use bad language. Think, for instance, of Simon Peter in the courtyard of the high priest's palace. The others around the bonfire said to him, "Surely thy speech betrayeth thee, thou hast been with Jesus, with Jesus of Galilee." Peter denied the allegation. They remained unconvinced; his tongue proclaimed him a disciple of Christ. Then Peter began to curse and to swear. The foul oaths of his unregenerate fisherman days poured out of his mouth. After that, they were convinced. No disciple of Christ would talk like that.

We can speak to *defraud*. We are not to tell lies. The lie is the idiom of Satan's language. Lying has become a way of life for millions of people. Children lie to their parents without conscience. Businessmen lie to each other and to their customers. Big government routinely lies to the public. The Communists used the technique of "the big lie" to destroy people whom they hated or feared. Their philosophy was, "Tell a lie big enough and often enough and people will believe it." That same philosophy lies behind modern propaganda. Christians sometimes tell lies. They will promise to do things that they have no intention of doing. We are to put off all such behavior.

(c) His evil ways (3:9b)

Seeing that ye have put off the old man with his deeds.

A good friend of mine, before his conversion, was a prizefighter. He was also an atheist. The man who led him to Christ first refuted all of his atheistic arguments and then turned the tables on him and forced him to face the magnificent logic of the gospel. His conversion to Christ took care of his atheism, but his love for fighting in the ring was something else. It was his life, his old life, and it died hard.

The new convert was full of the joy of his new life in Christ. He was regular in his attendance at the local church. He grew in grace and in the knowledge of God. But he went on boxing. The ring was in his blood.

One day, a choice saint of God asked this friend of mine how things were going with him. "Have a big fight coming up next week," he said. "I need to win."

"Have you prayed about it?" asked the wise old elder.

"Prayed about it?" echoed the pugilist, startled by the question.

"Yes, prayed about it. You ought to know by now that you can talk to your heavenly Father about all aspects of your life. Would you like me to pray with you right now about your coming fight?"

The young Christian was more than a little surprised. "Well, of course!" he managed at last.

"Kneel down," commanded the older man.

Then he began to pray, "Father in heaven, I come to You in the precious name of your Son. I thank You for Your love, for putting me in Your family, and for saving my dear young brother here. You know all about his fight coming up next week. He says that he needs to win that fight. So, Father, please help him to beat that other fellow to a pulp. May he batter him all over the ring. May he bash his face in, knock out all of his teeth, and smash up his nose. May he knock him down and then knock him out stone cold. In the name of Your Son, our Savior, Amen."

The converted boxer looked at this grave old elder in astonishment.

"You can't pray like that," he said.

"And you can't live like that," said the wise old saint.

The young Christian left the ring soon afterward. He put off "the old man" and his deeds. He went on to become one of God's choicest servants, a man whose ministry God blessed to the salvation of many souls.

"Ye have put off the old man with his deeds," says Paul. He takes for granted that once the Holy Spirit witnesses to something in our lives that is inconsistent with the Christ-life that we will put it off at once—"strip it off" is the more forceful original.

In 1665, the Great Plague, as it was called, raged with indiscriminate fury through the city of London. Those who could afford to do so fled. Those who remained lived in terror. Those who fled to the country were met by armed villagers who were determined to keep the plague out of their communities.

Because people did not know what caused the plague, the most elementary hygienic precautions were ignored. For instance, people in the city continued to send parcels of used clothing, often the property of the dead, to poorer relatives and relief agencies elsewhere. Even clothes stripped off the bodies of plague victims were thus dispatched.

Imagine a family's receiving such a parcel and proudly and gratefully putting on clothes much better in quality and style to their usual everyday wear. Then they discover that these attractive new garments had come from one of the plague houses. With what horror they would strip them off and consign them to the fire!

It is with the same horror that we should strip off the old man and his deeds; he has the plague.

b. The new man (3:10–14)
   (1) The new man's righteousness (3:10–11)
      (a) The creation of the new man (3:10)

> *And have put on the new man, which is renewed in knowledge*
> *after the image of him that created him.*

Every believer has this "new man." The Lord Jesus anticipated the day when this would be so. He told twin parables to that effect. One parable warned against sewing new cloth into an old garment, and the other parable warned against pouring new wine into old wineskins. They are a fascinating pair of parables (Matt. 9:16–17). The parable of the new cloth and the old garment points to a *new man*. God does not patch up the old nature. He replaces it throughout with a new one—the old man is replaced by the new man, the carnal nature by the divine nature. Ultimately, the old body is also to be replaced by a new body, the natural body by the spiritual body, the earthly one by the heavenly one (1 Cor. 15:44, 48).

Likewise, the parable of the new wine and the old wineskin points to a *new movement*. God has not patched up worn-out Judaism, He has replaced it entirely. Israel has been replaced by the church, a totally new entity. Judaism was of the earth, earthy; the church is seated in the heavenlies. The new wine of the kingdom is not to be found in the nation of Israel, although it, too, has a glorious earthly future, pledged to Abraham and David and guaranteed by the new covenant foreseen by Jeremiah. The new wine is to be found in the church. The church is not "spiritual Israel." It is a separate blood-bought creation, mystically united with Christ, destined to share His throne as His joint-heir. Any attempt to go back to Judaism is roundly condemned in Scripture. The Bible warns against what it calls "the synagogue of Satan" (Rev. 2:9).

Similarly, God is not going to reform society. No amount of education, psychology, reform, or political and religious activism is going to cleanse society. On the contrary, evil men and seducers will wax worse and worse as the end of the age approaches (2 Tim. 3:13). God intends, rather, to send His Son back to earth to overthrow the present order, inaugurate a millennial reign of righteousness, and enforce His righteous rule on men (Ps. 2). It will not be a patched-up version of the present order; it will be a new order altogether. Its constitution also will be the new covenant (Jer. 31:31; Heb. 8:8).

Paul has learned his lesson well. "[We] have put on the new man," he says, "which is renewed in knowledge after the image of him that created him." A new creation! "We are his workmanship, created in Christ Jesus unto good works, which God hath before ordained that we should walk in them" (Eph. 2:10). The new man is "created in righteousness and true holiness" (Eph. 4:24). The "old man" cannot be reformed. He is beyond all hope. Indeed, he has been put to death in the death of Christ, and he has been replaced by the new man, one who is righteous and holy and enabled to do true good works.

This is the new knowledge, God's great open secret. The verbs are instructive—"and have put on" is "did clothe yourselves." The verb expresses completeness and definiteness, as at conversion. It points to the regenerate man formed after Christ. But then there is a change—"which is renewed," or "which is being renewed," or "which is being ever renewed," or "ever maintained." The present passive participle is employed, suggesting that the process is always going on. God is ever bringing us into a fresh knowledge of Himself.

The supposed Gnostic "mysteries" once attained by the initiates of its innermost secrets would not satisfy. They would grow old and stale. They would exhaust their ability to excite and thrill the adept. Not so the new life that we have in Christ. It has the marks of eternal youth. It keeps on opening up before us ever-new vistas of truth. It is never exhausted. It is limitless, infinite, and eternal. As Jesus told the woman at the well, "Whosoever drinketh of this water shall thirst again: But whosoever drinketh of the water that I shall give him shall never thirst; but the water that I shall give him shall be in him a well of water springing up into everlasting life" (John 4:13–14). And as Paul told the Corinthians, quoting from an Old Testament Scripture, "Eye hath not seen, nor ear heard, neither have entered into the heart of man, the things which God hath prepared for them that love him" (1 Cor. 2:9; Isa. 64:4).

The "new man" is our entire re-creation in God's image, the restoration to the soul of all that God intended when He said, "Let us make man in our image and after our likeness." Adam threw all of that away for illicit knowledge. Now, in Christ, the doors of true knowledge are thrown open to us. The believer has spiritual knowledge of which the unregenerate know nothing and can know nothing.

And the goal? We have *received* this new life in Christ; now we must *reproduce* this new life in Christ. This is a daily process. The word for "renewed" here is found in only one other place in the New Testament—in Paul's second letter to the Corinthians, where he says, "though our outward man perish, yet the inward man is renewed [made new, different] day by day" (2 Cor. 4:16).

In his first Corinthian epistle, Paul reminds us that "as we have borne the image [the representation, the manifestation] of the earthy, we shall also bear the image of the heavenly" (1 Cor. 15:49). As the Lord Jesus was the "image" of the invisible God (Col. 1:15), so we are to be the image of the Lord Jesus. The process has already begun in the heart and life of the believer. It will be perfected at the Rapture when we receive our resurrection bodies. The new life that we already have in Christ will then have full and free expression. Meanwhile, the goal is the same. We have the indwelling Holy Spirit to enable us daily to manifest the life of Christ (1 John 3:2–3).

Jesus could say to Philip, "You want to see the Father? Then look at Me!" (see John 14:8–9). Likewise, we ought to be able to say to those around us, "You want to see what Jesus is like? Then look at us."

(b) The character of the new man (3:11)

> *Where there is neither Greek nor Jew, circumcision nor uncircumcision, Barbarian, Scythian, bond nor free: but Christ is all, and in all.*

In Christ, God has abolished all difference of *country*. There is "neither Greek nor Jew." The Jews divide the world into two classes, Jews and *Goyim,* Gentiles. In Paul's day, the Jew stood apart from all other people. God, the Jew felt, had spoken to him and to no one else. Paul put it thus: "Behold, thou art called a Jew, and restest in the Law, and makest thy boast of God, And knowest his will, and approvest the things that are more excellent, being instructed out of the law; And art confident that thou thyself art a guide to the blind, a light of them which are in darkness, An instructor of the foolish, a teacher of babes, which hast the form of knowledge and of the truth in the law" (Rom. 2:17–20).

No longer! The Law was merely a schoolmaster to bring people to Christ (Gal. 3:24–25). Now Christ has replaced Moses, Christianity has replaced Judaism, and the New Testament has replaced the Old Testament. The "middle wall of partition" between Jew and Gentile (Eph. 2:13–15) has been abolished in the church. National differences no longer count. Salvation is offered to Jew and Gentile on the same terms (Rom. 10:12–13). There is no particular advantage in being Jew—or for that matter, in being an American, a Frenchman, or an Englishman.

In Christ, God has abolished all difference of *creed.* There is "neither circumcision nor uncircumcision." "Greek and Jew" tells us that there is no advantage in *being* a Jew; "circumcision nor uncircumcision" tells us that there is no advantage in *becoming* a Jew. Up until Pentecost a Gentile had to become a Jew to come into the good of the Abrahamic covenant, meaning that he had to be circumcised. No longer! The Abrahamic covenant has been rivaled by the new covenant. Many Jews of Paul's day still thought that Gentiles had to become Jews to become Christians. "In Christ," Paul says, "there is neither circumcision nor uncircumcision." Rituals—even those hoary with antiquity and those sanctioned by a past revelation and rooted in the practice of centuries—are abolished now. Christianity is not centered in creeds, however ancient, but in Christ. It is not centered in a series of propositions but in a glorious living Person.

In Christ, God has abolished all differences of *culture*. There is "neither barbarian nor Scythian." The sophisticated and cultured Greeks and Romans regarded the Barbarians as uncouth and uneducated boors. The Mars Hill Greek intellectuals treated the brilliant apostle Paul with the utmost disdain. To them, he was a "babbler." The word used is *spermologos*, "a seed picker," used of birds and so applied to men who gathered scraps of knowledge from others (Acts 17:18). They do not seem to have recognized him as a Jew. Doubtless they were taken by surprise by his eloquence, polish, and flawless Greek, but that did not prevent the bulk of them from making fun of him (v. 32).

The word *barbarous* has entered into our language from this same source. Jews and Greeks alike regarded the Scythians as the lowest of the low. The word suggested savagery. In Christ, all cultural differences are abolished. The butcher, the baker, and the candlestick maker can sit at the Lord's Table alongside peers of the realm, college professors, and brilliant surgeons. Such distinctions are unknown in Christ. Indeed, the local chimney sweep or barber might be a much more brilliant man in the Scriptures than the brother sitting next to him who might be a famous engineer or an army general.

God has abolished in Christ all differences of *class*. There is "neither bond nor free." Rich and poor, slave and master, and intellectual and ignoramus—all are one in Christ. A common salvation reduces everyone to the same level of sinners in need of a Savior, then raises them to the same height as those who are called to be saints. Onesimus and Philemon meet at the Master's feet. Matthew the former publican and Simon the Zealot shared a common bond in Christ. In Christ, it is no more an advantage to have a college education than to have dropped out of school. Men of brilliant intellect and high social position are not thereby given special status in the church. Men barely literate by this world's standards may become giants of faith and mighty in the Scriptures, taught of God, and movers of men.

For instance, the church had many great and gifted men in the mid-nineteenth century. There were men of high social position such as the Earl of Shaftesbury, men of enormous gifts such as Charles Spurgeon, and men of outstanding faith such as George Müeller. It also had its D. L. Moody, a barely literate shoe salesman. Without higher education, he founded three schools. Without theological training, he reshaped Victorian Christianity. Without radio or television, he preached to one hundred million people. His influence continues to this day. One of his colleagues was Reuben A. Torrey, the first president of the Moody Bible Institute. Torrey graduated from Yale University and Yale Divinity School. He studied theology in Leipzig and Erlanger. He, the polished pastor and teacher, and D. L. Moody, the rough and ready and unconventional revivalist, were firm friends—one in Christ.

(2) The new man's robes (3:12–14)
    (a) Goodness (3:12)

Put on therefore, as the elect of God, holy and beloved, bowels of mercies, kindness, humbleness of mind, meekness, longsuffering.

"Put on!" "Put on!" "Put on!" Three times Paul reiterates the words. The new man is to be as much recognized by his robes (his habits) as the old man is by his rags. The words *put on* are in the imperative. This is not a suggestion but a command.

So, then let us look at the new man's robes, which we are required to wear. The believer *receives* holiness of character. He is "the elect of God." That has to do with what we are *positionally*. God has set us part from the unsaved. His purpose is and has been from all eternity that we should be like His dear Son. Accordingly, those who accept Christ as Savior are constituted holy. This is done by God's own sovereign will. It is not the result of human merit or attainment.

On the other hand, the believer *reveals* holiness of character. He is compassionate, kind, humble-minded, meek, and longsuffering. These are all characteristics that we associate with the Lord Jesus. We are to put them on as our own because they are given to us by God. By our own volition and deliberate choice, we put on Christlikeness of character. We are to put on goodness.

(b) Graciousness (3:13)

Forebearing one another, and forgiving one another, if any man have a quarrel against any: even as Christ forgave you, so also do ye.

Forebearance! Forgiveness! Here is the grave of all of our squabbles. In the home, at work, on the playing field, and in the church we are called upon to exhibit the spirit of the Lord Jesus.

In one of his sermons, D. L. Moody used to picture the Lord's saying to Peter, "Go, hunt up the man who put the crown of thorns on My head and tell him that I love him. Tell him that he can have a crown in my kingdom, one without a thorn. Find the man who spat in my face and preach the gospel to him. Tell him that I forgive him and that I died to save him. Find the man who thrust the spear into my side and tell him that there is a quicker way to my heart." That is how the Lord Jesus has forgiven us. Now it is our turn. We are to forgive others and make an end of our quarrels. The Greek word occurs only here and means "grievances."

c. Godlikeness (3:14)

Above all these things put on charity [love], which is the bond of perfectness.

The word for "love" is *agapē,* God's kind of love, the kind of sacrificing love that took the Lord Jesus to the Cross. That is to be our topcoat, the very love of Christ Himself, so sadly lacking in most of us most of the time. How often we go out without our overcoat!

Some time ago, I was preaching in an inner-city church and staying in a downtown hotel in a not too savory district. I decided to go out for a walk although I had been warned to "be careful."

Sure enough, before long I was accosted by a beggar, a wretched-looking man. I was tempted to give him something, then I remembered that the area had a bad name and the only money I had was in my wallet. I was reluctant to pull it out in full view. All I could think of was the possibility of being robbed, possibly assaulted. So I pretended not to hear him and left him standing.

His face haunted me. I had not gone a hundred yards before the Holy Spirit was convicting me. I felt like the priest and the Levite in the Lord's parable rolled into one.

I pulled out my wallet, took out a large bill, and retraced my steps with the money in my hand. But he was gone. I hung around the area for some time, but he was gone.

The man has troubled me to this day. The Lord would have given him something had He been me. I apologized to the Holy Spirit. I wished that I had put on my overcoat of love that day.

"Above all these things put on love *[agapē]*, which is the bond of perfectness." The word used for "perfectness" denotes the accomplishment of an end that God has in view—that of making us like Jesus. Why does such a gap exist between what we know and what we show?

So there's our wardrobe. It is ours to wear. We need to put on all of our clothes every day. Solomon in all of his glory was not arrayed like one of these, God's elect in full regalia. These clothes do us no good, however, if we leave them in the closet of God's Word. Let us ensure that we put them on. We will be the best-dressed people in town if we do. As Count Zinzendorf put it,

> Jesus, Thy blood and righteousness,
> My beauty are, my glorious dress;
> Midst flaming worlds in these arrayed
> With joy shall I lift up my head.

When I was a little boy growing up in Britain, a new suit was a great occasion. My parents were not affluent. The economic depression overshadowed the country, and money was scarce. So a new suit was a great occasion. The first place where a new suit was displayed was at church. In fact, with most of us in those days, it was known as our Sunday suit—to distinguish it from our everyday clothes. It was kept for going to church and other important occasions. The new robes we receive at conversion are not like that at all. They never wear out. They are for *all* occasions. They never get soiled, never get out of shape, and never fade or sag. We are to wear them everywhere, all of the time—at home, at work, at play, in church, and around town. Only thus can we be a credit to our Lord Jesus Christ.

2. In our church life (3:15–17)

Before we begin on this section, it is worth noting how very personal everything still is although the primary thrust is our life in the mystical body of Christ. Half a dozen times in three verses we have the personal pronouns *your*, *ye*, and *you*. Our church life, after all, depends very much on us. A local church is simply a collection of believers, each one born from above, each one indwelt by the Holy Spirit, each one added to the mystical body, each one gathered out of the world, each one seated with Christ in heavenly places, and each one related to all of the others in the body of Christ. So the local church is really the aggregate, the sum total of the spiritual experience, maturity, gift, and dependability of all of its members. How could it be anything else?

If the people who make up a given local congregation are mostly carnal, worldly, quarrelsome, selfish, critical, and unforgiving, that is what that local church will be like. Here and there may be found a different kind of believer, but the church itself will reflect the lack of spirituality of its members. If, on the other hand, a local church is comprised of members who are godly, consecrated, self-sacrificing, loving, praying, soul-winning, and missionary-minded, that is what that church will be like. It might include some carnal believers, some babes in Christ, but the church as a whole will radiate Christ.

Paul would have us ask ourselves as we go in and out among our brothers and sisters in Christ, "Am I wearing my new clothes to church?"

What kind of a church would the local church that I attend be if everyone was just like me? How long would the church be able to pay its bills, support its ministries, and back its missionaries? If everyone reacted as I do, how long would it survive? If everyone won as many souls as I do, would the church be growing or declining? Suppose that everyone supported the services the way I do, would there be any gatherings of God's people? If everyone studied their Bible and prayed as much as I do, what would the church be like? Suppose everyone followed my example when it came to visitation, teaching Sunday school, caring for the nursery, or helping with the chores—what kind of a church would it be?

Paul could use the personal pronouns *you*, *ye*, and *your* the way he did because he practiced what he preached. He was not afraid to have someone say, "Well, what about *you?*"

Paul was the best-dressed believer of all time. The occasions when we catch a glimpse of him in the "old man's" rags are exceedingly rare. Paul was a living example of the new man in action, dressed in his Sunday best. He realized that the best way to encourage other believers to use their new spiritual wardrobe was to make full use of his.

    a. The principle element (3:15)
       (1) The enthronement of Christ's peace (3:15a)

*And let the peace of God rule in your hearts, to the which also ye
are called in one body; and be ye thankful.*

Paul underlines three things here. First is the enthronement of God's peace. Scholars agree that the phrase "the peace of God" can be rendered "the peace of Christ." What a difference that makes to our understanding! It is like having a phrase from some foreign language translated into our own mother tongue. Often, authors like to air their scholarship by introducing foreign phrases into their writing—*laissez-faire*, for instance, or *coup de grâce*, or *ad hoc*. Many readers skip over such flourishes with a sense of grievance and annoyance. Few readers bother to look up the expressions in a dictionary to find out what they mean. To have them translated for him, however, makes all the difference.

The phrase "peace of God" sounds very good. Nevertheless, it is somewhat distant, ethereal, and remote. Of course, God dwells in an atmosphere of perfect peace. Nothing that could ever happen could ever disturb that sublime peace of His. He is in control of all of the factors of space, matter, and time. It's all very good to speak of "the peace of God" and to commend it to us as something that ought to reign in our hearts. But God is God, and we are but creatures of clay.

But to read instead, "Let the peace of *Christ* rule in your hearts," well, that clothes the whole thing in flesh and blood! It embodies it in a Person, One whom we know and recognize as being one of us. That brings things into focus. We can visualize the Lord Jesus enjoying perfect peace as a boy, as a teenager, as a young man at home, living in perfect peace at school, at play, in the synagogue, at the workbench, or on the highway. We can see that peace reigning when He was confronted by human foes and fierce demons from hell, when tossed on a wild and stormy sea, when surrounded by men who are determined to get rid of Him, and supremely when He was nailed to Calvary's tree. Then we can begin to grasp the peace of Christ.

And that was His last legacy. In the Upper Room—on this side of death, burial, and resurrection—He said, "Peace I leave with you, my peace I give unto you" (John 14:27). Peace! Peace! Peace! And what was "the peace of Christ" like? It was a peace that remained unruffled no matter what happened.

We see that peace in evidence throughout the book of Acts. That peace hushed Peter to sleep on the night before he was due to have his head chopped off (Acts 12:6). We see that peace shining in the face of Stephen as he faced the foes who were slavering for his death (Acts 6:15). We see that peace in that Philippian jail as Paul and Silas, their backs bleeding and torn and their feet fast in the stocks, fill that dismal place with song (Acts 16:23–25). We see that peace fill the heart of Paul on that stricken ship driven before the storm and headed for certain shipwreck on the approaching shore (Acts 27:1–15). We, too, are to let that peace reign.

The word translated "rule" occurs only here, although we have already met a kindred word in Colossians 2:18. Let us put the word in its natural setting. Most of us have watched a ball game degenerate into an uproar. One team claims that their man made it to the plate; the other team hotly disagrees. Angry words are spoken, tempers flare, and blows are exchanged. There is only one way to stop that kind of thing—bring on the umpire. The umpire knows the rules, and he has been watching the play closely. He is impartial, belonging to neither one side nor the other, and he has authority. When a disagreement arises, the umpire rules. That is how Paul uses the word for "rule" here. "Let the peace of Christ rule"—"let it umpire." The tense makes clear that it is to go on umpiring. The phrase can be rendered "Let the peace of Christ keep on acting the umpire in your hearts."

Two conflicting sets of emotions or two opposite opinions each clamor for control. We look to the Lord. We let Him be the Umpire. His peace settles the dispute. His peace is the most biased, partial, and arbitrary umpire that ever was. It will always rule on the side of Christ for that which is right and loving and pure.

Our reaction is, "Well, that sounds all very good. It is marvelous theology but does it work?" When Paul wrote this, he was chained to a Roman soldier awaiting a ruling from Nero as to the charges of treason that his foes had leveled falsely against him. But Paul did not allow such threatening circumstances to upset him. The peace of Christ was acting the umpire in his heart.

(2) The enlargement of Christ's peace (3:15b)

And let the peace of God rule . . . in one body.

The authority of that umpire extends not only to the individual believer but also to the whole mystical body of Christ.

One of the first evidences of a healthy body is that its various members dwell together in peace and harmony and exercise mutual care and concern for each other and are mutually helpful. If we see a man hitting himself on the head with a baseball bat, we conclude that he has serious problems. If we see a man biting chunks out of his leg, we lock him up; he's mad. That is not the way a sane man acts. Within the sphere of the mystical body of Christ in our fellowship one with another, there must be peace. And the peace of Christ is to umpire all disputes.

(3) The enjoyment of Christ's peace (3:15c)

. . . and be ye thankful.

Think again of Paul imprisoned at Rome, his liberty curtailed by the length of the chain that bound him to his jailer. His ministry has been greatly curtailed. He thinks of the plans that he had to make to evangelize Spain. The tin islands of Britain beckoned; so did the Germanic tribes beyond the Rhine. But his future is in the hands of a tyrant.

If we could hear him at prayer, we would hear something like this: "Thank You, Lord, for this prison; at least it is a house, not a dungeon. Thank You that I am still allowed to receive my friends like dear Epaphras here. Thank You, Lord, that I can still pray and write and thank You for the opportunities I have to tell these guards of mine about Christ so that now the entire Praetorian Guard has heard about You. Thank You for enabling me to meet runaway Onesimus who, but for my being here in Rome, might have died in his sins. . . ." And so on it would go. Paul could always find something for which to be thankful.

Handley Moule says, "The Sirens, by the sweetness of their magic songs, decoyed upon the rocks the mariners who sailed past their isles, and the shores were white with human bones. Ulysses with his crew and Orpheus by different means escaped the danger. Ulysses stopped the ears of his men with wax and (wishing himself to hear the song and to hear it in safety) caused himself to be fast bound to the mast. Orpheus took another method; he raised his voice in loud and long praises of the immortal gods and, thus, overcame the charm of the sirens with a better charm."[3]

The solution (to the problem of the seductive, siren voices of the world, the flesh, and the Devil) that the Gnostics advocated was that of Ulysses. We should bind ourselves with the chains of the law, with stern asceticism and a ceaseless round of ritual. Paul's answer was to sing! "Stop your ears," said the Gnostics to the Colossians, "bind yourselves, use every human device to resist the lure of lust, the whispers of the world, the devices of the Devil."

"Not so!" said Paul. "Sing! Use spiritual songs, sing with grace in your hearts to the Lord" (see v. 16). All of those things that seem to be over our heads are already under His feet! Sing! The thankful heart, the heart that can always find something for which to praise God, has little to fear from its foes.

---

3. G. Handley Moule, *Colossian Studies* (1897; reprint, Westwood, N.J.: Revell, n.d.), 130–31.

But we have a greater example than that of Paul. We have the example of our Lord Jesus Christ. On that dreadful night in which He was betrayed, He gathered with His own in the Upper Room, took bread, and gave thanks. Then He rent and tore that loaf. "This," He said, "is my body which is broken for you." Think of it! He gave thanks for Calvary, for the piercing of His hands and feet, for the searing pain, and for the dreaded darkness and torment. He gave thanks. There is nothing more to be said.

> b. The parallel element (3:16)
>   (1) The Word abiding in the life (3:16a)

Let the word of Christ dwell in you richly in all wisdom.

Thus, Paul links the peace of Christ with the Word of Christ. That Word is to dwell in us. The Greek word for "dwell" comes from "a house." The Word of Christ is to take up its *abode* in our hearts. The word of Christ is found within the covers of our Bible. The Gnostics were advocating "philosophy"; Paul advocates the Word. We need to get the Word out of our Bibles and into our hearts. The Word of Christ dwelling in our hearts becomes a vast treasury of wisdom upon which the Holy Spirit can draw as He guides us through the varying circumstances of life. Paul has already reminded his readers that in Christ "are hid all the treasures of wisdom and knowledge" (2:2–3).

We have all kinds of ways in which to get the Word of Christ where it belongs—into our hearts. We can memorize it. We can meditate upon it daily in our quiet time. We can study it using all available aids and helps. We can quote it in conversation, reinforcing its hold upon our hearts. We can live by it. It will fill our minds, control our lives, and become our constant counselor, companion, and guide.

> (2) The Word abounding in the life (3:16b)

. . . teaching and admonishing one another in psalms and hymns and spiritual songs, singing with grace in your hearts to the Lord.

The systematic input of the Word into our lives will result in the systematic output of the Word from our lives. Paul says that this will be expressed in two ways.

First, it will be expressed in *sermons:* "teaching and admonishing one another." That has to do with our public life. We will constantly minister God's Word to others in a helpful way. We will help others to understand the Scriptures and to apply its truths to their hearts. We will reveal its treasures, resolve its mysteries, relate its principles to life. We will rebuke error and confront moral and spiritual issues in the church and in society. We will "admonish." The idea behind that word is that of "training by word." It might be encouragement or reproof. Admonition is warning based on instruction. Eli contented himself with remonstrating with his wicked sons. That was mere expostulation and was worthless (1 Sam. 2:24). He failed to admonish them (3:13).

Paul admonished the Ephesian elders (Acts 20:29–31), putting them on guard against a coming incursion of wolves into the church over which the Holy Spirit had made them responsible overseers.

But that is by no means all. Christianity would be very dull if it consisted of nothing but sermons. The Word abounding in the life will be expressed just as much in *songs:* "in psalms and hymns and spiritual songs, singing with grace in your hearts to the Lord."

Spiritual experience goes hand in hand with spiritual exuberance. This is what is missing in much of Christianity. This lack of enthusiasm and joy makes the church and Christian life unattractive to the unsaved. To look at some Christians, one would think that they had been baptized in lemon juice! Christianity is a happy faith as well as a holy faith. That is why we have so many hymnbooks. The same was true of biblical Judaism. "Thus the LORD saved Israel," we read, "then sang Moses and the children of Israel" (Exod. 14:30; 15:1). This is the first mention of singing in the Bible. Only a redeemed people can really rejoice. This mention is in stark contrast to the second mention—one that describes graphically much of what passes for music today (Exod. 32:15–18). But by then Israel was in a thoroughly backslidden condition, one that bordered on apostasy. The antidote to that is to sing psalms, hymns, and spiritual songs.

c. The practical element (3:17)

And whatsoever ye do in word or deed, do all in the name of the
Lord Jesus, giving thanks to God and the Father by him.

The Christian life is not all singing. Indeed, we can put *too* much emphasis on joyful experience. Life is made up of decisions, some of them very hard ones indeed. Paul gives us a maxim, a rule of faith, a simple formula, to keep us in the mainstream. Everything we say and do must be linked to the peerless, ineffable name of the Lord Jesus. A danger always exists that the Christian life might become one of extremes—all sermons, or all songs, all intellect or all emotion, all exhortation or all exuberance. Both the intellectual and the emotional have their place. Paul here, however, stressed the volitional. Paul's formula is simple—do and say everything under the controlling influence of the saving, sovereign, safeguarding name of the Lord Jesus. If we say and do nothing that will dishonor that name, we shall not go astray. It will settle, for instance, all questions about doubtful vocations and amusements. If we cannot bring the name of the Lord Jesus into our conversation, then shame on us. If we cannot ask the Lord Jesus to endorse a decision and a line of conduct, then we have probably made a wrong decision.

Paul gives us three guidelines. First, everything should be done *proportionately:* "whatsoever ye do in word and deed. . . ." The Christian life is not all words (whether songs or sermons); it is also deeds. We have a Great Commission to fulfill (Matt. 28:18–20; Acts 1:8). We have a healthy balance to maintain. For too many people, Christianity is all talk.

Everything must be done *properly:* "whatsoever ye do . . . do all in the name of the Lord Jesus." Again we see Paul's balance. Good works are a part of the Christian life. Missionaries in underdeveloped countries know the value of establishing hospitals, schools, sanitariums, and leprosariums. But it is not a question of doing good works for their own sake. These things are a means to an end. We do them in the name of the Lord Jesus. We do them, hopefully, to win people to Christ. Social welfare in the church has a spiritual side.

Finally, everything must be done *prayerfully:* "giving thanks to God and the Father by him." The kind of life that Paul has been explaining, a life lived beneath the shadow of that lovely name, will be a life overflowing with gratitude to God. From such a life will ascend to God, like the fragrant incense from the golden altar in the Holy Place of the temple, a continuous outpouring of praise.

Thus, Paul describes Christianity as it relates to other Christians. How people would flock to the places where Christians meet if only we were all living the kind of life that Paul sets before us here.

3. In our domestic life (3:18–21)
   a. Our role as partners (3:18–19)
      (1) God's order in the home (3:18)

> *Wives, submit yourselves unto your own husbands,*
> *as it is fit in the Lord.*

The clue to what follows lies in what has just gone before. Paul is beginning a new subject, but it is by no means divorced from the preceding context. It is only as the Word of Christ dwells in us richly (the Greek word describes a wealthy person) that we can behave in a Christlike way toward one another in the various relationships of life.

In the parallel passage in Ephesians 5:18–25, Paul begins his discussion of family relationships by commanding us to be filled with the Spirit. Only as the Holy Spirit fills us can we live the Christ-life as wives and husbands, as parents and children, and as masters and servants.

The homes of our land are under attack. Our permissive society allows every form of pornography to be published and every form of perversion to be practiced. People generally accept a promiscuous lifestyle as normal. Chastity is scorned. Extramarital affairs are commonplace, wreaking havoc in homes.

In the United States, "no-fault" divorce has played havoc with marriage. It began in California in 1969 with the enactment of a statute allowing for "no-fault" divorce—in effect, divorce on demand—with no requirement to prove fault. One by one, the other states followed California's lead. South Dakota, the last to hold out, fell in 1985. In many families now the desires of the individual reign supreme. The very idea of binding commitments is viewed with disfavor. The old idea that marriage vows were sacred and sacramental and therefore binding has been thrown out of court. Now single-parent families are as common as two-parent families. Worse still, many "partners" just live together without even bothering with the formality of marriage. Many people regard marriage as a social institution that has failed dismally. Compounding the problem is the working wife. Traditionally women's primary functions in marriage were those of wife and mother. The husband was the breadwinner and the protector of the family. Today, wives either want to work or have to work. Many of them are as keen on their careers as are their husbands.[4]

Some years ago, Phil Donahue, a popular television talk show host, had Charles Schultz, creator of the popular "Peanuts" comic strip, and Tim LaHaye, a well-known Christian counselor, on his program. His guests were defending Christian standards of morality before an essentially hostile audience. One young man with a flushed and angry face wanted to know what difference a piece of paper (a

---

4. *Insight* magazine, 27 June 1994.

marriage certificate) made as long as he and his girlfriend had a mutual agreement. The audience approved of his view.

Yet, his contention was ludicrous and not one that he would care to carry through in other areas of his life. Suppose that the same young man were to buy a house or a car or buy a bank certificate of deposit. Would he not insist on having "a piece of paper" to document properly his transaction and give it status in the eyes of the law? Would he say to the seller, "Here's the cash. Now I own a house. We'll not be bothered about a mere piece of paper. After all, we are friends and we have an arrangement." Of course not!

The same is true of marriage, something infinitely more important than the purchase of a piece of property. The home is the basic building block of society. As the home goes, so goes the nation. A piece of paper neither makes nor breaks a marriage, although it makes it legal and adds solemnity to the "arrangement." The marriage certificate is a document recognized by society and by the law, just as marriage itself is an institution ordained by God of which the marriage certificate is a token. No amount of rationalization by today's libertarians alters the fact that God says, "Marriage is honourable in all, and the bed undefiled: but whoremongers and adulterers God will judge" (Heb. 13:4). So far as God is concerned, marriage involves a lifelong commitment (except in cases where He Himself sanctions divorce [Matt. 19:9]. And that "piece of paper," or whatever other proofs of marriage a given society accepts, of which the young man was so contemptuous, can be waived only at tragic cost for the individuals concerned, their children, and the society in which they live.

Let us look first then at our role as partners. Paul begins with God's order for the home—"Wives, submit yourselves unto your own husbands, as it is fit in the Lord." The women's liberation movement scornfully repudiates such a statement. Its advocates accuse the inspired apostle of being a woman hater, ignoring the fact that Paul wrote by direct inspiration of the Holy Spirit, not of himself. We must have order in the home as well as anywhere else in a stable society. We cannot have two heads of state in a nation, or we invite civil war. We cannot have two men running a corporation, each holding opposite views. We cannot have two commanders-in-chief of the country's armed forces. And we cannot have two heads of a family. God has ordained the man to be the head of his home. He is not the boss, but he is the head. Moreover, if he abdicates that headship, he does so to the detriment of himself, his wife, and his children. The Bible does not open up this issue for discussion or debate. It is part of God's plan in Creation (Eph. 5:22–24; 1 Cor. 11:3, 8–9), one made all the more necessary by the Fall (Gen. 3:16). The sensible man will listen to his wife, respect her views, and consider her best interests when making decisions regarding the home. God holds him responsible, however, to exercise his headship, and the woman is responsible to submit to it.

Charles Dickens, in his famous story *Oliver Twist,* gives us a telling glimpse into the home life of that old bully, Mr. Bumble. Evidently, God's order for the home was very much lacking in Mr. Bumble's domestic arrangements.

He had married the widow Corney in the hopes of acquiring her property. Instead, he acquired a partner who quickly reduced him to a state of abject servility. Mr. Bumble and his domineering wife entered into nefarious dealings with a man called Monks, dealings designed to bring harm to the poor orphan boy, Oliver Twist. When the plot was exposed, Mr. Brownlow, who had adopted Oliver, told Mr. Bumble that he and his wife would lose their position at the workhouse and that he would ensure that they were never employed in a position of trust again.

Like Adam, Mr. Bumble tried to transfer all of the blame to his wife. Mr. Brownlow cut him off, "Indeed you are the more guilty of the two, in the eye of the law; for the law supposes that your wife acts under your direction."

"If the law supposes that," said Mr. Bumble, squeezing his hat emphatically in both hands, "the law is . . . an idiot. If that's the eye of the law, the law is a bachelor; and the worst I wish the law is, that his eye may be opened by experience—by experience."

Well, regardless of whether the law supposes that a wife is under the direction of her husband, God does. The Bible lays down as the first principle of a harmonious home that wives are to submit themselves to their own husbands, as it is fit in the Lord.

W. E. Vine tells us that that the word for "submit" primarily is a military term, meaning "to rank under." Handley Moule prefers the rendering "be loyal" as best conveying the idea of submission in this husband-wife context. The wife is to acknowledge her husband's God-ordained role of leadership, but she is certainly not his slave.

Obviously, we must have order in the home as anywhere else. When a person buys an expensive appliance for his home, it usually comes with a guarantee and some instructions. Often buttons have to be pressed in proper order and so on. It is foolish to ignore the instructions. Failure to obey them might cause severe damage to the appliance and void the manufacturer's warranty.

Marriage is far more complicated than a mere machine. Marriage was God's invention. He performed the first wedding in the Old Testament, and in the New Testament the Lord Jesus Himself graced the first wedding—and made it the occasion of His first miracle. In the Bible, God has given us His instructions on how to make marriage work. It is foolish to quarrel with those instructions as many people are prone to do today.

(2) God's orders to the husband (3:19)

Husbands, love your wives, and be not bitter against them.

The instructions for the wife are addressed to her will; the instructions to the husband are addressed to his heart. He is to love his wife. In the parallel passage in Ephesians, the Holy Spirit adds, "As Christ also loved the church, and gave himself for it" (5:25). The word used for "love" is *agapē,* the highest form of love, the very love of God and of the Lord Jesus, Calvary love.

Husbands are not to become "bitter" toward their wives. The word used means to exasperate, to irritate, or to make bitter. It is used elsewhere in the New Testament only in the Apocalypse, where it is used to describe the effect that Satan will have on human life and society when he is finally cast down from the heavenlies. The imagery used to describe this coming fall is that of a falling star, "And the name of the star is called Wormwood: and the third part of the waters became wormwood; and many men died of the waters, because they were made *bitter,*" John says (Rev. 8:11). The word is also used to describe the effect that a certain "little book" had on John when he obeyed the angel's command to eat it. "It was in my mouth sweet as honey: and as soon as I had eaten it, my belly was bitter" (Rev. 10:9–10).

We must avoid allowing that kind of bitterness to sour our marriage. Most of us have irritating traits that exasperate others. Unless we deal with them, these traits, within the narrow walls of the home, can become destructive and turn the marriage to wormwood. The irritating things might be big or little. A sneering attitude by one partner toward the other partner's spiritual interests, economic needs, or emotional and physical desires will do it. On the other hand, it might be something as casual as the way one raises an eyebrow. The look on the face, perhaps, will do it, or the tone of the voice or the way a deaf ear is turned when the other is talking. These minor irritants might be done unconsciously, carelessly, and with no deliberate desire to annoy. They are, however, the little foxes that spoil the grapes. Solomon (with much experience of marriage and its problems) advises that these foxes be caught the moment they appear (Song 2:15).

"Don't become bitter against your wives," Paul tells all husbands. Cultivate a sweet, loving, tender spirit. Peter gives similar advice: "Consider your wife as the weaker vessel," he says (see 1 Peter 3:7). Perhaps Peter was thinking of his own wife and his own home back there in Capernaum. He would remember the day when he had invited the Lord into his home. The Lord had responded by working a miracle of healing right there in Peter's home (Matt. 8:14–15). Moreover, it would seem that thereafter the Lord made Peter's home His home for the duration of His Galilean ministry. Such is the blessing that comes to a home when Jesus is invited in and given His place.

Paul adds that a wife should submit herself to her husband because that is "fit in the Lord." The word means "to be befitting." The word suggests "arriving at," or "reaching" a goal. It came to denote doing one's duty—in this case, doing one's duty as a wife toward one's husband. Years ago, I saw a sign in the window of a dry cleaning establishment. It said, "If your clothes aren't becoming to you, they should be coming to us." Well said! God says much the same to us. If our conduct in the home is not becoming, we ought to be coming to Him.

b. Our role as parents (3:20–21)
    (1) The principle of parental rule (3:20)

Children, obey your parents in all things: for this is well pleasing
unto the Lord.

The whole encyclopedia of God's commandments for children and young people can be reduced to this one simple statement, "Obey your parents in everything."

Parental rule is the first circle of authority in God's moral government of this world. It is in the home that children are first confronted with the fact of authority and learn their first lessons in obedience. "In everything," says the Holy Spirit—in matters of diet, dress, and deportment; in matters of faith and morals. In everything, parents, under the authority of God themselves, are to set the standards, define the limits, and enforce the rules. Parents stand in the place of God with very small children.

A child has to learn to respect, fear, and obey parental authority. This learning prepares the way for other and larger types of authority as the child grows older and his spheres of interest enlarge. If a child does not learn obedience to parental authority, he will grow up to disrespect *all* authority—school authority, police authority, and eventually divine authority. Rebellion at home, if unchecked, grows up into brawling defiance of all authority.

God takes a serious view of disrespect for parental authority. In the Old Testament, a rebellious son was to be brought before the magistrate and condemned to death (Exod. 21:17). God declared rebellion to be as the sin of witchcraft (1 Sam. 15:22–23). The harsh law of the Old Testament has been replaced in the New Testament by the parable of the prodigal. Sooner or later, unrepentant rebels discover that God has not changed. However, in grace, He does not enforce the full penalty of the Law required under the Levitical code. He knows how to make rebels meet the consequences of their behavior. Incidentally, the hypocritical older brother in the Lord's parable was at heart just as much a rebel against parental authority as was the runaway prodigal—and much harder to reach (Luke 15:11–32).

The most glorious example of obedience is set before us, as we might expect by the Lord Himself. When He was a boy of twelve, Mary and Joseph took Him to Jerusalem. At the end of the festivities, the Nazareth party left for home, and Mary and Joseph went a whole day's journey just "supposing" Him to be one of the company. When they discovered their mistake, they went back to Jerusalem and scoured the city in search of Him. After three days of fruitless search, they found Him where they ought to have looked in the first place—in the temple. When Mary chided Him, He said, "Wist ye not that I must be about my Father's business?" (Luke 2:49). By then, He knew who His Father was and what His Father's business was—not that of a village carpenter but the work of the Cross— the business of procuring a judgment-proof salvation for sinners. Luke adds, "And *he* went down with *them,* and came to Nazareth, and was subject unto *them*" (v. 51). Think of it, *He,* the eternal Son of the living God, fully aware of who He was, was subject to *them*—to a carpenter and his peasant wife! The gulf between the "He" and the "them" was infinite. Yet, as a boy about to enter His teenage years, He put Himself absolutely under the parental authority of the woman whom His Father had chosen to be His mother and of the man whom He had chosen to be as a father to Him. Moreover, He was subject to them "in all things" we can be sure. There never was a more cheerfully obedient son on earth than He.

(2) The principle of parental responsibility (3:21)

Fathers, provoke not your children to anger, lest they be
discouraged.

The word for "provoke" here means "to rouse to anger," or "to fight." It can be rendered "to excite" or "to irritate." Often, parents forget that their children are what my father used to call "the little people." They are people, too, with feelings, thoughts, desires, hopes, and faults, just like grown-ups. The father's role is to be a dad, not a dictator. Just because at times he has to say, "No!" and enforce a "no" answer does not mean that he has to be nasty. Children need to be treated with the same courtesy shown to others. Nobody likes being bossed and bullied.

The word for "discouraged" means "to be disheartened" or "to have their spirit broken." We have to break a young child's will, especially when it is set in a defiant mode, but we must not break his spirit. Constantly nagging children can produce two opposite reactions. The child can become broken in spirit or belligerent in spirit. Parental responsibility involves setting standards and defining limits and enforcing discipline. But these things need to be done intelligently, reasonably, and lovingly. Being a parent involves awesome responsibility and ultimately accountability to God.

The "Word of Christ" dwelling in us richly along with the filling of the Holy Spirit will enable us to be the persons, partners, and parents God wants us to be. True wisdom is to be found in God's Word. The books of Ecclesiastes and Proverbs are full of down-to-earth advice along these lines. In Proverbs, Solomon looked at life from the standpoint of his maturity; in Ecclesiastes, he looked at life from the standpoint of his mistakes. Both books are valuable. The New Testament Epistles are also treasure chests of practical wisdom.

> 4. In our business life (3:22–4:1)
>   a. Men and their tasks (3:22–25)
>   (1) The measure of their service (3:22a)

Servants, obey in all things your masters according to the flesh.

The Holy Spirit now addresses the often stormy area of management-employee relations. We are all familiar with modern confrontations between giant unions and multinational corporations. The resulting strikes and lockouts affect all of our lives. Much of the strife between employers ("masters") and employees ("servants," literally "slaves") would vanish if both sides observed these simple rules. Certainly so far as the Christian is concerned, the principles laid down here by the Holy Spirit should be the rule in the marketplace.

Here and elsewhere (Eph. 6:5–8; 1 Tim. 6:1–2), Paul addresses himself to slaves. It is noteworthy, however, that he devotes twice as much space to the problems of slaves here in Colossians than he does in the other passages. That is probably because of his interest in Onesimus and Philemon. We would use the term *employee* today, of course, but in Paul's day the vast majority of the workforce throughout the Roman Empire was made up of slaves, people who had no rights whatsoever under the law. They were not people but property.

"Servants, obey in *all* things your masters according to the flesh." This was not the place for Paul to deal with the social problem of slavery; he would do that in his accompanying letter to Philemon. The Holy Spirit's word to slaves was sweeping: obey your masters in everything. Peter endorses that command, adding the unpalatable fact that the rule applied to harsh masters as well as to kind ones (1 Peter 2:18).

The human master, or employer, is to be obeyed in all things that do not contradict the express commands of the heavenly Master. Employees are to render faithful, diligent, Christlike service—the kind of service Joseph rendered to Potiphar and later to the prison warden and later still to Pharaoh. For the hours of the day he is on the job, an employee's time and talents belong to his employer. We live in a kinder age than did Paul. If a person does not like his employer, he can always leave. A Christian cannot honestly continue in his employment and complain about this, that, and the other thing. He cannot continue in his employment and laze around, do shoddy work, and expect God to bless him. An employer deserves diligent, loyal service from those who work for him.

(2) The manner of their service (3:22b–23)

Not with eyeservice, as menpleasers; but in singleness of heart,
fearing God: And whatsoever ye do, do it heartily as to the Lord,
and not unto men.

Paul tells Christian employees that they should be the best, the most trustworthy, the most loyal, faithful, and industrious people in the workforce. Their employers ought to be able *to leave them.* Their service is to be "not with eye-service." This is, they should work just as hard when the boss is away as when he's looking over their shoulder. The Lord's eye is on them. They should need no other motivation to do their best.

Their employers ought to be able *to load them.* It should be the Christian employee's goal to do his own job well and to shoulder extra duties. He should not go around complaining, "That's not my job." The union policy of "feather-bedding" should be abhorrent to a Christian employee. That word *whatsoever* covers all of the ground of employment and claims it all for God. Here, too, Paul shows his genius. He centers his appeal in a person. He does not say, "Make yourself indispensable so that you will get promoted or so as to develop your skills, or so as to develop good Christian character, or even so as to maintain a good testimony," worthy though any of these motives might be. No, indeed! Nothing so cold and calculating could ever inspire the enthusiasm of thousands upon thousands of slaves. A cause must live in some powerful name. It must be incarnate in flesh and blood. Thus, Paul, with unerring and inspired genius, gathers up all abstract arguments for doing one's best on the job and sets them all aside. "Do it," he says, "heartily as to the Lord." The boss might be fair or unfair, a bully or a benevolent employer. That is a side issue. The Christian keeps his eye on Christ. *He* is the One for whom he is working, not some man.

(3) The motive of their service (3:24–25)

Paul lifts the whole idea of service, even forced service in a slave labor camp, to a higher plane. First, he puts it on an *eternal* plane, *"Knowing that of the Lord ye shall receive the reward of the inheritance."* We divide work into secular and sacred. God does not do such a thing. All work for the believer is elevated to the eternal plane and will be rewarded at the judgment seat of Christ. There will be a reward for the man who followed the plow, just as for the man who filled the pulpit. There will be a reward for the man who worked in the factory, just as for the man who went to the mission field. There will be a reward for the man who gave his life for science, just as for the man who gave his life in sacrifice. Not for nothing did the Lord of glory sanctify human labor when He entered into human life. Not for nothing did He toil year after year at the carpenter's bench in Nazareth. All diligent, faithful service, done as to the Lord, will be acknowledged in the crowning day that's coming bye and bye—acknowledged and rewarded by One who chose to spend most of His life in a shop as a workingman.

Then, too, He lifts it to the *evangelical* plane, *"For ye serve the Lord Christ,"* Paul adds. We are in reality employed by Christ, not just some human master or corporation. Who would not put in a full day for Jesus? Who would not do his best for Him? Suppose you could actually see the Lord Jesus in the office of the president of the corporation, or in the manager's office, or walking down through the lathes as shop foreman?

Paul has just reminded us that "whatsoever ye do in word or deed, do all in the name of the Lord Jesus" (v. 17). Now he reminds us that in the workplace the same rule applies—only there it is even more personal. Jesus is there. Ultimately, He is in charge. We serve the Lord Christ as believers. Others might see some unscrupulous, sarcastic, uncouth boss; we see Jesus. Or, to be more accurate, we see the Lord Christ. The unsaved man doesn't see Him and has no concept of the evangelical plane where Christ is Lord. But we see Him, and that changes everything.

Finally, Paul lifts it to the *ethical* plane, *"But he that doeth wrong shall receive for the wrong which he hath done: and there is no respect of persons."* Shining service will be rewarded; shoddy service will be punished. God does not have one set of standards for sinners and another for saints. The Lord is not impressed by the fame and fortune of some successful business tycoon. Nor does He show favoritism to a man on the job just because he happens to be a believer. When it comes to judgment, it is what we do and what we say and what we are that matters, not who we are. Salvation is always on the basis of faith, judgment is always according to works—good or bad.

> b. Masters and their trusts (4:1)
>> (1) The man in authority (4:1a)

Masters, give unto your servants that which is just and equal.

The absolute impartiality of God is now revealed in a different way. If men have their tasks, masters have their trusts, their responsibilities under God. It is not a one-sided affair. The employer has a right to expect the best kind of work out of his men, a full day's work for a full day's pay. But workers have a right to the best kind of welfare from their employers. They have a right to expect that they will be fairly and adequately paid, that their work conditions will be safe and hygienic, and that benevolence will be shown toward their general social welfare. "Masters, give unto your servants that which is just and equal."

"The labourer is worthy of his hire" is a fixed biblical principle (Luke 10:7). Centuries of injustice meted out to employees has now caught up to employers. They have to deal with hostile unions and with government regulations of all kinds, covering every facet of employment and often entailing endless discord and red tape. The Bible warned that this would be so (James 5:4–8). How much better it would have been and would still be if these simple biblical principles were followed. The Communist specter that haunted the world for the best part of a century stemmed directly from the terrible injustices in the workplace which accompanied the industrial revolution and from the creation of soulless joint-stock corporations. Giant and impersonal corporations were formerly owned by stockholders who were interested in profits, not workers. Workers were expendable. Management and labor were completely divorced. Corporate enterprises had no soul. Marx and Engels found an eager audience and a ready response to their slogans—"from each according to his ability, to each according to his need" and "workers of the world unite."

What kind of an employer would Jesus be? Suppose that you had lived in those days when He was running the carpenter's shop in Nazareth and had been hired to work for Him. Well, we can be sure that you would have been paid generously and treated magnificently. Jesus would have become your best Friend. He would have taken a personal interest in you and genuine and continuing interest in your spiritual and financial and social welfare and that of your family. That is the kind of employer the Lord Jesus expects the Christian employer to be.

(2) The man under authority (4:1b)

Knowing that ye also have a Master in heaven.

A Master in heaven! Yes, indeed, and One who knows all about the pressures of being in the marketplace. He knows all about the stiff competition you face. He is aware, too, that you are running a business, not a charity.

Just the same, the employer must face the fact that he is not only *in* authority, he is *under* authority and directly accountable to God for his behavior. This is true of all employers. It is particularly true of Christian employers. What an opportunity the Christian employer has to witness of Christ to all of those who work for him! What an opportunity to show a Christlike spirit and, thus, earn the right to speak for Him to those whom he employs.

The man who comes to mind is Robert Laidlaw. Some time ago, my wife and I were in New Zealand. The person who met us at the airport knew that we had some time to wait before going on to the South Island, so he gave us a quick tour around Aukland. A sign caught my eye. It was a large sign being taken down from an old but impressive building. I just caught the name on that sign as it was being lowered—ROBERT LAIDLAW.

It sparked a host of memories. I had once heard Robert Laidlaw preach in

South Wales at the height of the Second World War. A crusade was being held in downtown Cardiff despite the fact that bombs rained down nightly. That did not stop the crowds from coming. With Robert Laidlaw, successful New Zealand businessman, as the featured crusade speaker, you could not have kept them away. And preach he could! I was working in a bank at the time not far from the rented auditorium, so I took the opportunity to go and hear him. The place was packed. The gospel was preached. Souls were saved.

As a young man, Robert Laidlaw saw in his travels abroad a Montgomery Ward mail-order catalog. It caught his interest. Because there was nothing like it in New Zealand, he decided to start a mail-order house. His first catalog was a modest 125 pages and his place of business a small thirty-by-twenty-foot room. He boldly promised to supply country folk with anything they could possibly want, from socks to farm equipment. The response was immediate and overwhelming. The bargain prices, the easy access to an ever-expanding list of goods, caught on. Orders poured in. The new company had to move time and again to bigger buildings. Soon Auckland's largest commercial building was built. It was five stories high and had floor space covering more than seven and a half acres. That was in 1914. It was in 1996 that I saw the sign coming down.

But that is not the end of the story. Robert Laidlaw had a burden to win to Christ the people who worked for him. When the Chapman-Alexander evangelistic team arrived in New Zealand in 1913, Laidlaw had Wilbur Chapman address his staff, already numbering about two hundred people.

Shortly afterward, he wrote *The Reason Why*, probably the most widely used and effective gospel booklet ever written. It has been translated into some thirty languages. Millions of copies have been sold. Countless thousands have come to Christ in response to its reasoned and interesting presentation of the gospel. It was originally written to give Robert Laidlaw's personal testimony of the saving power of the Lord Jesus to each one of his employees. It is a readable booklet, full of telling illustrations and designed to bring readers to a personal decision.

In the early 1960s, I was in charge of course development in the Correspondence School of the Moody Bible Institute in Chicago. We decided at that time to expand the number of courses offered on the popular level that could be used for evangelistic purposes. I suggested that we adapt *The Reason Why* as a correspondence course. I wrote to Mr. Laidlaw and received his cordial blessing on the project. Many people found Christ by studying this booklet in its correspondence course format.

And the booklet itself is still being used. Just the other Sunday, I was browsing through the large and well-stocked bookstore of the Bellevue Baptist church in Memphis, Tennessee, and my eye was caught by that old familiar title, *The Reason Why*. This particular slim-line edition was attractively produced with a hard cover! So Robert Laidlaw, successful businessman, gifted evangelist, and committed soul winner with a heart for his employees, "being dead, yet speaketh."

That is the kind of thing, surely, that the apostle Paul had in mind.

  5. In our secular life (4:2–6)
    a. We are to be prayerful in character (4:2–4)
      (1) The great habit of our lives (4:2a)

Continue in prayer. . . .

"Them that are without" (4:5). That is the key to what Paul has to say in this closing part of this section of his epistle. The expression first meets us in our Lord's words to His disciples, "Unto you it is given to know the mystery of the kingdom of God: but unto them that are without, all these things are done in parables" (Mark 4:11). Thus, the Lord Himself drew the line. He made the difference. Some people are His disciples, others are "them that are without," a cold and terrible place to be.

Similarly, Paul tells the Corinthians, "For what have I to do to judge them also that are without? do not ye judge them that are within? But them that are without God judgeth" (1 Cor. 5:12–13).

In closing both the Apocalypse and the Bible, John draws the line for the last time. He describes the bliss of those who are within, those who have access to the celestial city and "to the tree of life, and may enter in through the gates into the city." Then he makes the solemn contrast with those who are without—"For without are dogs, and sorcerers, and whoremongers, and murderers, and idolaters, and whosoever loveth and maketh a lie" (Rev. 22:14–15).

The believer is to have these outsiders in mind in all of his secular contacts. He is to so live that those on the outside might come to Christ and so join those who are on the inside. The great resource available to us in all of this is prayer.

Paul was a great believer in prayer. Prayer is what links us with God's throne. It is by prayer that we do business in the heavenlies. It is the most purely spiritual of all of our exercises. Yet, there is nothing that we neglect more. Most people would rather do anything than pray.

Prayer, Paul says, is to be the great habit of our lives. "Continue in prayer," he says. The statement could be rendered, "Be strong toward prayer." One suggested rendering is "persist in the siege." For we are up against all of the might of Satan's invisible principalities when we pray. Satan lines up his big battalions when we pray. We need the whole armor of God when we pray (Eph. 6:11–18). We need the Holy Spirit's help when we pray (Rom. 8:26–27). We must fight drowsiness, distractions, and discouragement when we pray.

If the wife is to submit properly to her husband, if the husband is to love his wife as Christ did the church, if the young person is to submit to his parents, if parents are to keep from discouraging their children, if men are to serve their human masters as rendering service to the Lord Christ, and if masters are to care for the well being of their employees as those accountable to God, then they must pray.

(2) The guarded habit of our lives (4:2b)

Continue in prayer, and watch in the same.

"Watch and pray," Jesus told His companions in Gethsemane. They promptly fell asleep. In fact, they kept on falling asleep. They neither watched nor prayed. No wonder they took to their heels when the soldiers showed up.

It was in this area of watchfulness that Elijah tested his servant. He announced that they were going into partnership for revival. "You watch," he said, "and I'll pray." He sent his servant up to the crest of Carmel to watch while he stayed down below and prayed. Up and down, back and forth that servant went but without the slightest expectation that God would answer Elijah's prayer. It was not until his seventh trip back to the mountain peak that he finally saw what Elijah had known all along would be there (1 Kings 18:43–44). That kind of "watching" is of no value at all. Shortly afterward, Elijah replaced that servant with Elisha, a true watcher indeed! He received a double portion of Elijah's spirit because that was so (2 Kings 2:9–12).

From then on, there was a man on earth (Elisha) and a man in heaven (Elijah). The man in heaven once trod the path of obedience on earth. Now he was living the life of a man in Glory.

The man on earth (Elisha) had observed the path of obedience trodden down here by the man in Glory (Elijah). Now he (Elisha) coveted to be the true copy on earth of that man in Glory—to tread the same path of obedience, to exhibit his spirit and his power. But everything depended on his keeping his eye on that man in heaven. All of which is a parable of us on earth and of Jesus in heaven. We are to live with our eyes fixed on Him—beholding Him and beseeching Him.

(3) The grateful habit of our lives (4:2c)

Continue in prayer . . . with thanksgiving.

How grateful we should be that at Calvary Jesus tore aside the temple veil and blazed the way for us right into the very presence of God. We can come to Him whenever we like, stay as long as we like, talk to Him about anything we like, no matter who we are or where we live or what we do. The blood of the Lord Jesus cleanses us from all sin and gives us access into the throne room of the universe. There is not a man on earth who will give us either the time or the understanding or the help that Jesus will. We should come to Him gratefully.

Suppose that the privilege of prayer were suddenly to be withdrawn—as it will be at one point during the Apocalypse (Rev. 15:8). Right after that, wrath will be outpoured. It was withdrawn from wicked King Saul (1 Sam. 28:6). So desperate did Saul become when he could no longer knock on heaven's door, he went and knocked on the door of hell and consulted a witch. God simply opened that door and let him fall through it into a lost eternity.

Truly prayer should be the grateful habit of our lives. We should thank God every day that we can come before His throne, bow our hearts before Him, and make bare our innermost souls.

(4) The grandest habit of our lives (4:3–4)

Withal [at the same time] praying also for us, that God would open unto us a door of utterance, to speak the mystery of Christ, for which I am also in bonds: That I may make it manifest, as I ought to speak.

Such is the power of prayer. It can open prison doors, a sinner's heart, or an apostle's mouth as God wills. Paul was the greatest of all messengers with the greatest of all messages. He had long since come to terms with his incarceration, two long years at Caesarea and now, year after year, at Rome. That would be enough to shut any smaller man's mouth. Not Paul! He saw opportunities everywhere. Felix, Festus, and King Agrippa all heard the gospel because of his chains.

So, we believe, did Nero. Paul's converts were found in the royal palace itself. And he still had visitors, those daring souls such as Onesiphorus, who was not intimidated by Paul's chains (2 Tim. 1:16; 4:19). And he still had his pen! Paul's prison was more like the corporate headquarters of a global enterprise than anything else. And he could still preach! Even if only to an audience of one, the Roman soldier at the other end of his chain.

But he was still human. He needed the Holy Spirit to fill his heart and to loose his tongue. And he needed the supporting prayers of God's people, great and gifted and godly apostle that he was. In this he was like Queen Esther, who pleaded for the supporting prayers of God's people to back her up in her daring venture to become the mediator for God's people with the king (Esther 4:16–17).

So there at Rome, writing to Colosse, Paul says to the saints, "Come! Share with me in this great opportunity I have of testifying to the truth to those in Caesar's palace. I need your prayers. It is only as you pray that I will know what to say when my time comes." That, the mystery of prayer, and how and why it works, is part of the even greater "mystery of Christ." Prayer gives us our opportunity of sharing in the ministry of others of like precious faith. It is a gracious provision that God has made for us, not only to aid in another's ministry but also to lay up treasure in heaven.

> b. Prudent in conduct (4:5)
> (1) We must guard our testimony (4:5a)

Walk in wisdom toward them that are without.

So often our behavior as Christians does not commend the gospel to the unsaved. How far would Peter have gotten, we wonder, if he had tried giving a word of testimony to Malchus, had he met him in the high priest's garden after just cutting off his ear? The Lord had performed a special miracle to put that ear back on again. He is constantly doing the same for us to those whom we offend and attack and whose ears we so often cut off.

Here, for instance, is a woman who wants to see her husband saved. So what does she do? She nags him because he does this and that and because he goes here and there and because he won't go to church. Then she wonders why he shows so little interest in the things of God.

Or here is an employee who wishes his boss would get saved. But he slacks off the job, pads his expense account, loses his temper, or occasionally uses bad language. Then he wonders why his boss declines an invitation to come to an evangelistic crusade.

Here is a neighbor who wishes that he could win the fellow next door to Christ. But he borrows his ladder or his lawn mower and fails to return it. He responds to his neighbor's overtures of friendship by saying, "No thanks, I don't drink." Or, "Can't do that. I don't play cards." Then he wonders why his neighbor holds him at arm's length.

"Guard your testimony," says Paul. Put yourself in the other fellow's shoes. Be wise, especially in your dealings with the unsaved.

(2) We must guard our time (4:5b)

Redeeming the time.

We are stewards of our time. Time is a nonrenewable resource. It slips past us at an alarming rate. Once it's gone, it's gone. It can never be recalled. We invest each fleeting moment with something even if it is only idleness. Solomon had a well-developed appreciation of the value of time (Eccl. 3:1–8). It was sad that he wasted so much of it in personal aggrandizement and desecrated even more of it by his carnality and worldliness! Solomon does not seem to have practiced much of what he preached.

"Redeem the time," says Paul. Suppose that a wealthy man were to give someone $1440 a day to spend. He had to spend it. The gift did not allow him to save it, still less to hoard it. At the end of each day what was not spent was lost. The same sum would arrive every day until the end of life. Then an accounting would be made of what the recipient had done with the sum. There it was $1440 a day to spend or squander, to be used buying things for oneself or in helping others, to be wasted on trifles or invested for eternity.

Every day God gives us 1440 minutes to be spent by us and us alone. We have to spend it. We cannot save up some of today's time for tomorrow. We have none of yesterday's time left over for today. All of these precious minutes are ours. However, when life is over, there will be a strict accounting of what we have done with that time. We, as Christians, will give our accounting at the judgment seat of Christ. The unsaved will render account at the Great White Throne. But an accounting will be made. "Make the best possible use of your time," Paul says. Paul might have wasted his time moping over the restrictions placed upon his liberty. Not him! He invested that time in writing immortal books, in praying for the furtherance of the gospel, in talking to those who came or were sent to him about the things pertaining to the kingdom of God, in meditating upon the Scriptures long since committed to memory, and in preparing himself for new missionary journeys should he be released or to meet the Lord in Glory should Nero order his execution.

      c. Pungent in conversation (4:6)
         (1) Adding sweetness to our conversation (4:6a)

Let your speech be alway with grace. . . .

Paul urges us to add three things to our conversation—and he has "them that are without" in mind. All too often, we alienate people with our tongues. Paul has a recipe for changing that. We should add grace to our speech. That rules out all harshness, all criticism, all gossip, and all unkind, ungracious talk. It is said of the Lord Jesus that people marveled at the gracious words that proceeded out of His mouth (Luke 4:22). That's our model.

How often we have spoken hastily only to wish immediately afterward that we could recall those words. In the old days when train travel was common and people on long journeys paid for a sleeping car, a train was roaring across the United States. It was nighttime. Most passengers were in their bunks. But in one of the sleeping cars the passengers were being kept awake by the cries of a small child.

One of the sleepless passengers could stand it no longer. He raised an angry voice. "Can't you keep that child quiet?" he demanded. "Surely the child's mother ought to be able to control all this crying."

A man's voice replied. "I'm very sorry, Sir. I'm doing the best I can. But the child's mother can't keep the poor child quiet. She's in her coffin in the baggage van at the end of the train. She died yesterday."

The angry passenger apologized. We can be sure Jesus never spoke like that exasperated man on that train.

Some years ago, a popular magazine used to run a column titled "The Perfect Squelch." The column was concerned with the way in which some objectionable person was put in his place by a clever retort.

One such story told of a man who was standing at an airline counter. The airport was crowded because bad weather had caused the cancellation of numerous flights. The two airline ticket agents were having trouble fitting everyone into the limited space available on the few flights that were still running. Most of the disrupted passengers patiently and politely accepted the situation, but one man, a business executive, was loudly complaining and criticizing. He verbally attacked the efficiency of the airline, the incompetence of the management, and the stupidity of the staff at the counter. He demanded immediate reservations, and when the clerk patiently tried to explain that he would have to wait for a much latter flight, the angry man, filled with his own importance and used to ordering his subordinates around, burst out, "Young man, do you know who I am?" The clerk turned to his colleague. "Fred," he said, "here's a man who really needs help. He's forgotten who he is!"

Most of us take sardonic satisfaction in "the perfect squelch." Jesus never squelched anyone. His speech was always with grace. Paul insists that we add the same kind of sweetness to our conversation. After all, more people are won with honey than are won with vinegar.

(2) Adding seasoning to our conversation (4:6b)

Let your speech be . . . seasoned with salt. . . .

So much of our conversation is flat and insipid. And so much of it when it is spiced up is seasoned with anger. Many people use profanity and obscenity to season their speech.

The Christian is to add salt to his conversation. Salt does three things. It adds tang. Many foods would be tasteless were it not for salt. We are to add pungency to our speech. We are to aim at being interesting conversationalists and communicators. We should draw on our experiences, our reading, and our Bibles to spice up our speech. The Lord's conversation and teaching were thoroughly laced with Old Testament truth and with illustrations drawn from all walks of life and the everyday events all around.

Think of the countless expressions and phrases from the Bible that have passed into the common coinage and currency of the English language. Common phrases from the Bible include "the salt of the earth," "signs of the times," "the powers that be," "a thorn in the flesh," "the handwriting on the wall," "the fat of the land," "all things to all men," "the fly in the ointment," and many more.

My father's thought life was saturated with the Scriptures, and it came out constantly in his everyday conversation. When I visited him in Chicago after I had left a small congregation in far-off northern British Columbia, he said, "With whom hast thou left those few sheep in the wilderness?" When he was introduced to a popular preacher, he said, "Ah! the man whose praise is in all the churches." When he introduced me to a well-known soloist, he said, "Meet the sweet singer of Israel." When he met a doctor friend, he said, "Here comes the beloved physician." It was not artificial or forced or obtrusive. It was as natural as daylight. He dwelt in the Scriptures day and night and it was reflected in his speech.

Salt not only adds a tang but also arrests corruption. The Christian's conversation should be a constant rebuke to those who use profanity and take the Lord's name in vain.

And salt creates thirst. Our talk should make people thirsty for the water of life. That is what the Lord's conversation did for the women at the well until, at last, she blurted out, "Sir, give me this water, that I thirst not" (John 4:15). It was the same with Nicodemus. When confronted with his need to be born again, he was so convinced by Jesus that he did not ask "why" but "how." "How can a man be born when he is old?" (John 3:4).

(3) Adding spirit to our conversation (4:6c)

That ye may know how ye ought to answer every man.

The vast majority of people around us are lost. They might be kind, thoughtful people and they might be religious, friendly people, but they need Christ. Our conversation should get them asking questions, and when they do, we need to know how to answer them. For this we need the enlightenment of the Holy Spirit. Some people are looking for an argument, some are looking for answers to heart needs, some are idly curious, and some are victims of wrong teaching. The Holy Spirit knows the hearts of all and what passage of Scripture should be used. So we are to be ready.

We must not be like the Irishman who, when he was asked what he believed, replied, "I believe what the church believes." When asked, "And what does the church believe?" he replied, "The church believes what I believe." Then when asked, "And what do you *both* believe?" he declared, "Why to be sure we both believe the same!"

No! We should know how to give an answer to every man. That is part of being a Christian. To that end we should "give attendance to reading" (1 Tim. 4:13). And we should study the great doctrines of the faith so that we can be ready ministers of the Word, instruments available for the Holy Spirit to use.

PART 5

Conclusion

Colossians 4:7–18

V. CONCLUSION (4:7–18)
   A. Tychicus: the faithful man (4:7–8)
      1. His character (4:7)
      2. His commission (4:8)
   B. Onesimus: the fugitive man (4:9)
   C. Aristarchus: the fearless man (4:10a)
   D. Marcus: the forgiven man (4:10b)
   E. Justus: the friendly man (4:11)
   F. Epaphras: the fervent man (4:12–13)
      1. His practical fervor (4:12a)
      2. His prayerful fervor (4:12b)
      3. His personal fervor (4:14)
   G. Luke: the famous man (4:14a)
      1. The healer
      2. The helper
      3. The historian
   H. Demas: the floundering man (4:14b)
   I. Nymphas: the fruitful man (4:15–16)
      1. The local ministry (4:15)
      2. The larger ministry (4:16)
   J. Archippus: the faltering man (4:17)
      1. The remembered gift of his ministry (4:17a)
      2. The required growth in his ministry (4:17b)
   K. Paul: the fettered man (4:18)

V. CONCLUSION (4:7–18)

Paul now begins a roll call of his companions and colleagues in the ministry. The cultists at Colosse are now completely ignored. They were way off course. We know from history that Paul's epistle went unheeded by the budding Gnostics. They had their own agenda. Paul leaves them to their apostasy. Rather, he embraces those of like precious faith. The names ring out! Tychicus, Onesimus (yes, even Onesimus, babe in Christ that he was, has his place in this inspired list of names) along with Aristarchus, Marcus, Archippus, and the rest. They stood for the truth, for the apostolic faith. They were by no means all. Doubtless, Paul could have included many more people on his list. The full roll call awaits Judgment Day, when all of those who have marched to the beat of Paul's drum—rank after rank, age after age, members of the true church of God—will be named.

These men were not perfect. Indeed, one of them became a noted backslider and another needed a word of rebuke. But Paul lines them up, representative people, all of them, taking sides with the Truth against the Lie. They represent orthodox, fundamental, evangelical mainstream, historic Christianity. Paul lines up these men in protest against those people at Colosse who had broken from the ranks to trail after Gnostic fantasies.

The mainstream, after all, provides us with a good test at all times and on all issues. It does not give us an infallible test, perhaps, but it gives a valuable test just the same. On controversial issues, where has the mainstream flowed, where has the main body of God's blood-bought saints stood?

When the so-called "charismatic" movement first began to make inroads into the orthodox churches, it raised its head on campus at Moody Bible Institute. It was during the annual Founder's Week Conference. The infiltrators hired a building just a few blocks from the Moody campus and held rival meetings. Some students and a faculty member were involved. A few others were drawn away, lured by the prospect of speaking in tongues and receiving gifts of the Spirit long since withdrawn from the church.

Nothing was said during the week but when Founder's Week was over, a special meeting of the entire Institute was called. Faculty, students, and staff were summoned into the Torrey-Gray auditorium and Dr. Culbertson, the Institute president, addressed them.

First, he rehearsed the historic position of mainline Christianity on the person, work, and gifts of the Spirit. Then he issued the ultimatum. "Here we stand!" he said. He referred to the rival meetings. "We are not going to have that kind of thing here," he continued. "If that is what you want, that is your business. But you are *not* going to have it here. So make up your minds. No matter who you are or how long you've been here—be you faculty, student, or staff—if that's what you want, then leave."

He concluded with words that I have remembered from that day to this: "We want fire at Moody Bible Institute," he said "but we are not going to have any wildfire."

In essence, that is what Paul was saying as he lined up this list of believers who stood by the fundamentals of the Christian faith. "Keep in step with these!" That was his unwritten word.

Going through the Bible and getting acquainted with all of the people and places that it mentions is a study in itself. Christianity was not born and bred in ivory towers and behind cloistered walls. It is not just a collection of theological propositions. Its great truths are incarnated in people. Its dogmas are clothed with flesh and blood. Paul, therefore, ends this epistle by mentioning by name ten people and then by adding his own name to the list and saying his final farewell.

In one sense, there is something almost pathetic about these shadowy names that appear for a moment on the sacred page only to be swallowed up instantly, it would seem, by the black night of obscurity. These were real people. Like us, they lived and loved, suffered and sorrowed, laughed and cried. They, too, had their moments of bliss and their ambitions, aspirations, hopes, and fears.

And now it is all over. The hot fire has burned down to such a little handful of white ashes. They are gone. Tychicus, Onesimus, Aristarchus, Justus, Mark, Epaphras, Luke, Demas, Nymphus, Archippus—and Paul. Shadows that once were men! As they are, so shall we be. It remains for us to get ourselves honorable mention in the book of God.

These men, after all, are no mere shadows. Nor was it only ashes that they left behind. They are men, still alive forevermore, living in another Land where Glory reigns supreme. They are numbered now and named over there as God's Immortals. And they have left behind them an example for God's people for the rest of time.

A.   Tychicus: the faithful man (4:7–8)

All my state shall Tychicus declare unto you, who is beloved brother, and a faithful minister and fellowservant in the Lord: Whom I have sent unto you for the same purpose, that he might know your estate, and comfort your hearts.

We first meet Tychicus toward the end of the book of Acts. He is mentioned briefly as one of Paul's companions on the apostle Paul's third missionary journey. Likely, he was saved at some time during Paul's lengthy stay at Ephesus. Paul had been forced to leave Ephesus in a hurry because of a riot. He crossed over to Europe and then decided that he would go on to Jerusalem. He was accompanied on this long trip by a remarkable group of friends, mostly delegates from various Gentile churches that he had founded. These men were bearing financial aid to the impoverished Jerusalem church. Seven men were named, and Tychicus was one of them.

During the long journey to Jerusalem, doubtless Paul came to know Tychicus very well. He marked him down as a man of promise in the things of God. Then followed Paul's arrest at Jerusalem, his long detention at Caesarea, his witness before governors and kings, his eventful voyage to Rome, and his house arrest there. We do not know whether Tychicus was with Paul all of this time, but we do know that he was with him for at least part of this captivity and that he rendered Paul devoted service at that time.

Now Paul sends him off to Colosse to tell the believers there all that has been happening. "You go, Tychicus," Paul said, "you come from those parts."

Paul gives us a twofold glimpse of this man. He gives us a look at his *character*. He was a beloved brother, a faithful minister, and a fellow servant in the Lord. Paul valued this man's *friendship*. Few titles are more endearing in the New Testament than that of "beloved brother." It speaks of a kinship of spirit closer than any earthly ties. Here was a man who not only earned Paul's commendation, he earned the Lord's as well. Jesus said, "I was in prison, and ye came unto me" (Matt. 25:34–40). Such a man, Jesus said, was "blessed of my Father" and that such a man was to "inherit the kingdom prepared for you from the foundation of the world." Paul had a way of attracting such people to himself. Tychicus did the very thing that the Lord blessed—he visited Paul in prison. He stood by Paul in the face of danger and death. To befriend a political prisoner such as Paul was no light thing, especially when he was under the eye of Nero, who doubtless had his own toadies and spies among Paul's guards. No wonder Paul called Tychicus "a beloved brother."

Paul valued this man's *fellowship* also. He was a "fellowservant" in the Lord— literally, a fellow slave, sold out to the same Master. And he was a "faithful minister." Paul knew that he could trust him to follow diligently the plow to the end once he put his hand to it. He is mentioned in the companion epistle to the Ephesians (6:21). He is named also in connection with Trophimus (Acts 20:4), a fact that suggests that, like Trophimus, Tychicus was an Ephesian. He was with Paul, too, later on during his second imprisonment, when the danger was acute. Paul appreciated the death-daring loyalty of Tychicus and sent him back to Ephesus out of harm's way (2 Tim. 4:12).

But that was later. Paul now gives us a look at the *commission* he gave to Tychicus at the time of his first imprisonment. Paul sends his faithful partner to Ephesus and on to Colosse. Onesimus was with him (Col. 4:9). Paul knew that he could trust Tychicus. Tychicus seems to have carried both the Ephesian and the Colossian letters with him, and Onesimus carried one of his own—the epistle to Philemon.

Because the epistle to the Ephesians was a circular letter, doubtless as soon as he had delivered it to that church, he took copies of it to all of the other churches in the area. It does not call for a great deal of imagination to picture Tychicus in church after church—at Ephesus, in danger of losing its first love; at Smyrna, about to face fiery persecution; at Pergamos, where the damnable doctrine of Balaam would eventually take root; at Thyatira, where "that woman Jezebel" would soon make her evil presence felt; at Sardis, a church boastful of its reputation; at Philadelphia, where revival fires still burned; and at Laodicea, where love of money was already becoming the root of all evil. But doubtless to Colosse was where Tychicus headed first as he began his circuit from Ephesus.

And everywhere Paul's converts, friends, and supporters would be full of questions about the beloved apostle. "Is he well? Do you think he will be released? Is the Roman church standing by him? Does he need anything?"

Basically, Tychicus was given a twofold commission. First, he was to *gather information* about the Colossians. Paul probably had heard no more from the church in that little market town since the arrival of their pastor with his tale of woe. Paul would be eager for more information. "How great had the cult's inroads been? How many people had defected, and who were they? Had other churches in the area taken sides?" Paul would have a hundred questions. Most of all, Paul would want to know what the response had been to his letter—and to the memo tucked away in Onesimus's bag.

Second, Tychicus was to *give inspiration* to the Colossians. He was to comfort their hearts. The heresy would leave its scars. Families would be divided. Friends would be on opposite sides. Loved ones would become traitors to the cause of Christ. Paul knew enough about Tychicus to know that his very presence in Colosse when the epistle was delivered and read would be a blessing to the believers. And Tychicus was an old campaigner; he would stiffen the resistance of the church to the cult.

Such a man was Tychicus. He represents some ten years of faithful service, part of it during the apostle's detention at Rome, much of it spent in dangerous and wearisome journeys. Paul regarded him as his fellow slave, as if to say, "I have *composed* this epistle, Tychicus, but you are the one who *carried* it. Your part is as important as mine. We stand on the same ground before God. We are both willing captives of our Lord."

How astonished Tychicus would have been that morning as he boarded the ship with Onesimus and put out to sea had he known that the piece of parchment in his purse would outlast the Roman Empire, that it would be translated into thousands of languages, and that it would be read and studied and proclaimed among men for some two thousand years—and that millions of people would read about *him!*

B. Onesimus: the fugitive man (4:9)

> *With Onesimus, a faithful and beloved brother, who is one of you.*
> *They shall make known unto you all things which are done here.*

Onesimus was a runaway slave with a price on his head and the shadow of death by crucifixion lying upon him. Cruel masters had been known to devise the most horrible deaths for slaves returned to them after running away. Slave owners just assumed that any master who recovered a runaway would make a terrible example of him to discourage other slaves from doing the same.

Onesimus, however, had one hope: he had become a Christian, and his master was a Christian. Both he and his master owed their conversion to Paul. And in his purse, Onesimus carried a letter from Paul to Philemon, from whom he had run away. Onesimus was a free man in Christ, but he was still Philemon's runaway salve. He had been pardoned by God for all of his sin, but he still had to face the consequences of the wrong that he had done to Philemon. Conversion does not cancel moral, financial, and social debts.

Like Tychicus, Onesimus is "a beloved brother." And with a broad public hint to Philemon, a member of the Colossian church, he is "one of you." That is, he is a fellow member of the body of Christ by virtue of his conversion. Moreover, however unfaithful he might have been in the past, he was now "faithful." Paul had put him to the test. The fact that he was now on his way back to Philemon to face the music, as we say, is an indication of his new trustworthiness.

"They shall make known unto you all things which are done here," Paul says. Winning souls such as Onesimus to Christ was one of those things. Great things were going on, as Paul told the Philippians in a letter written about this same time (Phil. 1:12–18).

C. Aristarchus: the fearless man (4:10a)

> *Aristarchus my fellow prisoner saluteth you.*

Aristarchus was a native of Thessalonica and a faithful companion of the apostle Paul. He became a companion of the apostle Paul on his third missionary journey. He accompanied him to Ephesus. He was captured and almost killed by the mob in the riot raised by Demetrius and the silversmiths (Acts 19:29). He accompanied Paul to Greece and from there back to Asia Minor (Acts 20:4). He accompanied Paul to Rome (Acts 27:2), sharing in the dangers of the voyage and in the shipwreck.

We do not know at what point he was made a prisoner, but evidently that was the price he paid for his allegiance to the apostle. Tradition has it that he was martyred by Nero. One suggestion is that Paul's friends took turns in keeping him company at Rome but were permitted to do so only by becoming prisoners themselves.

The name of a loyalist such as Aristarchus, included in this letter, would be another nail in the coffin of the cultists at Colosse. It would help strengthen the hands of those who were fighting the cult.

D. Marcus: the forgiven man (4:10b)

And Marcus, sister's son to Barnabas (touching whom ye received commandments: if he come unto you, receive him).

Some years earlier, John Mark had disappointed Paul badly. Shortly afterward, Paul and his best friend, Barnabas, had disagreed so hotly over Mark that they had parted company. Paul had gone his way and Barnabas, taking Mark with him, had gone another way. The story evidently was well known, and a stigma had become attached to Mark's name although Paul had long since forgiven Mark. It is at least possible that Mark's gospel was already in circulation, that Paul had read it, and that it had his heartiest commendation, transforming his opinion of Mark altogether; hence, Paul's concern here that Mark's name be cleared. Be that as it may, Mark was with Paul at Rome, and that would be commendation enough. Mark was a converted Jew, so he was one of the few Hebrew Christians willing to be by Paul's side during his imprisonment.

Mark probably had been converted through the ministry of Simon Peter. His mother's home in Jerusalem was one of the meeting places of the early church. We are not told how or why or when Mark joined Paul at Rome, but some people have speculated that his uncle Barnabas might have died and that Mark felt afresh the tug of Paul's personality. Paul had a certain magnetism about him. Their first meeting after so many years must have been emotional.

Perhaps Mark had reacted against the ungracious behavior toward Paul that the Jerusalem church had displayed under the leadership of James. If so, then naturally thereafter he gravitated toward Paul. It must have taken no little grace and courage on Mark's part to seek Paul out and put things right between them.

Now Paul trusts Mark enough to suggest that he go to Colosse on his behalf. In case some people might have been inclined to give him the cold shoulder, he calls for Mark's ready reception by the Colossian Christians. Paul was astute enough to know that Mark would be a valuable man to have at Colosse. He was a close confidant of Simon Peter, whose name carried enormous weight in the early church. Mark, though Jewish by birth, would no longer be Judaistic by belief. He could help counter the Judaism of the cult. Moreover, any man who could write a Holy Spirit-inspired *gospel* must be a man well thought of in heaven.

To round out Mark's story, he later was with Peter at Babylon. At the time of his second and fatal Roman imprisonment, Paul had such a high estimate of Mark that he urged Timothy to bring Mark with him to Rome (2 Tim. 4:11) because he was profitable to the ministry.

So Mark is the forgiven man. We can always make amends if we will.

E.   Justus: the friendly man (4:11)

And Jesus, which is called Justus, who are of the circumcision.
These only are my fellowworkers unto the kingdom of God, which
have been a comfort unto me.

It is startling to come across the name "Jesus" as a common name. Such was the name of this particular colleague of Paul, Jesus Justus. It helps us remember that it was a common enough name among the Jews in those days. It reminds us, too, that the Lord Jesus bore an ordinary, everyday name. It was a transliteration of the name Joshua, or Yeshua. The name was not particularly holy then, although it is now. The surname, Justus, marks this man, perhaps as having belonged to a rigorous form of Judaism before his conversion. Paul notes that, like Mark, he was "of the circumcision," that is, a Jew.

Paul had suffered much from "the circumcision," as he calls the legalistic, Judaistic members of the Jerusalem church and its followers. Extremist members of this group had campaigned against him far and wide. They had dogged his footsteps, subverted his converts, spread legalism, and done their best to undermine him. Had it not been for James and "the circumcision," Paul might yet have been free instead of in prison facing extremely serious charges (Acts 21:18–40).

But here were Mark and Justus standing shoulder to shoulder with Paul as his firmest friends. Paul says that these men had been "a comfort" to him. The Greek word is used only here in the New Testament, but it was a common enough medical term. Our English word *paregoric* comes from it. Paregoric is a soothing drug.

Justus had been a Good Samaritan to Paul, pouring soothing balm into his soul and ministering to his physical needs. Would that all of those of "the circumcision" had so valued Paul.

F.   Epaphras: the fervent man (4:12–13)

Epaphras had come to Rome to acquaint Paul with what was going on at Colosse. Paul had three things to say about this brother and his fervor for the cause of Christ.

First, it was a *practical* fervor. He says, *"Epaphras, who is one of you, a servant of Christ, saluteth you."* A servant of Christ! A slave! His fervor for Christ was manifested in self-sacrificing service. That fervor had taken him to Rome. We can imagine the long discussions among the elders at Colosse when the cultists had finally begun to show themselves in their true colors and when their teachings became more and more subtle and successful. Nobody in the neighborhood seemed to have the ability to cope with them or the necessary authority to excommunicate them. In the course of the discussions, someone would raise the name of Paul. But Paul could not come. He was in prison—in Rome—charged with high treason.

Well, what was to be done? Someone would have to go to Rome. It would need to be someone capable of explaining the gist of the cultic dogmas. And it would have to be someone with courage. It would be dangerous to go walking around Rome inquiring about Paul.

Epaphras was the one who went. He braved the hazards of the journey. He braved the looks and evasions that he encountered when he explained that the man for whom he was looking was under house arrest. He braved the guard at the door when finally he found the house. He gladly proclaimed himself a friend of the prisoner. Such was his fervor. It was a *practical* fervor.

Then, too, it was *prayerful* fervor. Paul says that Epaphras was *"always labouring fervently for you in prayers, that may stand perfect and complete in all the will of God."* Epaphras had evidently impressed Paul (a big-time prayer warrior himself) with the frequency and the fervency of his prayers. He waxed warm and eloquent. He poured out his heart. He wanted them to rise in triumph over the cult and to be perfect and complete in the will of God. One wonders what the Roman guard made of all of this. Who was the captive—Paul on one end of the chain, deprived of his liberty, or the Roman soldier on the other end of the chain, ushered—like it or not—into an apostolic prayer meeting?

Moreover Epaphras had a *personal* fervor for his brethren back home: *"For I bear him record, that he hath a great zeal for you, and them that are in Laodicea, and them in Hierapolis."* No doubt, this faithful pastor-teacher had labored among all three churches. Hierapolis, like Colosse and Laodicea, was located in the Lycus River valley. It was noted for its hot baths. It was also the wealthy center of the dye industry. It had a cosmopolitan population that included a considerable number of Jews. We are not told how it was evangelized. Similarly, Laodicea was in the same area, near Colosse and about forty miles from Ephesus. The same cult that was plaguing Colosse was also subverting the saints at Laodicea.

So why did Epaphras, having accomplished his mission at Rome, not return himself to Colosse with the great epistle that Paul had written? Because he couldn't. He had paid the price of which he had long since counted the cost. He was now Paul's "fellowprisoner" (Philem. 23).

G.   Luke: the famous man (4:14a)

Luke, the beloved physician . . . [greets] you.

Paul was not a well man. He had been beaten and battered times without number. He had been arrested and imprisoned in various places, sometimes treated harshly. He had been shipwrecked more than once. He carried with him some kind of handicap that he called his "thorn in the flesh." By the time Paul wrote Colossians, he seems to have needed the constant services of a physician. So we think of Luke as a *healer.* He did not have the spiritual gift of healing; that gift had about died out because of the Jews' persistent rejection of the gospel. Tongues and miracles and the other foundational, temporary, and transitional gifts were also being withdrawn. Instead, Luke was a medical man. Paul needed such a man near him. He was grateful for his "beloved physician."

We think of him, too, as a *helper.* Paul calls him his "beloved" physician.

Lightfoot suggests the rendering, "Luke the physician, my very dear friend." Luke remained with Paul through thick and thin. He followed him all over the Roman Empire. He chronicled his missionary activities. Paul was Luke's hero. There was nothing that he would not do to help. He remained with Paul when all other helpers were gone (2 Tim. 4:11).

But we think of him most as a *historian*. Luke has bequeathed to the church two of the most interesting books of the New Testament—his gospel and the book of Acts. He wrote like the trained scholar he was, with meticulous care. He carefully consulted people who could fill in the gaps in his knowledge. His gospel is a masterpiece. He portrays the Lord Jesus as a very warm, loving human being, One who, at the same time, was God. It is the longest of the Gospels. He probably wrote it at Caesarea, or at least commenced it there and finished it at Rome. It is likely enough that he and Mark compared notes. In any case, he seems to have omitted much that Mark had already written. He begins at an earlier point in the gospel story than Mark or Matthew and ends at a later point with the ascension of the Lord.

His brief history of the early church is also of great interest and bears equal testimony to Luke's investigative skill where he was not actually an eyewitness. Its pages are crowded with people (some seventy-six of them) and places (some fifty-three of them). It chronicles the main advance of the gospel from Jerusalem, the Hebrew capital, to Rome, the heathen capital of the world. Luke shows us how Paul chose strategic places for the delivery of his message on the principle that if Christianity were to be established in the center, it would spread to the circumference.

H. Demas: the floundering man (4:14b)

And Demas. . . .

Paul placed Luke and Demas side by side here, perhaps to accentuate the contrast. Paul has something praiseworthy to say about all the people whom he mentions—except Demas. In the companion letter to Philemon, Demas is listed along with Mark, Aristarchus, and Luke as a "fellow laborer." But here, in Colossians, he is allowed to stand alone. It would seem that Paul had already sensed a flaw in Demas's commitment. The word that he used for "forsaken" means literally "to leave in the lurch." Perhaps Paul was doing here what Jesus did to Judas in the Upper Room when He gave him the sop. It was a last attempt to call him back to honor and duty. Paul here lists Demas with the others, but he puts him between Luke on the one hand and Paul himself (a few names later) on the other hand as though to hedge him in. But having done as much as he could for him, he left it at that. Demas was allowed to send greetings to the Colossians, something anyone could have done, but beyond that Paul had no more to say about him—yet.

A few years later, when Paul was back in Rome, imprisoned again under the harshest of circumstances, he would have one final comment about Demas, and a sad comment it turned out to be: "Demas hath forsaken me, having loved this present world, and is departed unto Thessalonica" (2 Tim. 4:10). He had not departed because he had denied the faith or abandoned the truth but because the world, this world, had gotten the better of him. When Paul wrote thus about "this world," he was facing *that* world, the world to come. His execution was only a short time away. Demas, it would seem, had no stomach for martyrdom. It is always with us all a question of "this world" or "that world."

Jesus warned of the two kinds of thorns that choke out the wheat: "the care of this world" and "the deceitfulness of riches" (Matt. 13:22). Both represent worldliness. Worry chokes spiritual growth and so does wealth. Perhaps with Demas it was worry. He still hung around Paul, but his heart wasn't in it. He was too conscious of that Roman soldier listening to everything that was said and watching every move that was made. Or maybe, after all, it was wealth that did it. Perhaps some wealthy congregation offered him a lucrative pastorate in a fashionable and safe part of a town far enough away from Rome to have been comparatively secure.

    I.   Nymphas: the fruitful man (4:15–16)
        1. The local ministry (4:15)

> *Salute the brethren which are at Laodicea, and Nymphas, and*
> *the church which is in his house.*

Nymphas is the only believer in Laodicea whose name we know. The church became famous in the next generation for its wealth and worldliness (Rev. 3:14–15). It is a wonder that Demas didn't go there. In John's day, at the close of the first century, the Laodicean church had become rich, influential, and self-sufficient. The Lord, however, describes it as wretched, poor, and blind and depicts Himself as being outside it altogether. In contrast with the other half dozen churches in the surrounding towns, John describes the Laodicean church as "the church of the Laodiceans."

We do not know how many congregations were in Laodicea. Just one is mentioned here, and it met in the home of Nymphas. Paul acknowledges that congregation. He refers to "the *brethren* which are in Laodicea" and to "the church which is in his [Nymphas's] house."

If Nymphas lived up to his name ("bridegroom"), then he was still very much in love with the Lord. No wonder Paul found him to be a kindred soul! He was a fruitful man. Within the walls of his home, a group of God's blood-bought people met for prayer, worship, and Bible study. Doubtless, too, souls were led to Christ in that home. What better use could be made of a home than that?

2. The larger ministry (4:16)

And when this epistle is read among you, cause that it be read also in the church of the Laodiceans; and that ye likewise read the epistle from Laodicea.

There it is again—"the church of the Laodiceans." Evidently, the trend that we meet full grown in the Apocalypse had already begun. Paul knew that something was wrong at Laodicea. Probably Epaphras had told him all about all of the churches in Asia Minor. Paul would have been keenly interested. He had been so concerned about it that he had written to the Laodiceans. Evidently, whatever the trouble was, it was affecting the Colossian church, too. Similarly some of the things that Paul addressed in the Colossian church were infiltrating the Laodicean church, too. He called for a mutual sharing of the two letters.

J.   Archippus: the faltering man (4:17)

And say to Archippus, Take heed to the ministry which thou hast received in the Lord, that thou fulfill it.

Archippus seems to have been the son of the slave owner Philemon, evidently a man of means. Paul's comment to Archippus includes a number of things about his ministry for the Lord.

Paul mentions, for instance, the *giving* of that ministry. To be a ministry, it had to be "received in the Lord." The Holy Spirit is the One who distributes the gifts, directs their use, and develops the scope and success of their use. The Lord's work is not a career but a calling. We do not get into the ministry by going to Bible school and on to a seminary, graduating with distinction, and being called by a church to manage its affairs. It is not a business. We receive whatever ministry we have from the Lord. The Lord often bypasses the system and puts His hand upon a most unlikely person and equips him for a ministry owned and blessed by God. Church history is full of the stories of such men. For examples, Moses had to unlearn most of the things that he had been taught in Egypt before God could use him. David was just a shepherd although taught of God. Elisha followed the plow, and Peter was a fisherman. Paul, although an intellectual, learned his theology alone with God amid the solitude and silence of Sinai. So trained or not, let us ensure that we have "received" our ministry.

Furthermore, Paul mentions the *guarding* of one's ministry. He says to Archippus, "Take heed" to your ministry. It is a serious thing to neglect the Spirit-given gifts and ministry with which we have been entrusted by God. The Lord's parables of the talents and the pounds teach a similar lesson (Matt. 25:14–30; Luke 19:11–27).

Archippus seems to have been neglecting his ministry. Perhaps his family was making heavy demands on him. Perhaps he was discouraged and out of his depth because of the cult. Paul did not go into details. A word to the wise is sufficient. Remember that Paul had never been to Colosse, but he certainly knew Philemon and doubtless knew Archippus. He had been grieved to learn of his discouragement.

Paul mentions also the *growth* of one's ministry. "And fulfill it," he says. Fill it full! He was to regard his ministry as a vessel into which he was to pour his whole life. Nothing else must be allowed to come first. The Lord Jesus could say to His Father, "I have finished the work which thou gavest me to do" (John 17:4). His ministry lasted just three and a half years, but into that short span of time He poured everything. And what a life it was that He poured into His ministry— and what a ministry! The world itself could not contain all of the books that could be written about it (John 21:25). There is our example. Such a ministry will grow.

K. Paul: the fettered man (4:18)

> *The salutation by the hand of me, Paul. Remember my bonds.*
> *Grace be with you. Amen.*

As Paul took the pen in his hand once more to sign this letter, an iron fetter chafed his wrist, and a long chain stirred upon the floor. With this touching reminder, this noble warrior brings this letter to a close.

He ends with an invocation that in the face of all of the upset caused by the cult, God's grace might be the portion of his own. "Amen!" Then Paul put away his pen, and the chain rattled again.

Tychicus would recall that sound. So would Onesimus, who might soon be in chains himself. Demas would remember it with a shudder. The remembered sound would wake him up at night.

Clang! Clang! went that chain day and night, at mealtime and at bedtime. It was the background music of Paul's whole life in Rome. It would gall his wrists. That chain would get in his way. And always he had to move with care so as not to hurt or irritate the soldier at the other end.

"Remember my bonds!" Clang! It was Paul's last word to this church and to the church at Laodicea. As the reading of this letter came to an end at Colosse, the clang of that chain would be heard. The sound of that fettering iron rang up and down the Wolf River. Paul was not handing out advice from an ivory tower; he was proclaiming truth purchased at great cost.

My chains! The cultists were busy forging chains to bind the unwary. Chains are the stock-in-trade of every false religion. Paul would not have exchanged his chains for theirs for all of the wealth and power of Rome. Paul, riveted by his chains, was a far freer man than those at Colosse who were propagating a dead religion, a far freer man than those who were being recruited by them. Yes indeed! Paul would much rather have his chain than theirs—an empty philosophy, fruitless rituals, satanic mysteries, binding legalism, and all.

"Remember my bonds!" It was his parting shot. Yea, rather—take a good look at your own bonds.

"Remember my bonds! Grace be with you. Amen."

APPENDIX

The Gnostic Heresy

In closing this section of our study, we can do no better than quote D. M. Panton one more time:

> In the study of Gnosticism it is vital, for the adjustment of all truth, to master what Scripture says on prohibitions of every kind; and we learn at once that personal abstinences, so long as they are not elevated into dogmas binding the consciences of others, are to be freely conceded by all to all in the happy fellowship, profoundly tolerant, of Christian love.
>
> In different ages the abstinences have been different. In our day there are Christians who avoid all drugs (medicines), refusing even opium (deadening drugs) to dying agony; others eschew tobacco . . . others never touch or taste flesh food, some not even milk or eggs. Still others refrain from marriage, as forbidden on the same ground as the other prohibitions, namely as evil in itself.
>
> To all these, and totally apart from the reasons, whether good or bad, why they so abstain, Christian love grants a mutual and perfect liberty.
>
> But, while this gracious forbearance meets all the practical requirements of Church life, manifestly it is no solution of the problem itself. It is a joy to discover a lonely revelation (Col. 2:8–23), supreme and unique, which solves the problem of all pledged abstinences as seen from the viewpoint of God: and in this passage, peculiarly apt, the Spirit opens with a challenge by which He seeks to arouse our careful thinking and alertness.
>
> *"If ye died with Christ"*—symbolized in the funeral ritual of baptism— *"from"*—so utterly died that you are severed from the world by the breach

of an open grave—*"the rudiments of the world"*—the elements of natural religion; the religious maxims and morals of the unregenerate; rules of life that are childish groupings in a moral twilight—*"why, as though living in the world"*—as though still finding your true life there; as though the baptismal corpse had risen and crossed back into a dead world—*"do ye subject yourselves"*—allow yourselves to be dogmatized, submit to the enslaved by decrees—*"after the precepts and doctrines of men"* (Col. 2:20)—commandments which God never made? Why are you reenslaving yourselves to worldly creeds and moral dogmas from which Christ *died* to deliver you? or why are you fastening again to the legalisms—Nazarite prohibitions, or restrictions in Levitical diet—that were nailed to the cross? and why are you forfeiting your standing in the new and living world, and going back to the old carcase [sic] of a dead world's obsolete authority?

For, be it carefully observed, the samples given by the Spirit are all negatives, prohibitions, abstinences—that is, a holiness lodged in external refusals; and though these particular "dogmas" named reveal asceticism, they are purposely so vague—and therefore especially valuable—as to cover *all* prohibitions that are not found in the Word of God.

Handle not! Nor taste! Nor touch! "Handle not"—the dead, or the Pariah; "Nor *taste*"—forbidden foods; "Nor *touch*"—Paul himself (1 Cor. 7:1) uses this word of marriage. The Essenes (to state but one example) would not touch oil, or a stranger, and were pledged against all wine and flesh. (Marriage was, to the Essene, an abomination. So also, when an Essene was excommunicated, he often died of starvation, being bound by his oath not take food prepared by defiled hands—Lightfoot).

It is hardly credible, but it is a fact, that Ambrose and other Latin Fathers, as well as some modern Christians, suppose these words to be *Paul's* prohibitions, in which he was laying wide abstinences upon the Church of God! Laid down as religious dogmas, such negatives are taken bodily out of the world; the prohibition of the touch of the outcast is common to the whole Brahmin world; the prohibition of flesh is common to the whole Hindu world; the prohibition of alcohol is common to the whole Mohammedan world; and the prohibition of marriage is common to the whole Roman Sacerdotal world, as it was to the priesthood of Babylon, whence it came.

"The world and the flesh," as Dr. A. Maclaren has said, "are willing that Christianity should shrivel into a religion of prohibitions and ceremonials, because all manner of vices and meanness may thrive and breed under them like scorpions under stones." Such are among the great world-ordinances imposed by human decree, and generally the decree of false religion, on the masses of mankind.

Now the Spirit, following in the footsteps of Christ, in an appended remark, almost casual, reveals the futility, the unspirituality of such prohibitions. "All which things"—the things prohibited—"perish"—even marriage, as such, does not survive the grave—"with the using"—leaving nothing *spiritual* behind them. That is, they *are* to be used: but perish—that is, have fulfilled their purpose—with their use: they were *made* to be handled, tasted, touched—"which God *created* to be *received* with thanksgiving" (1 Cor. 6:13), but were made to be used *up*—the term means *full* use (Eadie)—and have no purpose whatever, and no effect but a physical.

As Paul says elsewhere: "Meat will not commend us to God: neither, if we eat not, are we the worse; nor, if we eat, are we the better" (1 Cor. 8:8). That which is physically nourishing can hardly be spiritually poisonous: the poison, if poison result, is already in the man. Exactly so our Lord says, "Perceive ye not, that whatsoever from without goeth into the man, it *cannot* defile him; because it goeth not into his heart, but into his belly, and goeth out into the draught?"—it never touched the spirit at all: but "that which proceedeth *out* of the man, *that* defileth the man" (Mark 7:18).

The Spirit next shows that a religion is only skin-deep whose regulations go no deeper than the skin. "Which things have a *show* of wisdom"—an air, an appearance, a pretension of morality; they enjoy a reputation for goodness—"in will-worship"—that is self-imposed, self-invented worship; worship originated by man, not by God; authorized, and therefore unaccepted, devotion—"and humility"—a monkish self-degradation—"and severity to the body"—unsparingness, rigour, self-laceration: not control of the body but contempt of the body; not grace enthroned over passion, but passion throttled, nature strangled, and manhood debilitated or destroyed.

Prohibitory pledges and rigorous abstinences, often profoundly well-meant and superficially most wise, appeal with extraordinary power to large classes of men. The whole of sacerdotal (monastic living) has sprung from this root. For asceticism is the miscarriage of noble principle, which confounds the BODY with the FLESH; and prohibiting what can be hallowed, assaults and batters the temple of the Holy *Spirit,* instead of enthroning the divine Lord within all the precincts.

So the Spirit closes with a simple, profound, final dissuasion from all attempt to find or maintain holiness by abstinences. "But" (as in the Revised translation) "(which) *are not of any value against the indulgence of the flesh.*" Paul is not quarreling with the *end,* but with the *means:* the cure of gluttony, drunkenness, fornication, cocaine or morphia intoxications, as well as minor objectionable habits that may be perfectly lawful but are not wise or expedient, is the admirable goal of us all: what he denies to prohibitory abstinences is their fundamental efficacy—if practical regulations do not secure their end, they are worthless. The monasteries of the Middle Ages were hotbeds of vice. . . . And abstinence may prevent *this* indulgence, but not *that:* in suppressing one sin, it too often creates worse: it dams a tributary, only to swell the flood.

The Divine solution is other and profounder: "I will put MY SPIRIT within you and CAUSE you to walk in My statutes" (Exod. 36:27). . . .[1]

---

1. D. M. Panton, *Present Day Pamphlets: "Gnosticism: The Coming Apostasy"* (London: Thynne & Jarvis, 1925), 7–11.

Exploring
PHILEMON

PART 1

Introduction

One can study a book such as Philemon in numerous ways. For instance, we could examine the epistle through the eyes of *Philemon* himself. With Philemon, the dominant issue would be slavery, which was so much taken for granted by the world of his day. The Romans had conquered most of the known world and had reduced whole populations to bondage. Some slaves were exceedingly valuable, being artists, scholars, and highly skilled craftsmen. Others were little more than beasts of burden, and all were useful as a source of cheap labor. From the standpoint of a slaveowner, to upset such an entrenched social institution was unthinkable. Paul's letter, at first reading, must have come as a shock to Philemon. He might, as an unusual act of appreciation for some singular and extraordinary service, set a slave free. But free a runaway slave like Onesimus? Paul's demand was revolutionary.

We could examine the epistle though the eyes of *Onesimus*. He knew the other side of slavery. He knew the indignity of being mere chattel, of being always at another man's beck and call. He knew the fear of the lash, the terror of death by crucifixion. He knew that even a benevolent master such as Philemon could change, in a fit of temper, into a tyrant. Or, even if that fear were to be removed, there was always the possibility of the good master's death and of being put back up for public auction. He could have no life of his own. He could be torn from wife and child, from family and friends, sold and shipped off to some distant province. He could fall into the hands of a monster, a sadist, whose chief delight was to torment a slave and against whom the law offered no redress.

We can well imagine with what trepidation Onesimus approached Colosse notwithstanding Paul's letter in his hand. We can picture his quailing before

Philemon's eye, trembling as Philemon exclaimed aloud again and again at this line or that in the letter. His life hung in the balance.

We could examine the epistle through the eyes of *Paul.* He was no stranger to slavery. He has been familiar from childhood with the benevolent form of slavery permitted under Hebrew law and with the safeguards built into the system to protect the slave from abuse. Paul had been raised in a Roman city and knew well enough the horrible abuses to which a slave could be exposed under Roman law.

Paul looked at slavery from the standpoint of Calvary. The cross changed all human relationships. Man or master, it made no difference; all were one in Christ. In Him, there was neither Jew nor Gentile, bond nor free, Greek nor barbarian; Calvary reduced all men to the same level—all must come to God by way of the Cross. Christ lifted all men to the same dizzy heights, made them equally sons of God, joint-heirs with Jesus Christ.

Paul was too wise to make a frontal attack on slavery. He had no intention of involving the church with the state. Politics was not the answer, and no social conscience existed in Paul's day as far as slaves were concerned. The answer was love—brotherly love in Christ, which would make it impossible for one man to abuse the rights of another man.

Finally, we could examine the epistle through the eyes of *Tychicus* (Col. 4:7), who accompanied Onesimus to Colosse. Tychicus was not personally or emotionally involved. He must have taken the keenest interest in the whole situation. He could be much more impartial and objective than Philemon, Onesimus, or Paul. Onesimus had not robbed and run away from him as he had Philemon. His life and liberty did not hang in the balance as did that of Onesimus. He was concerned for God's people, but he had neither the authority of an apostle nor the care of all the churches as did Paul.

To Tychicus, the affair must have been a fascinating study in psychology. What would be the outcome of these struggles of mind, heart, conscience, and will?

PART 1: THE CAUTIOUS APPROACH (vv. 1–7)
  A. Greetings (vv. 1–2)
    1. Who they were from (vv. 1a–b)
      a. Paul and his condition (v. 1a)
      b. Paul and his companion (v. 1b)
    2. Who they were for (vv. 1c–2)
      a. Philemon and his family (vv. 1c–2a)
        (1) How Paul claims them

        (2) How Paul commends them (vv. 1c–2a)

            (a) Philemon the saint

            (b) Apphia the "sister"

            (c) Archippus the soldier

     b. Philemon and his fellowship (v. 2b)

B. Grace (v. 3)

    1. Not just unaccompanied grace (v. 3a)

    2. Not just unaccredited grace (v. 3b)

       Paul directs Philemon's thoughts to:

     a. The Father of the Christian family

     b. The focus of the Christian faith

        (1) The Lord: His power

        (2) Jesus: His person

        (3) Christ: His position

C. Gratitude (vv. 4–6)

    1. When Paul prayed for Philemon (v. 4)

    2. Why Paul prayed for Philemon (v. 5)

     a. Philemon's love for the Savior (v. 5a)

     b. Philemon's love for the saints (v. 5b)

    3. What Paul prayed for Philemon (v. 6)

     a. The outward flowing of his Christian life (v. 6a)

     b. The inward flourishing of his Christian life (v. 6b)

D. Gladness (v. 7)

    1. The personal experience of Philemon's love (v. 7a)

    2. The practical expression of Philemon's love (v. 7b)

Part 2: The Comprehensive Appeal (vv. 8–19)

A. Along the line of desire (vv. 8–13)

    1. Paul states his rights (v. 8)

    2. Paul surrenders his rights (vv. 9–13)

     a. In favor of higher ground (v. 9)

     b. In favor of higher gains (vv. 10–11)

        (1) I have gained a new son (v. 10)

        (2) You have gained a new slave (v. 11)

     c. In favor of higher goals (vv. 12–13)

        (1) For Philemon: the question of receiving or not receiving (v. 12)

        (2) For Paul: the question of retaining or not retaining (v. 13)

B. Along the line of duty (vv. 14–17)
   1. The duty of Paul: a legal restoration (v. 14)
   2. The duty of Onesimus: a life redemption (v. 15)
   3. The duty of Philemon: a love relationship (vv. 16–17)
      a. The negative (v. 16a)
      b. The positive (v. 16b)
      c. The superlative (v. 17)
C. Along the line of debt (vv. 18–19)
   1. What was owed to Philemon (vv. 18–19a)
   2. What was owed by Philemon (v. 19b)

PART 3: THE COMPELLING APPENDIX (vv. 20–25)
A. A personal word (vv. 20–22)
   1. Provide me relief (v. 20)
      a. Rejoice me in the Lord (v. 20a)
      b. Refresh me in the Lord (v. 20b)
   2. Prove me right (v. 21)
      a. By simple obedience (v. 21a)
      b. By superlative obedience (v. 21b)
   3. Prepare me room (v. 22)
      a. Plan on it
      b. Pray for it
B. A public word (vv. 23–24)
   1. A greeting from the man in prison with Paul (v. 23)
   2. A greeting from the men in partnership with Paul (v. 24)
      a. Marcus
      b. Aristarchus
      c. Demas
      d. Lucas
C. A parting word (v. 25)

Philemon was a prosperous slave owner who lived at Colosse. He had a slave named Onesimus who, having helped himself to some of Philemon's wealth, had run away to bury himself amid the multitudes who thronged the streets and slums of Rome. Rome, a cosmopolitan melting pot, provided a convenient hiding place for anyone wishing to disappear from public view. There, Onesimus was sure that he would be safe. Instead, he was destined to be saved!

In some way, his path crossed that of the apostle Paul, a man hungry for souls. Paul promptly led him to Christ and proposed returning him to his master, also a Christian, who had been introduced to Christ by Paul. Because Paul had never been to Colosse (as far as we know), the likelihood is that Philemon had been saved sometime during Paul's remarkably successful evangelistic crusade at Ephesus.

Naturally, Onesimus must have been very much alarmed at the prospect of being sent back to his master, who, understandably, could be expected to deal with Onesimus with the utmost severity. The law was harsh. Mutilation or scourging would be the least of the terrors that would loom in Onesimus's mind: crucifixion or even some more horrible death was very likely. But Paul preached no cheap gospel. It was the clear duty of Onesimus to return to Philemon and throw himself on his mercy. Perhaps at this point in his talk with Onesimus Paul rattled his own chains. A bribe to Felix years ago would have secured his release (Acts 24:25–27). Instead, he was awaiting the alarming uncertainties of an appearance before Nero simply because he had done what was right. Now Onesimus must return to Philemon; it was his duty. He could not begin his new life in Christ by ignoring a debt that he had accrued in his unconverted days. What kind of salvation would that be?

To still the fear of his new convert, Paul offered to write a covering letter to Philemon. And so he did. It is in our Bible to this day as the epistle to Philemon, Paul's polemic against slavery and the Holy Spirit's answer to all social ills. It is a marvelous little memo, full of tact, persuasion, personal glimpses, and Christian grace. No Roman general planning the best way to subdue a city could have covered all of the approaches with more meticulous care than did Paul when laying siege to Philemon's soul.

We can divide this memo (for it is little more than that) into three main parts. We have, first, *Paul's cautious approach* (vv. 1–7). He did not demand instant submission to his apostolic authority; indeed, he does not mention his apostleship at all. He began with words of greeting and grace. Then we have *Paul's comprehensive appeal* (vv. 8–19), in which Paul leaves no moral or spiritual stone unturned in his quest for his friend Philemon's positive response to all that Christian love and duty could urge. Finally, we have *Paul's compelling appendix* (vv. 20–25), in which Paul cautiously seals off any loopholes through which an unwilling or unworthy believer might slip.

PART 2

The Cautious Approach
Philemon 1–7

I. THE CAUTIOUS APPROACH (vv. 1–7)
    A. Greetings (vv. 1–2)
        1. Who they were from (vv. 1a–b)
           a. Paul and his condition (v. 1a)

Paul, a prisoner of Jesus Christ.

*P*aul! The very name was an argument in itself. It would be fascinating to know when, where, and how Philemon had first met Paul. Perhaps news of what was happening at Ephesus had reached Colosse. Three months of ministry in the synagogue shook Ephesus to its foundations and caused a sharp division among the Jews. This was followed by two years in the schoolhouse of Tyrannus. All kinds of miracles had been performed. An attempt by a phony exorcist to cast out demons in the names of Jesus and Paul had resulted in sensational physical attacks by the ferocious, demon-possessed man upon those making the attempt. A public bonfire of priceless books on the occult had been staged. News of these startling happenings must have spread in all directions. It would not be at all surprising if Philemon had not found some excuse to go to Ephesus to see for himself what was taking place just as people, at the turn of the twentieth century, came from all over Britain to see what was happening in Wales at the time of the Welsh Revival. However it came about, Philemon and Paul had met. It had been a truly momentous meeting. Thereafter, the name of Paul was high on the list of people whom Philemon and his family held in special esteem.

Paul, *a prisoner!* That was almost as potent an argument as the bare mention of his name. Who of those who loved and admired Paul would not give the world itself to alleviate the hurt and hindrance of Paul's chain, especially since he was "the prisoner of Jesus Christ"? Paul never regarded himself as merely the prisoner of Rome; he was really the captive of his Redeemer's will, an ambassador in bonds. It was for the sake of the *gospel* that he was kept bound. He threw the same blessed bonds around Onesimus in sending him back to Philemon, also a prisoner of the Lord's will. He slipped the bonds of Christ gently and firmly on Philemon's wrists. He, too, must be the Lord's bondslave, the prisoner of Calvary's love.

b. Paul and his companion (v. 1b)

> *. . . and Timothy our brother. . . .*

Timothy had been with Paul at Ephesus (Acts 20:4), was one of Paul's most loyal and diligent coworkers (Phil. 2:19–23), and was a man whose praise was in all of the churches. In six of his epistles, Paul joins Timothy's name with his. Probably, if Philemon had met Paul at Ephesus, he had also met Timothy. Possibly he had a warm regard for him as well.

Paul describes Timothy as "our brother"; thus, on the very first line, in the very first verse, in the very first sentence, he planted firmly the seed of that wondrous new relationship, one with another, that we all have in Christ. It is in the gospel alone that we find the universal brotherhood of man because it is only in the gospel that we find the Fatherhood of God. Before he is through, Paul will be calling Philemon his "brother" (vv. 7, 20), along with Onesimus (v. 16). He is forging already the chains that he intends to fasten on Philemon's wrists.

2. Who they were for (vv. 1c–2)
a. Philemon and his family (vv. 1c–2a)
(1) How Paul claims them

Underline the repeated personal pronoun *our* here—"our dearly beloved," "our beloved," "our fellowsoldier." Paul has a genius for making friends and for bonding them firmly and fervently to himself. His love was like that of the Lord—a love that will not let one go, a love that many waters cannot quench, a love that never fails, and that believes all things and hopes all things, that never falters or fails, and that suffers long and is kind (1 Cor. 13).

(2) How Paul commends them (vv. 1c–2a)

> *Unto Philemon our dearly beloved and fellowlabourer, and to our*
> *beloved Apphia, and Archippus our fellowsoldier. . . .*

Paul now speaks of Philemon's family in the highest terms of praise. This was not flattery. Such a man as Paul would scorn to stoop to that cheap method of securing favor. This was a commendation based on high regard, rooted in real achievement in the things of God. Doubtless Philemon, having been won to

Christ by Paul, had flung himself, heart and soul, into the evangelization of his hometown of Colosse. In this he had been heartily supported by his family.

Paul mentions "our beloved Apphia." The word for "beloved" is taken by some to read "sister," which could be more in keeping with Paul's habitual guardedness in addressing women. There can be little doubt, however, that she was Philemon's wife, just as Archippus was Philemon's son. Paul calls Archippus a fellow soldier. Archippus was evidently one of the ministers of Colosse. In the absence of Epaphras (Col. 1:7), temporarily with Paul at Rome, and whom Paul later describes as his fellow prisoner (Philem. 23), no doubt the full burden of the ministry at Colosse had fallen on this young man's shoulders. This was no light burden in view of the struggle going on with the cult. In the less personal letter to the Colossian church, Paul charged Archippus to "take heed to the ministry which thou hast received in the Lord, that thou fulfill it" (literally, "fill it full") (Col. 4:17). He was to regard his ministry as a vessel into which he was to pour all of his life, talents, energy, and power. Here, however, the reference to Archippus is one of warm commendation. He was standing to his post of duty like a valiant solider, one of Paul's fellow soldiers.

b. Philemon and his fellowship (v. 2b)

. . . and to the church in thy house.

Philemon's house was one of the gathering places of the church at Colosse. Probably, it was the chief meeting place, perhaps the only one, in light of the fact that Colosse itself was only a small town. We gather from all of this that Philemon was an active and influential member of the Colossian church.

Paul is laying his foundations with care. If Philemon was such an outstanding and leading member of the Christian community, it would not be too much to ask, at the appropriate time, that he act like it in his treatment of Onesimus.

B. Grace (v. 3)
1. Not just unaccompanied grace (v. 3a)

Grace to you, and peace. . . .

Not just grace, although grace alone would be all of the argument that was really needed. Grace in the New Testament is unmerited favor; getting something we don't deserve. Grace is the very essence of the gospel, what we have all received through Christ.

Suppose that you were to look out of your window just in time to see a young fellow making off with your car. You phone the police and report the theft, giving the car's make, model, color, and license number. Then you sit back and await developments, not too hopefully perhaps. But the unexpected happens. You receive a phone call from the local police station. The sergeant says, "Sir, we have recovered your car and also have the young man in custody. Can you come down?"

You arrive at the police station and examine the car. No damage has been done. You go inside and the officer says, "Here's the young man. Do you want to press charges?" At this point, you have three alternatives. If you say, "Yes, he stole my car, he deserves to be punished," that would be *justice*. If you say, "Well, look here, officer, he doesn't seem to have done any harm. I don't think I want to have him booked," that would be *forgiveness*. But suppose that you were to say to the young man, "Look here, son, you don't need to steal a car. I have two. I'll give you one of mine. Also, I'll fill it up with gas for you and buy you a year's insurance." That would be *grace*. That would be giving him something that he did not deserve. That is exactly how God has treated us—with grace!

Paul uses the word because, in a paragraph or two, he is going to ask Philemon to treat Onesimus on this very principle of grace. He is going to ask him to give Onesimus something that he did not deserve.

But it is not unaccompanied grace here. It is grace *and peace*. Peace means that the war is over. We have "peace with God through our Lord Jesus Christ." Once we were rebels, runaway slaves, and our hearts were filled with harsh thoughts against God. We had declared war on God's claims, but now the war is over. We have peace.

Again, Paul uses the word deliberately, carefully laying his approaches to Philemon's soul. He is going to tell him that whatever state of war existed between him and Onesimus is now over. He is surrounding Philemon with subliminal arguments of an incontrovertible nature—and Philemon has no idea yet of what's coming. Paul, however, is hedging him in with reminders of all that he has received at God's hands.

2. Not just unaccredited grace (v. 3b)
   Paul wants Philemon to think of:
   a. The Father of the Christian family

From God our Father. . . .

The concept of God as a Father is almost unique to Christianity. The concept occurs in the Old Testament, but only very rarely. Pagan religions know no such God. The gods of the pagans are fierce, demanding, often blood-thirsty, vengeful, and cruel. Pagan religions sometimes postulated a mother, but pagan theology often exalted a female goddess who was as lustful as the male gods were lawless. Jesus taught men to pray, "Our Father which art in heaven, Hallowed be thy name." We find the name "Father" in His first recorded utterance, "Wist ye not I must be about my Father's business" (Matt. 6:9). It was a name on His lips just before the darkness fell at Calvary, "Father, forgive them, for they know not what they do" (Luke 23:46). The name was back on His lips immediately after the darkness was over: "Father, into they hand I commend my spirit." He spoke the name immediately after His resurrection: "I am not yet ascended to my Father" (John 20:17). It was almost the last word on His lips before His ascension: "Wait for the promise of the Father . . . It is not for you to know the times or the seasons, which the Father hath put in his own power" (Acts 1:4, 7).

Paul underlines this great, revolutionary concept of Christianity—God is the Father of all of those who believe. God was *Paul's* Father, He was *Philemon's* Father, and He was the Father now of *Onesimus.* Paul does not say that yet, but he is planting seed thoughts, reminding Philemon of some essential basic truths.

> Paul wants Philemon to think of:
> b. The focus of the Christian faith (v. 3b)

> *. . . and the Lord Jesus Christ. . . .*

Christianity is Christ, so Paul focuses Philemon's attention on Him. Indeed, he mentions the Lord Jesus by name six times in this memo before he even comes to Onesimus.

First, Paul emphasizes *the power of Christ*—He is *Lord,* Jesus Christ, a title of special interest here. The word is *Kurios,* which literally means "owner" (so translated in Luke 19:33). It carries the idea of that kind of authority with arises from and pertains to ownership. Paul is subtly reminding Philemon that Jesus is his Lord, his Owner. He was just as much a possession of the Lord Jesus as Onesimus was a possession of Philemon.

Then Paul emphasizes *the person of Christ*—He is the Lord *Jesus* Christ. When reference is made to Him in the New Testament, the order of the names is always of importance. When the name "Jesus" comes first, as here, it means Jesus, the

One who humbled Himself but who is now exalted and glorified as the Christ, and the emphasis is on His essential humanity. By becoming a man, Jesus has forever glorified humanity and added an incredible dimension of dignity to human life. That is another of Paul's oblique blows at the whole concept of slavery.

Also, He is the Lord Jesus *Christ*. In this title Paul emphasizes *the position of the Lord Jesus*. He is the anointed One, supremely a royal priest, now seated at God's right hand in heaven in a human body that still bears the scars of Calvary. Once men scourged and crucified this Christ of God—in view of that, how could Philemon, or any true Christian, ever consider scourging and crucifying another human being? Which on every human count by right and custom of Roman law, was all that Onesimus could expect, possibly the least that he could expect at the hands of a slave owner. And, as yet, Paul has come nowhere near his subject.

C. Gratitude (vv. 4–6)
  1. When Paul prayed for Philemon (v. 4)

I thank my God, making mention of thee always in my prayers.

Paul's prayer life was such that he could actually and honestly assure Philemon that he prayed for him *always*. He had prayed for him from the day that he led him to Christ. He prayed for him, his wife, and his son. He prayed for him constantly and continually. He had prayed for him with added fervor, surely, in recent days now that his name had been especially brought to his mind. No doubt Epaphras, who came from Colosse, had mentioned Philemon when he had first come to Rome brimming with news about the Colossian church (Col. 1:7). And now the matter of Onesimus had come up. We can be quite sure that before Paul ever put pen to paper he had spent some extra time in prayer for Philemon and his loved ones, praying over Philemon's personal spiritual life, his place in the assembly of God's people, his business responsibilities, and his duties to his household establishment and those who owned him as master, praying fervently that Philemon would do the Christian thing when he set eyes on Onesimus.

Paul says, too, that he prayed with genuine gratitude to God each time he thought of Philemon and his family. He was thankful to God for them.

Paul was one of those rare Christians who had learned the secret of being thankful. He could find things for which to be thankful in all of the circumstances of life. It is an attitude that we would do well to cultivate. It is so easy to fall into the habit of complaining. Paul scorned such carnality. He was a thankful person. And in this case, he was devoutly thankful that he was addressing this particular letter to a man of Philemon's character and Christian worth.

He told Philemon how thankful he was for him and how often he prayed for him. It was another paving stone, carefully laid down by Paul in his approach to Philemon's response to his coming plea for Onesimus. It is hard not to want to please a person whom you know thinks highly of you and whom you know prays for you always, especially when you know that person to be a particularly effective prayer warrior.

2. Why Paul prayed for Philemon (v. 5)
   a. He had heard of Philemon's love for the Savior (v. 5a)

Hearing of thy love and faith, which thou hast toward
the Lord Jesus.

Love and faith! Love comes first. Love is what the Christian life is all about; faith is what makes our new life in Christ *effective*. Faith is what releases the power. All of the glory of God's eternal plan—rooted in eternity; thought out before time began; brought down to earth by Jesus; translated into a sinless life, an atoning death, a glorious resurrection, and an amazing exaltation to the right hand of power in glory—is made available to us by faith. All of the glory of that redemptive plan, made clear to us by the Holy Spirit in the Scriptures and available to regenerate us, is available to us by faith. All the Holy Spirit's power to make us new creatures in Christ Jesus, sons of God, heirs with Christ of the resources of the Godhead, and destined to reign with Him above all principalities, all powers, over every name that is named, not only in this life, but also in the life to come, is made *effective* in our lives by faith. Faith is the link that completes the chain, the switch that closes the circuit, the activating principle that allows the whole wondrous process to go into effect.

But love is what makes it *evident*. Love for the Lord Jesus is the proof that the light has been turned on in the soul, that new life now flows where once death ruled. Love for the Lord Jesus is the ultimate test, the proof that our faith is real, that ours is a faith that works. Not just a sentimental attachment that contents itself with singing hymns, but love that bows to the Lord's own definition: "If ye love me, keep my commandments." Before long, Paul was going to put that "love and faith" that Philemon had "toward the Lord Jesus" to the test. Perhaps, as he read these words in this memo, Philemon already suspected what was coming and cast a sidelong glance at Onesimus standing there watching every expression on his master's face.

b. He had heard of Philemon's love for the saints (v. 5b)

. . . and toward all saints.

Paul has not yet told Philemon that Onesimus is now one of those saints. But there could be no exceptions. If Philemon's love for the Lord Jesus proved itself real, as it did by his love for all saints, then he was under divine obligation to love this guilty and apprehensive runaway slave of his, one who had resented his authority, abused his kindness, stolen his property, and fled from his presence but who was now one of the saints.

All natural feelings of resentment, indignation, and outrage must be swallowed up by love. All legitimate appeals to the provisions of the law must be disarmed by love. Did Philemon love all of the saints? Did he love dear Paul there in that Roman prison? Did he love beloved Epaphras whose pastoral ministry at Colosse had been such a benediction? Did he love Timothy for his unswerving loyalty to Christ and the apostle? Did he love *all* saints? Paul had no doubt that he did. Then he must now love Onesimus. Paul does not say so yet. He is still hedging Philemon in.

3. What Paul prayed for Philemon (v. 6)
a. For the outward flowing of his Christian life (v. 6a)

That the communication of thy faith may become effectual. . . .

The word translated "communication" here can better be rendered "fellowship." Handley Moule suggests that the word, as used here, refers to Philemon's generous financial fellowship prompted by the dear brother's love for the Lord Jesus. Perhaps Paul himself had profited from Philemon's generosity. One way that Philemon translated his faith and love into action was by sharing his material wealth with others.

This was no doubt a noble and commendable thing to do; but, ordinarily, human love can prompt mere philanthropy. Many a successful, unsaved businessman has been generous with his money. Many charities are made possible through such men. Moreover, generous giving to the Lord's work and God's people does not in itself necessarily denote a vital state of soul. Paul does not want Philemon to show kindness and charity to Onesimus on merely human grounds. So he goes on.

b. For the inward flourishing of his Christian life (v. 6b)

. . . may become effectual by the acknowledging of every good thing which is in you in Christ Jesus.

Good works can be prompted by outside stimuli. For instance, modern television programs show heartrending pictures of the victims of famine, disaster, or persecution, and, at once, generous people respond. Millions of dollars can be raised in support of relief organizations very quickly. Most people will respond to an emotional appeal.

Or good works can be prompted within. Most people have generous impulses and respond to appeals to their better nature, to their natural, humanitarian feelings. Many people have a strict sense of duty toward the underprivileged and do good works as a result and often from a variety of motives.

Good works that count with God, however, originate with the indwelling Lord Himself. Thus, Paul prayed that Philemon's good works might have their wellsprings, not in his own generous nature, but in the Lord.

Then, and only then, would his good works be of such a startling, supernatural, and purely spiritual nature that people all around would be forced to take notice. They would be "effectual by the acknowledging [by those looking on] of every good thing which is in you in Christ Jesus." They would not just see Philemon's being kind and generous. They would see something much more startling than that; they would see Christ in action in a man's life. They would see not just the natural but the supernatural. They would see God in the man.

In a paragraph or two farther on into his memo, Paul will tell Philemon one way by which he can give evidence of such a supernatural life to a wondering world. He can show it by what he does to Onesimus. And, as we shall see, Paul intends to suggest to Philemon a course of action that goes far beyond the call of duty, far beyond any merely human concept of charity, and far beyond anything a carnal or worldly Christian might be prepared to do. He is going to suggest such a demonstration of the indwelling Christ-life as would make anyone but a truly spiritual Christian gasp. Paul prays that the inward flourishing of Philemon's Christian life will be revealed by the outward flowing of the Christ-life within.

  D. Gladness (v. 7)
    1. The personal experience of Philemon's love (v. 7a)

For we have great joy and consolation in thy love. . . .

What a joy it is when those whom we lead to Christ go on well with the Lord. Paul there at Rome, with so much against him, had experienced a real lift in his soul at the news that Epaphras had brought. We can picture the scene: Paul chained to a Roman solider who may or may not have been favorably disposed toward him, the knock at the door, and the news that a friend had arrived from Colosse. We can imagine the eager exchange of greeting, how Epaphras would inquire after Paul's well-being, the state of his lawsuit, his prospects for release or possible harsher detention, even death. We can picture Paul's inquiries about this one and that one at Ephesus and places all around that great center. His thoughts would have been busy wondering just why Epaphras had come, wondering if something was wrong at Colosse. Possibly he would not inquire too closely at first about the Colossian Christians, not even about his "dearly beloved Philemon" and his family. Possibly he would wait for an opportune moment. Then would come the serious news about the inroads of the cult, and Paul would be taken up with that for awhile, shaking his head as Epaphras revealed more and more of the complex doctrinal issues involved. "Give me time, Epaphras," Paul would say. "I'll pray about it and write a letter. This thing has to be nipped in the bud."

Then, "And what about Philemon and Apphia and Archippus? Where do they stand in all of this?"

And Epaphras would say, "They're as solid as a rock. Thank God for Philemon. He has been a tower of strength in all of this. My! What a dear man he is. What a generous, warmhearted, hospitable brother!" Possibly Philemon had financed Epaphras's visit to Rome.

So Paul could write, "For we have great joy and consolation in thy love." For doubtless Philemon had sent word by Epaphras of his love for Paul. "Epaphras, be sure and give our love to Paul. Tell the dear man that he reigns in our hearts."

Paul intended to put that love to the test. He had experienced it in the past. He was going to make a great demand upon it in the immediate future.

2. The practical expression of Philemon's love (v. 7b)

. . . because the bowels [hearts] of the saints are refreshed by thee, brother.

It was not just Philemon's love for him that moved Paul to what he calls "great joy." It was also the fact that Philemon's practical brand of Christianity was such an encouragement to many of the Lord's people. Philemon was a second Barnabas, a true son of consolation, a son of encouragement. He had a word of encouragement for every believer and a helping hand for all who loved the Lord. He did not allow himself to be discouraged by the schemes or even the success of the cult. He did not quit but threw himself all the more earnestly into the task of strengthening the things that remained, encouraging and consoling those who were struggling to remain true to the Lord.

News of this blessed Paul's heart. Such a man would be sure to lend a sympathetic ear to what Paul was soon going to write about Onesimus.

Thus, Paul laid his approaches to Philemon's heart and mind and will. His approach was cautious but relentless.

PART 3

The Comprehensive Appeal
Philemon 8–19

II. THE COMPREHENSIVE APPEAL (vv. 8–19)
  A. Along the line of desire (vv. 8–13)
    1. Paul states his rights (v. 8)

Wherefore, though I might be much bold in Christ to enjoin thee
that which is convenient.

B y this time Philemon must have had a good idea at the direction in which
Paul was heading, although he has not yet come to the point and bluntly
stated his purpose in writing. With Onesimus standing there, however, Philemon
would have been dense indeed not to have put two and two together. Paul was
going to make some kind of a request for this prodigal slave.

The apostle with this verse takes a bold step in the direction of his ultimate
objective. He says, in effect, "Philemon, I'm going to ask you to do something
for me, though, of course, as your spiritual father, I could command you to do it.
That would be well within my rights, especially as I am an apostle of Jesus Christ."
The word *convenient* translated here could better be translated "befitting." Paul
says, "I could boldly, in Christ's name, command you to do what was right and
fitting."

But to stand upon one's rights and take advantage of one's position to enforce
a line of behavior from another person is never very satisfactory. A person can be
made to follow a given line of behavior from one of three reasons—out of a sense
of discipline, out of a sense of duty, or out of a sense of desire. Discipline says, "I
have to"; duty says, "I ought to"; desire says, "I want to." Paul could coerce, but
that is never the Holy Spirit's way. However, just as an added collateral argument,
he states his rights.

    2. Paul surrenders his rights (vv. 9–13)
      a. In favor of higher ground (v. 9)

Yet for love's sake I rather beseech thee, being such an one as Paul
the aged, and now also a prisoner of Jesus Christ.

What an emotion-packed statement! Paul will not command; he will appeal.

But he will not hesitate to use every argument he can, even the argument of his age and his bonds. Although Paul refused to order Philemon to do what he should do to Onesimus, he did not hesitate to use every weapon he had to take Philemon's will by storm. Not the least powerful of the weapons at his disposal was the emotional one. He mentions two things that he was sure would make a great emotional appeal not only to Philemon but also to Philemon's wife and son.

First, he mentions his age. He describes himself as "Paul the aged." That was still a day when age had its privileges. In actual fact, Paul was probably about sixty years of age. His poor, battered body, however, had lived through experiences that must have aged it much more than that. It had been beaten again and again, had been scourged, and had suffered in the stocks. It had been exposed to fierce summer suns and bitter winter cold. It had been inflicted with a chronic disability described by Paul himself as a "thorn in the flesh," something so severe that he could describe it as "a messenger of Satan to buffet me." He had suffered through four shipwrecks and, on one occasion, had been at the mercy of the sea for a whole night and day. His years of missionary activity had been marked by constant peril. He was a man so broken in body as to need the constant care of a physician. All of these things had taken their toll. He was "Paul the aged."

Who would not want to do something to bring a little sunshine into the life of such a notable veteran in a beloved cause? There might not be many more opportunities to render a service to "Paul the aged." Death could not be far away, even if Nero's headsmen were kept at bay. Surely Philemon would do something for "Paul the aged."

Then, too, he was a prisoner. True, he put the noblest possible connotation on the fact by calling himself the "prisoner of Jesus Christ," and this, too, for the second time in this brief memo. But the fact remained that he was a *prisoner.* His wrists were galled with fetters. He had lost his freedom and could not come and go as he pleased. He appealed to Philemon along that line. Surely, if he had the power, Philemon would be only too willing to set him free! If the decision rested with Philemon, those bonds would soon be broken! Well! Philemon could not set Paul free, but he could set someone else free instead.

"For love's sake I beseech thee!" Only a hard-hearted man could resist such an appeal, and Philemon was certainly not that. He was a tenderhearted man, and he loved Paul. Paul has taken higher ground. He will not command, although he could. Instead, he will appeal to Philemon's love, to his love for "Paul the aged," his love for "Paul the prisoner." And, thus, he completes his encirclement of Philemon. He is ready now to state his case bluntly.

Paul has surrendered his rights in favor of higher ground. He has surrendered them also for another reason.

> b. In favor of higher gains (vv. 10–11)
>   (1) I have gained a new son (v. 10)

I beseech thee for my son Onesimus, whom I have begotten
in my bonds.

There it is at last! Paul is more than a third of the way through his letter before he even mentions Onesimus. When at last he does write down that name, it is in terms of tender endearment. He is Paul's son ("my own child" is one rendering). He is Paul's son, begotten to new life in Christ, begotten while Paul was still in bonds. Onesimus was just as much Paul's spiritual son as Philemon was Paul's spiritual son.

The order of the words in the original text reads, "I appeal to you about my own child, whom I begot in my bonds, Onesimus." The name comes at the very end of the sentence, dramatically, with a touch of inspired genius. There it is at last! The name that Paul has been saving up for this moment—Onesimus!

"Why!" Philemon might have exclaimed, "That's my *slave!* My worthless, thieving, runaway slave!"

"Never!" says Paul, "Not any more! That's my *son,* my own child, the child of my old age, the child born of my bonds."

> (2) You have gained a new slave (v. 11)

Which in time past was to thee unprofitable, but now profitable
to thee and to me.

Well, admits Paul, if you insist on keeping him as a slave, then please note, Philemon, that you will have a *new* slave. At this point, Paul makes a play on the name of Onesimus. The name means "profitable." "There was a time," Paul says, "when Onesimus was indeed unprofitable, but now you have a new Onesimus, a profitable Onesimus. He will work his fingers to the bone for you. You will find him a living example of what I have written to the church at Colosse: 'Servants, obey in all things your masters according to the flesh; not with eyeservice, as menpleasers; but in singleness of heart, fearing God: and whatsoever ye do, do it heartily, as to the Lord, and not unto men; knowing that of the Lord ye shall receive the reward of the inheritance; for ye serve the Lord Christ'! (Col. 3:22–24). You will find, Philemon, that the new Onesimus will be a living example of *that*."

Paul had already put Onesimus to the test on that score. "But now profitable to thee and to me," says Paul. He had kept Onesimus with him long enough to know that if Onesimus was to remain a slave to the day of his death, he would be the best slave a man ever owned. Philemon could expect nothing but gain if he took Onesimus back just as a slave.

>   c. In favor of higher goals (vv. 12–13)
>   (1) For Philemon: the question of receiving or not receiving
>   Onesimus (v. 12)

Whom I have sent again: thou therefore receive him, that is, mine
own bowels [heart].

To receive or not to receive—that was the question!

Under Roman law, a slave was mere chattel, without any civil rights whatsoever and wholly at the mercy of his master. A slave suspected of treachery or a crime, when caught, could expect to be tortured without mercy. A slave owner could do anything he wanted with the full approval of the law and with the hearty approval of other slave owners. A slave could be scourged and crucified, or he could literally be killed by inches. Fiction cannot conceive more terrible atrocities than those actually done to offending slaves. Vedius Pollio, a friend of Caesar Augustus, allegedly kept conger eels in a tank in his garden and to which he threw offending slaves to be killed and eaten. The most trifling blunders would bring down his master's wrath on the terrified slave. In one recorded incident, Vedius condemned a slave to the tank for dropping and breaking a crystal cup.

About the time that Paul was in Rome, four hundred slaves, men and women, were executed because their master, Pedanius, had been murdered by a member of his establishment. Tacitus called this mass retribution "an old custom."[1] Petty thievery merited death by crucifixion for a slave.

Slave owners had a vested interest in seeing that offending slaves were summarily punished. The slave revolt under Sparticus highlighted the need (from the slave owners' point of view) of swift and terrible punishment for rebellious slaves. After all, slaves far outnumbered slave owners.

---

1. Tacitus, *Annales* 14.42.

Thus, Philemon would be under considerable social pressure from his peers to make a summary example of Onesimus. They would regard leniency as a betrayal of their privileged class. Now that Onesimus had shown up at his master's house, he was exposed to the full weight of the law, custom, and social pressure. His only protection, for what it was worth, was this brief note from Paul, addressed to Philemon, urging him to act, not as a Roman patrician, but as a Christian believer.

We can be sure that all heaven watched with bated breath to see what Philemon would do. And we can be sure that poor Onesimus was on tenterhooks waiting for his master's reaction.

But Paul has only just begun. He has come out into the open at last and named Onesimus and confronted Philemon with his choice: to receive or not to receive! But Paul had a choice, too.

(2) For Paul: the question of retaining or not retaining Onesimus (v. 13)

Whom I would have retained with me, that in thy stead he might
have ministered unto me in the bonds of the gospel.

"In fact," Paul continued, "I have found Onesimus so useful a man, I wish I could keep him here to serve me. I could use a man like Onesimus, like the new Onesimus. And, dear brother Philemon, I have had experience of your generosity. I know you would willingly serve me yourself and put all that you have at my disposal. So, in a sense, if I'd kept Onesimus, which I was tempted to do, you could have ministered to me through him, by proxy, so to speak. I cannot tell you how tempted I was to do this."

Onesimus would have liked that idea, too, very much more, we can be sure, than he liked the idea of going back to Philemon to face whatever music awaited him in Colosse, to be condemned to the arena, perhaps, to be torn to pieces by wild beasts, to help make a Roman holiday for the masters of the world.

So Paul argues along the line of desire. His rights, along with personal wishes, are all brought into play only to be resigned because there was something better. There was higher ground, higher gains, and higher goals. Paul resolutely refused to put this matter of slavery on any ground but that of Christian love. Everything must be dealt with in the light of Calvary.

There was, of course, inspired genius in all of this. God does not settle social issues on the low ground of human rights, but on the high ground of Calvary's love. The Lord and the apostles resolutely refused to resort to political agitation, militant reaction, social revolution, or civil disobedience. That was low ground. That kind of thing degenerates a spiritual issue into a political issue. God does not challenge political force on its own ground; He takes higher ground.

Paul did not organize the slaves of Rome or promote mass demonstrations against the gross injustices and the glaring wrongs of slavery. Slavery was the universal social injustice of the day; it was dehumanizing and destructive. But Paul did not organize marches on the Forum, mass disobedience, and armed resistance. He did not campaign among the more humane and liberal members of Roman society or the Roman Senate for orderly change of the laws governing slavery. He refused to allow a spiritual movement to become a political or social movement. He fought for the abolition of slavery from the standpoint of Calvary. It is Calvary's love that provides the only lasting answer to social ills. First change the man; changed men no longer want to enslave other men.

The church should always be wary of seeking political answers to what are essentially spiritual questions. God's answer to social and political ills is revival. We must work at winning people to Christ and teaching them Christian love, life, and law. Lesser issues will be resolved sooner or later. Social reformers work on changing the environment to change the individual; God works at changing the individual to change the environment. In the wake of every genuine spiritual awakening has come social reform. Holy Spirit revivals always clean up society.

Paul, then, deliberately took his stand on the question of slavery, not by trying to abolish it on the grounds of its gross unfairness, but by accepting the existing laws regarding slavery as the law of the land and by raising the whole issue to the realm of the spiritual. Along the line of desire, he desired to keep Onesimus. He could have written quite a different letter.

Dear Philemon:

A remarkable thing has happened. Here, at Rome, I have run into a slave of yours by the name of Onesimus. He has become a Christian and has been a tremendous help to me. Would you let me have him? If you cannot see your way clear to give him to me, maybe you would sell him to me.

Love in Christ,
Paul

That would have been one way of doing it. It would have spared Philemon a very difficult decision and solved the problem of his possible estrangement with his neighboring fellow slave owners. He would probably have been delighted to give or sell his unprofitable slave to his beloved Paul. And, once he was his, Paul could have set Onesimus free as an example of what a Christian should do to a slave. No rocking the boat! No confrontation! A gentlemanly settlement of an awkward issue.

Paul, however, lifted everything to higher ground, for higher gains, and to achieve loftier goals. His desires, the desires of Onesimus, and perhaps even the desires of Philemon must be passed through the prism of the Lord's desires. Paul now shifts to another position. He argues:

B.   Along the line of duty (vv. 14–17)
    1.   The duty of Paul: a legal restoration (v. 14)

But without thy mind would I do nothing; that thy benefit
should not be as it were of necessity.

Onesimus, according to Roman law, was Philemon's property, and Paul had no right to keep him. He wanted to keep him. He could have talked himself into keeping him. He could have found some kind of technicality that might have justified his keeping him—it was too risky to send Onesimus back, it could cost Onesimus his life, Onesimus was only a new convert and might run away somewhere between Rome and Colosse, it would be to the benefit of Onesimus to stay in Rome and learn more New Testament truth in the apostle's school, or Paul needed him and he knew Philemon well enough to know that he'd gladly donate Onesimus to the cause.

Paul set all such rationalization aside. He had a duty to send Onesimus back to Philemon. Like it or not, that was his clear duty.

Besides, he did not want Philemon to feel pressured to give Onesimus to him. Paul had no compunction in putting the pressure on Philemon to do what was right in the sight of the Lord in his own relationship to his regenerated slave. But he refused to put pressure on Philemon to make a donation of Onesimus to the work of God in Rome as represented by himself, Paul. He could have done so, but he would not do so.

The best kind of giving is that which is spontaneous, spiritual, systematic, and free from coercion. Nobody likes to feel that he *has* to give to this or that. Most believers are willing enough to give to the Lord's work, but "not as it were of necessity." Nobody likes to feel as though he has been backed into a corner, that he is under pressure, or that someone has taken advantage of his generosity.

Paul knew where *his* duty lay. He must send Onesimus back to Philemon. Legally, morally, and spiritually that was where his duty lay. Paul was not the kind of man to allow his desires to overrule his duty.

2. The duty of Onesimus: a life redemption (v. 15)

For perhaps he therefore departed for a season, that thou shouldest receive him for ever.

When Paul first broached the subject to Onesimus, that he had a Christian duty to return to Philemon, the poor fellow more than likely was greatly alarmed. But Paul preached no cheap gospel. Salvation did not absolve Onesimus of his moral obligations. It never does.

In his testimony, Jim Vaus tells how for years he ran away from God and worked as a wiretapper for the crime syndicate. He was won to Christ at a Billy Graham Crusade. His prayer was unorthodox but real: "Lord, if You mean business with me, I mean business with You." Immediately, he ran into the moral obligations that accompany salvation. He had to break with the mobsters, a most dangerous undertaking, which almost cost him his life. He had to go to prison. He had to face a former employer and restore thousands of dollars worth of stolen equipment and face the possibility of arrest. Salvation is free; the moral obligations that accompany it can often prove to be very expensive indeed.

Onesimus must go back to Philemon. Paul writes, "For perhaps he therefore departed for a season, that thou shouldest receive him for ever." Said Paul, "He'll never run away again."

There was, under the Mosaic Law, the remarkable provision of the trespass offering. The sin offering had to do with the *principle* of sin; the trespass offering had to do with the *practice* of sin. When a guilty person brought his trespass offering to the priest, he was required, under law, not only to make full restoration for the wrong he had done to the offended party but also to make an added payment of 20 percent to the person he had wronged.

Getting right with God involved getting right with men. It always does. Any presentation of the gospel that fails to take this principle into account is wholly inadequate. Onesimus must go back to Philemon. And Philemon would not only regain his property but also get his bonus. He would receive back a new man in Christ, and he would have him forever!

Again Paul is striking harder than the surface appearance might indicate: "Receive him back *for ever.*" "My dear, Philemon," Paul says, "Onesimus is yours for all eternity. You and he will spend the endless ages together. You are both going to live forever with your Master in heaven. Think of that, my beloved brother, when deciding what you intend to do with your born-again slave."

But for Onesimus there could be no compromise. No matter what, he must go back to Philemon. He must not go back resentfully or with reservations. As a new man in Christ, he must do what duty demanded. He could have no guarantees. Paul would do what he could for him, but, in the last analysis, his fate lay in the hands of Philemon.

3. The duty of Philemon: a love relationship (v. 16–17)
   a. The negative (v. 16a)

Not now as a servant, but above a servant. . . .

Now Paul comes out bluntly with the issue at which he has been hinting all along. Philemon's treatment of Onesimus should be colored not only by the fact that he, Philemon, was a Christian but also by the fact that Onesimus, too, was a Christian. The legal relationship must be set aside; grace, not law, must prevail. He must not treat Onesimus as a slave; he must treat him as something more than a slave. Surely, the implication is that he should set him free. He should treat him as a freed man. "Not now as a servant." That was Philemon's duty stated in the negative. It was the lowest, the most basic, thing, the very least that Philemon could do. That was heaven's irreducible minimum. Christian love could accept no less than that. That Philemon could even think of doing less than cease to think of Onesimus as a slave was inconceivable.

b. The positive (v. 16b)

. . . above a servant, a brother beloved, specially to me, but how much more unto thee, in the flesh and in the Lord?

That statement rang the death knell to slavery in the Christian community. Paul said, in effect, "Onesimus is not to be treated as one of your slaves;

he is to be treated as one of God's saints." He is "a brother beloved, specially to me."

More! If Onesimus was "a brother beloved" to Paul, he should be all the more brother beloved to Philemon. Philemon should be prepared to esteem Onesimus highly *"in the flesh."* On the purely human level, that is, as a compassionate human being, as a dear friend of the apostle Paul, he should be prepared to welcome someone whom Paul regarded as a very dear brother. But that was only part of it. Philemon should be prepared to esteem Onesimus highly "in the Lord." How does one Christian treat another Christian highly esteemed and beloved in the Lord? Certainly not as a slave.

c. The superlative (v. 17)

If thou count me therefore a partner, receive him as myself.

What more could he ask? Suppose that Paul was the one who was coming to Colosse. Suppose that it was Paul who was arriving at Philemon's home. Would he assign *him* to the slave shed? Would he treat Paul like a slave? Of course not! He would run out to welcome Paul with open arms. He would warmly embrace him, inquire diligently after his health, and escort him solicitously into his home. He would kill the fatted calf for him. He would put him in the finest room in the house. He would see to his comfort and take prompt care of all of his needs. He would sit him at the place of honor at his own right hand at the table. He would treat him as a member of his family, give him the run of the house, put his means at his disposal, try to anticipate his needs, and keep him happy in every way.

"If thou count me therefore a partner, receive him as *myself.*"

Paul could ask for no more. If Philemon did what Paul requested, then there was an end of slavery. If everyone would do as Paul suggests, then there is an end to all social ills.

C. Along the line of debt (vv. 18–19)
1. What was owed to Philemon (vv. 18–19a)

If he hath wronged thee, or oweth thee ought, put that on my account; I Paul have written it with mine own hand, I will repay it.

Apparently, Onesimus had stolen from Philemon. Probably he had taken the money that he needed to get to Rome and to establish himself in the city. Paul now addressed himself to the question of this debt. It could not be ignored. Evidently, Onesimus did not have any means of repaying Philemon, so Paul said, "I will repay."

"I Paul have written it with mine own hand," he says. Evidently at this point, he took the pen out of the hand of his amanuensis and wrote the pledge in his own handwriting. That was his signature to the bond, his acknowledgement that the debt had been transferred to him, his guarantee—signed with his own name, in his own hand—of payment in full.

So, if something was owed to Philemon, and if that debt stood, in any way, between Philemon and his Christian treatment of Onesimus, then now that debt was legally transferred to Paul's account, and payment was promised by the most honest man in the world.

2. What was owed by Philemon (v. 19b)

Albeit I do not say to thee how thou owest unto me even thine
own self besides.

And that was Paul's last word in the second segment of his letter, his comprehensive appeal. He had now taken care of everything. Now it was up to Philemon to act—either like a Roman slave owner or like the Lord Jesus Christ. Paul's closing thrust was overwhelming: "I don't remind you," he said (even as he did!) "that you owe me your own soul. Where would you be if it had not been for me? You would be a lost sinner. You would be still in your sins. You would be without God and without Christ and without hope. You would be on your way to hell. Think of what you owe me. I led you to Christ. Now you are a child of God, born from above, your name written in life's eternal book, and on your way to heaven. You are a joint-heir with Jesus Christ, seated with Him in the heavenlies." "And," Paul could have added, "so is Onesimus." It would be hard to win an argument with Paul!

PART 4

The Compelling Appendix
Philemon 20–25

III. THE COMPELLING APPENDIX (VV. 20–25)
    A. A personal word (vv. 20–22)
       1. Provide me relief (v. 20)
          a. Rejoice me in the Lord (v. 20a)

Yea, brother, let me have joy of thee in the Lord. . . .

Paul now returns to the more oblique type of argument. As in the opening section, Paul writes about other things, but he never lets Philemon forget that Onesimus is standing by. And, as in the opening section, he includes constant references to the Lord. "Let me have joy of thee *in the Lord,*" he says. In these closing verses, he is going to keep the *Lord* ever in the forefront of Philemon's thinking. He must not act out of benevolence to Onesimus or out of pity for Paul. He must act out of direct responsibility to the Lord.

Yet, Paul does not neglect the emotional: "Yea, brother, let me have *joy* of thee." The word that Paul used was *oninēmi,* the root word from which comes the name Onesimus. Paul is saying, "Let me have profit from thee, seeing that I am sending back Onesimus ('profitable') to you."

          b. Refresh me in the Lord (v. 20b)

. . . refresh my bowels [heart] in the Lord.

The word for "refresh" is "rest." Evidently, the suspense was very great so far as Paul was concerned. After all, Paul was not made of iron. He certainly knew how to rest in the Lord, but at the same time he was not immune to life's pressures. The possibility existed that Philemon might not respond to this letter meaning that Paul had sent Onesimus to his death. Then Paul would have to sorrow over both Philemon's spiritual condition and the death of Onesimus.

"Rest my heart in the Lord," Paul pleaded. "Don't add to my burdens."

       2. Prove me right (v. 21)

Having confidence in thy obedience I wrote unto thee, knowing
that thou wilt also do more than I say.

"I know you won't let me down!" Paul said. Then, with magnificent daring, he added, "You will do more than I say."

Now Paul had asked Philemon to receive Onesimus, not as a slave, but above a slave—as a freed man. He had asked him to treat him as a brother, or more, as "a brother beloved." He had asked him to treat him in exactly the same way that he would treat the great apostle himself. How could he possibly do *more?* Well, he could adopt Onesimus as his own son! That would be the ultimate act of Christlikeness.

3. Prepare me room (v. 22)

> *But withal prepare me also a lodging: for I trust that through*
> *your prayers I shall be given unto you.*

No doubt, like all of Paul's other numerous friends around the world, Philemon was praying for Paul's release from prison.

"I have a feeling," said Paul, "that your prayer is about to be answered." Opinions differ as to whether Paul actually was released from prison about this time. The likelihood is that he was set free and that he continued in his evangelistic activities for a season, only to be arrested again when the Neronic persecution broke out, at which time his prison conditions were much more severe, as described in 2 Timothy.

In any case, at this time Paul was optimistic. Perhaps the failure of his Jewish enemies to press their charges, together with the warm reports about him from Roman officials, caused his case to be dropped. Or perhaps he did actually appear before Nero and bore testimony to that wicked man before Nero committed his final barbarities.

"Prepare me a lodging, Philemon," said Paul. "I hope to be coming your way one of these days." It was another nail hammered home in his pleas for Onesimus. The thought that the beloved Paul might show up in person would be an added powerful incentive for Philemon to comply with Paul's wishes. It is always much easier to ignore or refuse a request when the suppliant is far away and not likely ever to be personally present than it is to do so when one is expecting a visit from that person, especially if it is a person for whom we have a warm affection and a high regard and to whom we owe an incalculable debt.

B. A public word (vv. 23–24)
1. A greeting from the man in prison with Paul (v. 23)

There salute thee Epaphras, my fellowprisoner in Christ Jesus.

Epaphras! Paul calls him his fellow "prisoner of war." It is an impressive title. A war was going on. Onesimus was a new recruit on the side of the Savior. Epaphras, beloved pastor of the Colossian church, was a dear friend of Philemon, his loved coworker. He had gone to Rome to consult with Paul about the cult and, no doubt, to take to him gifts of a material nature to help support him in the work, along with the love and greetings of the Philemon family. Epaphras was now a prisoner of war. He was now sharing Paul's chains.

Epaphras! Maybe that was how Paul had come in contact with Onesimus. It is unlikely that Paul, under house arrest, could have bumped into Onesimus on the streets of Rome. It is also unlikely that Onesimus would have voluntarily sought out Paul unless he had been in desperate financial straights or suffering from unbearable pangs of remorse. But, perhaps Epaphras had seen him, recognized him, talked to him, and persuaded him to come to talk to Paul. "Epaphras, my fellow prisoner of war, salutes you." "Epaphras! My beloved fellow bondsman in the sacred slavery of Christ greets you!" It was another weight thrown on the scales in favor of the forgiveness and manumission of Onesimus. How could Philemon face Epaphras again if he failed to do the Christian thing regarding Onesimus? The only kind of slavery that a true Christian could tolerate after reading a letter like this was the voluntary slavery of a soul to Christ.

2. A greeting from the men in partnership with Paul (v. 24)

Marcus, Aristarchus, Demas, Lucas, my fellowlabourers.

Marcus was a Jerusalem Jew, Aristarchus was a Thessalonian, and Luke was possibly a Macedonian or a Syrian. Mark and Luke both wrote gospels—Mark the gospel of Jesus as God's Servant; Luke the Gospel of Jesus as Man's Savior. Aristarchus, like Epaphras, was Paul's "fellow captive." Demas—well, Demas was soon to defect because he loved this present evil world. The stark brevity of Paul's reference to him in the accompanying letter to the Colossian (4:14) might be a hint that already he was becoming restless. Who would want to be another Demas just to win the approval of the world? Would Philemon? Never!

"The Christian world is looking on, Philemon," said Paul. "We are all watching you. You are now in the arena." One almost feels sorry for Philemon.

But Paul has not quite finished. He had one last parting shot. If all else fails, surely this will prevail.

C. A parting word (v. 25)

The grace of our Lord Jesus Christ be with your spirit. Amen.

For the last time, Paul lifted the whole matter from the secular, the social, the moral, and the material to the spiritual. Philemon was to think of the *grace* of the Lord Jesus Christ. He was to think of what that grace had now done for Onesimus. He was to think of how that grace was manifested at Calvary. He was to look at Onesimus in the light of the grace of our Lord Jesus Christ.

Philemon was to think, too, of the Lord Jesus Christ. Again, Paul spells out the whole lovely name so that Philemon can think again of the glorious person, power, passion, and position of the Savior. He was to look at the Lord Jesus Christ, then he was to look at Onesimus. He was to look at Onesimus, then he was to look back at the Lord Jesus Christ. Then he was to decide what to do.

And he was to remember that he is *our* Lord Jesus Christ—Philemon's, Epaphras's, Mark's, Luke's, Aristarchus's, Demas's, and even Onesimus's Lord Jesus Christ. The whole body would be effected by his decision.

"The grace of our Lord Jesus Christ *be with your spirit.*" The decision, in the final analysis, was spiritual. It would affect Philemon's own spiritual life. He might be richer or poorer materially by his decision regarding Onesimus, but that was neither here nor there. He would certainly be richer or poorer spiritually.

"Amen!" says Paul. "That's an end of it!"

What do you think that Philemon did? What would you have done? What are you doing with similar issues in your life where a conflict of interest exists—where the claims and considerations of this world clash with the claims and considerations of the world to come?

"The grace of our Lord Jesus Christ be with *your* spirit. Amen."